CYBER THREATS AND NUCLEAR WEAPONS

CYBER THREATS AND NUCLEAR WEAPONS

HERBERT LIN

STANFORD UNIVERSITY PRESS
Stanford, California

Stanford University Press
Stanford, California

Printed in the United States of America on acid-free, archival-quality paper

Library of Congress Cataloging-in-Publication Data

Names: Lin, Herbert, author.
Title: Cyber threats and nuclear weapons / Herbert Lin.
Description: Stanford, California : Stanford University Press, 2021. |
    Includes bibliographical references and index.
Identifiers: LCCN 2021021374 (print) | LCCN 2021021375 (ebook) | ISBN
    9781503630390 (paperback) | ISBN 9781503630406 (ebook)
Subjects: LCSH: Nuclear weapons—United States. | Nuclear weapons—Security
    measures—United States. | Computer security—United States. | Command
    and control systems—Security measures—United States. | Cyberspace
    operations (Military science)—United States.
Classification: LCC U264.3 .L56 2021 (print) | LCC U264.3 (ebook) | DDC
    355.8/25119028558—dc23
LC record available at https://lccn.loc.gov/2021021374
LC ebook record available at https://lccn.loc.gov/2021021375

Cover illustration: shutterstock | Maha Heang
Cover design: Rob Ehle

Contents

Preface

Information and communications technologies now pervade all aspects of life, both civilian and military. That most people in civilian life struggle with getting those technologies to work properly is commonly understood. Most of us have watched a speaker struggling to get his or her computer to work properly with a projector for an entirely routine presentation. Most of us have had a help desk tell us, "Let's try X to solve your problem. If that doesn't work, we'll try Y, and if that doesn't work, we'll try Z." Most of us have stared at our computers in disbelief at one time or another, saying out loud, "Huh? Why did you [the computer] do *that*?"

What is less commonly understood is that things are no better with military applications of information technology. Military information technologies were once far more sophisticated than the technologies available to the civilian world, but those days lie decades in the past. Today, the most advanced information technologies are first developed for use in the private sector, and most military applications of information technology are years behind those in the private sector. Most important, military personnel face many of the same kinds of problems that ordinary civilians face.

Computer security, or cybersecurity, is no exception to this rule. Military personnel and civilians alike find cybersecurity to be an inconvenience that gets in the way of doing real work. It may be marginally easier to order military personnel to follow security procedures that civilians would not tolerate, but the underlying urge to ignore security is the same, and the security outcomes for civilian and military computer systems are often more similar than might be expected.

Moreover, as weapons systems are brought into the internet age, they may well become more vulnerable to attack than older ones. Each electronic component, each wireless communications link, each contractor-supplied software system used in a weapons system is a potential vulnerability as well as an asset. National leaders who command "the red button" (a very common metaphor for a trigger that could set into motion the use of nuclear weapons and the end of the world) have unvetted Twitter and Facebook feeds to inform their decision-making as well as vetted intelligence feeds and diplomatic telegrams and letters.

Many of the existing components of the U.S. nuclear enterprise—that is, the entire array of activities and operations that have some significant connection to any aspect of nuclear explosive devices (i.e., nuclear weapons), whether in production, acquisition, operations, organization, or strategy—were developed before the Internet of things, the World Wide Web, and mobile computing and smart cell phones became ubiquitous throughout society. Today, the United States is embarking on a nuclear modernization program, and unlike in the past, cyber technologies will play a much larger part in it.

How, if at all, could increasing dependencies on modern information technologies lead to a nuclear war that no sane person would want? This is the question that motivates this book.

A cyber-enabled world affords many benefits to individuals, businesses, and society at large, as well as to the military. Today, U.S. military forces are unparalleled in the world, in part because of their use of information technology. But the growing use of modern information technologies has a downside as well, and where nuclear weapons are concerned, it behooves us to examine that downside and to mitigate it where possible.

Thus, in an age of increasing dependence on information technology, cyber risk is one element of the risk profile against which U.S. decision-makers, both civilian and military, must prepare, anticipate, and mitigate. This book addresses the relationship to and possible impact of cyber technology on all aspects on U.S. nuclear forces and operations. Most of the work done in this area relates to nuclear command and control, and that is a very important topic. Loosely, command and control refers to the processes and arrangements that enable the president and senior military leaders to decide upon the actions of military forces and provide these individuals with the information needed to make good decisions; a more precise definition will be presented in the main text of this book. It is with command and control that "the button" is usually associated.

But the forces must be acquired and organized before they are ordered into action, and once they are ordered into action, they must be able to operate so that they can achieve their mission objectives. Cyber technology is an integral element both of force acquisition and of force operations. In short, cyber technology affects all aspects of the nuclear enterprise. Hence, a multiple-button metaphor is more appropriate. One button orders nuclear forces to operate; after that, a variety of different cyber buttons are needed to operate the various weapons systems and information-gathering systems as those orders are put into effect.

The bottom line? Cyber risks across the nuclear enterprise are poorly understood. As a result, a number of aspects of the nuclear modernization effort may well exacerbate rather than mitigate these risks, and the incoming administration will have to find ways to effectively manage tensions between new nuclear capabilities and increasing cyber risk. Senior U.S. decision-makers are aware of these problems to some extent, but they face two important challenges. The first is that limiting cyber risk may require some hard choices about what nuclear capabilities to give up; the second is closing the large gap that exists between that awareness and remedial actions on the ground.

The rationale and intended audience for this book

A public discussion of the cyber risks to the nuclear enterprise is essential if they are to receive any kind of sustained attention. The management of cyber risks and cybersecurity is almost always a poor stepchild to other aspects of technology acquisition (such as cost, scheduling, and performance) and operations (such as military efficacy, resource allocation, and adaptability). Acquisition and operations managers have every incentive to say cybersecurity is receiving adequate attention while in fact doing the minimum necessary to keep security auditors off their backs, because cybersecurity just gets in the way of doing their jobs, which is to deploy a working system or to use it to accomplish some important task.

As for every new U.S. administration, policy on nuclear weapons is a major national security issue for the incoming Biden administration. Guidance for such policy is generally provided in what is called the *Nuclear Posture Review*. A Biden-endorsed *Nuclear Posture Review* may emphasize or de-emphasize various aspects of the Trump-endorsed *Nuclear Posture Review* released in 2018. But the requirements of the Biden-endorsed nuclear force structure are not likely to differ much from those of the Trump-endorsed force structure, which did not differ much from those of the Obama-endorsed force structure, and the likelihood of the new team abandoning the fundamental philosophy underlying the structure of the U.S. nuclear enterprise is virtually zero. For example, the Biden administration's U.S. nuclear weapons strategy will surely emphasize the role of deterrence, just as every other administration has done.

Thus, even though this book is based on documents and statements regarding the nuclear enterprise from the Trump administration for authoritative statements about nuclear policy, it is directed primarily at those in the Biden administration and the new Congress who will formulate and oversee that policy in the coming years.

A note on secrecy

Two of the most highly classified areas in U.S. national security involve nuclear and cyber issues. Despite this fact, the broad outlines of how

cyber issues might affect nuclear ones can be derived from first principles and what has been published on an unclassified basis. For example,
the structure of the U.S. nuclear enterprise is described in considerable
detail in an unclassified Department of Defense (DoD) publication
called the *Nuclear Matters Handbook*.[1] In addition, there is a voluminous
literature on nuclear strategy and matters related to nuclear deterrence,
including considerable discussion of certain issues related to nuclear
command and control.[2]

As for the technical side of cyber issues, the simple fact of the matter
is that both the civilian and military worlds use more or less the same
information technology. Indeed, one could easily make the argument that
the information technologies used by the military are considerably less
advanced and sophisticated than those used in the civilian sector, rather
than more advanced, as some might believe. Thus, the military sector is
unlikely to have more sophisticated or advanced technical solutions to
problems faced by the civilian sector.

What are secret, for good reasons, tend to be specific examples. For
example, the range of a Minuteman III ICBM (intercontinental ballistic
missile) is "in excess" of 5,218 nautical miles, according to a public fact
sheet published by the U.S. Air Force.[3] Consideration of the content in
any first-year physics textbook would indicate that the amount in excess
depends on the precise trajectory the missile flies and the payload the
missile carries. The specific relationship of those factors to the actual range
is classified, but it could probably be derived based on public information—after all, the laws of physics are the same whether one is performing
a classified or unclassified calculation.

The answers to certain specific questions (e.g., can a Minuteman III
based at Warren Air Force Base (AFB) in Wyoming destroy a Russian
ICBM silo based at Aleysk, Russia?) depends on the precise latitude and
longitude of the silo in question and the hardness of the silo: the former may be difficult to find using unclassified techniques, and the latter certainly counts as classified information. However, the answers to
other questions (e.g., approximately how long would it take for a missile
launched from one site to hit the other?) are unclassified—it is widely

known that it would take about 25 minutes. Perhaps the true answer, based on knowledge of specific mission profiles and other classified information is 27 minutes. That two-minute difference matters for some purposes, but not for others.

The same kinds of arguments are true of cyber operations. The fundamentals of how computers and networks operate are widely known to technically trained people. For example, computers must be programmed, and correct operation depends on the specifics of the software developed for those computers. All complex software has bugs in it, and sometimes an adversary can take advantage of those bugs to compromise the operation of the computers on which such software is running. What *might* be classified is the knowledge that entering a particular command sequence into a particular public-facing DoD database will cause the unauthorized deletion of data in that database or the specific cybersecurity measures protecting a DoD computer that is not directly connected to the Internet; what might be *highly* classified is the fact that a particular tool for cyber attack could make use of such classified knowledge, or that China has used that particular tool.

Again, classified information is necessary to answer certain questions, such as "Can China penetrate that particular DoD database?" or "Can Russia reach this particular non-Internet-connected computer? But classified information is not necessary to point to the frequent existence of such vulnerabilities and to express a concern that such vulnerabilities often exist without anyone knowing about them, often because they have not made the effort to investigate that possibility.

In short, analysis based on first principles and officially unclassified information, coupled with a variety of studies that examine the history of nuclear command and control, provide a reasonable unclassified basis for sketching the broad outlines of the cyber risks facing the U.S. nuclear enterprise. Those tasked with specifically managing and mitigating those risks will of course require access to classified information.

Acknowledgments

I gratefully acknowledge contributions and commentary on earlier drafts from James Acton; Sonja Amadae; Paul Bracken; Linton Brooks; David Clark; Grace Butler; Robert Butler; Lynn Eden; James Ellis; Matt Ellison; Steve Fetter; Maggie Gray; Peter Hayes; Rachel Hirshman; David Holloway, Jill Hruby; Robert Jervis; C. Robert Kehler; Austin Long; Alix Myerson, Joseph Nye; Scott Sagan; Jacquelyn Schneider; Sharon Squassoni; Leslie Sussan, James Timbie; Frank von Hippel; James Waldo; and Amy Zegart. Two reviewers of the draft manuscript also improved its quality tremendously.

None of the above individuals bear any responsibility for errors or misstatements found in this book. However, such errors or misstatements will inevitably be found to be the result of an adversary cyber attack on the integrity of the manuscript or a malign influence operation on me, rather than anything for which I should be held responsible.

CYBER THREATS AND NUCLEAR WEAPONS

1   Introduction and Background

Early in his administration, President John F. Kennedy told his science adviser, Dr. Jerome Wiesner, that he had looked around the Oval Office and could not find the "red telephone" that was supposed to inform him of a Soviet attack.[1] Wiesner told him that the previous President (Dwight Eisenhower) had kept the phone in a drawer in his desk. However, even after Kennedy and Wiesner had pulled out all of the drawers, they still could not find it.

The implications of this discovery are staggering—for at least a short time near the start of his term, President Kennedy did not have access to the telephone that was specifically intended to inform him of a Soviet nuclear attack while he was in the Oval Office.

The explanation was entirely mundane. In taking charge of redecorating the White House, Jacqueline Kennedy had found an elegant desk made from the timbers of the HMS *Resolute* that had been given to President Rutherford Hayes in 1880 by Queen Victoria. She had directed that this replace the desk that President Eisenhower had used, and in the replacement process, the red telephone was disconnected and removed.

What might have happened if the Soviet Union had in fact launched a nuclear attack when the phone was missing? It's highly unlikely that word of the attack would never have reached the president, but almost certainly there would have been some delay, perhaps a few minutes, while the people calling Kennedy tried to figure out why he was not answering the phone. Given the actual nuclear balance at the time (substantially favoring the United States), such a delay may not have mattered very much. But it's very hard to argue that the lack of the red telephone in the Oval Office at the time was a positive contribution to U.S. national security.

That telephone was cyber technology in 1960, and this is one of the first known indications that not all was necessarily well at the U.S. cyber-nuclear nexus.

Standing at the Cyber-Nuclear Nexus

In December 2020, the American public became aware of a major cyber attack to hit the United States: the SolarWinds incident. Described as a "significant cyber incident" and "a serious compromise that will require a sustained and dedicated effort to remediate" by the U.S. intelligence community,[2] this incident has been described in much stronger terms. Senator Richard Durbin (D-IL) described it as "virtually a declaration of war by Russia."[3] Senator Mitt Romney (R-Utah) said: "The cyber hack [SolarWinds] is like Russian bombers . . . repeatedly flying undetected over our entire country."[4] Senator Chris Coons (D-DE) said: "[I]t's pretty hard to distinguish this from an act of aggression that rises to the level of an attack that qualifies as war."[5] Thomas Bossert, President Trump's former homeland security adviser, wrote: "The magnitude of this ongoing attack is hard to overstate."[6] Brad Smith, president of Microsoft called it "the largest and most sophisticated attack the world has ever seen."[7]

From an international legal standpoint, espionage—even cyber-enabled espionage—is not prohibited. The intelligence community statement said that "this was, and continues to be, an intelligence gathering effort," and if true, claims that analogize the incident as an "act of war" are a big step too far. But these claims have a kernel of truth to them in the sense that the incident, however it is characterized, points to dangerous holes in the U.S. national security posture, while the other comments from non-politicians point to the highly sophisticated and advanced nature of the cyber attacks launched using these holes.

This book is focused on the risks of adversary cyber attacks that could have a negative impact on the most important and significant military capabilities the United States maintains—its nuclear capabilities. For example, one major concern is that such attacks might push U.S. decision-makers across a threshold that they deemed strategically significant, thus increasing the possibility of a nuclear response. Thus, this book addresses cybersecurity issues across all aspects of the modernizing nuclear enterprise, specifically nuclear weapons design and upgrades; nuclear delivery systems and platforms carrying such systems; the nuclear tactical warning and attack assessment (TW/AA) system; nuclear command, control, and communications (NC3); the planned modernization of U.S. NC3 systems; nuclear planning; and nuclear decision-making and escalation.

On cybersecurity and offensive cyber operations

This section reviews some of the basic elements of cybersecurity and offensive operations in cyberspace.[8] For those familiar with these elements already, this section can be regarded as a reminder of some of the terms and concepts that will be used later in this book. For those unfamiliar with them, this section will serve as a primer on these terms and concepts.

Security concerns associated with cyber technology (which includes the hardware components of a computer, the software modules that run on it, and the people who operate and use it) revolve around adversary manipulations of the technology that cause it to act in a way that results in a loss of confidentiality, integrity, and availability of the information and/or services or capabilities that the technology affords.[9] (Note that "information" includes both data processed or handled by the computer and programs or applications that run on the computer.)

- Confidentiality. A secure system will keep protected information away from those who should not have access to it. Examples of failures that affect confidentiality include data breaches that improperly reveal sensitive personal information of people with electronic medical records or credit files or classified war plans and the loss of intellectual property such as confidential technical documents from businesses or the manufacturers of key weapons systems.

- Integrity. A secure system produces the same results or information whether or not the system has been attacked. When integrity is violated, the system may continue to operate, but under some circumstances of operation, it does not provide accurate results or information that one would normally expect. The alteration of data in a database, the insertion of a virus into a document file that is subsequently opened, or a "poisoned" website that infects all visitors to it could have this effect.
- Availability. A secure system is available for normal use even in the face of an attack. A loss of availability may mean that an important e-mail message does not get through, or the computer freezes, or its response time becomes intolerably long (possibly leading to catastrophe if a physical process is being controlled by the system).

The targeted computer or network may not be the ultimate target of interest to the attacker—it may merely be a means to an end. The ultimate target may be the radar system connected to the computer, or the wing surfaces on the airplane that the computer controls, or even the human operator of the nuclear platform looking at a computer display.

In most cases, a party intent on compromising any of these attributes—that is, a party intent on conducting a cyberattack—needs to establish access to the computer system in question and then to exploit a vulnerability in the system that allows the delivery of a payload to cause the desired effect.

- Access may be remote (e.g., through the Internet, through a dial-up modem attached to the computer, through penetration of the wireless network to which the computer is connected, or through the radio receiver on the satellite). Alternatively, access may require close physical proximity (e.g., trusted insiders who have been bribed or blackmailed or persuaded to violate that trust; spies acting or serving as operators, service technicians, or vendors). Close access is a possibility anywhere in the supply chain (e.g., during chip fabrication, assembly, or loading of system software, during shipping to the customer, during operation).[10]

- A vulnerability is a design or implementation flaw in the computer that is accidentally or unknowingly introduced or is deliberately introduced (i.e., implanted by the adversary somewhere in the supply chain). An unintentionally introduced flaw ("bug") may open the door for opportunistic use of the vulnerability by an adversary. Vulnerabilities may be present in or introduced into applications or system software; hardware (e.g., microprocessors, graphics boards, power supplies, peripherals, storage devices, network cards); communications channels (e.g., fiber-optic cables or Wi-Fi broadcasts); and configurations (e.g., pathways for communication between a computer and the outside world improperly left open, weak passwords allowed, insufficient bandwidth on communications channels).

- The payload determines the scope and nature of the attack's effect after access has been used to take advantage of a vulnerability. For example, once a software agent (such as a virus) has entered a computer, its payload can be programmed to compromise information in the computer for many purposes—reproducing and retransmitting itself, destroying files on the system, altering files, changing program code and so on. In general, the payload can be programmed for attack (i.e., an action that degrades, disrupts, destroys, or denies system/network capabilities or information therein) or for the usually surreptitious exfiltration (theft) of confidential information, also known as espionage or intelligence gathering. (Exfiltration is similar but not identical to theft. Theft is meaningful with tangible objects—that which I steal from you becomes available to me but unavailable to you. But when intangible information is at stake, that which I exfiltrate from you is still available to you.) Also, in some cases, the payload is for all practical purposes the actions of a human being at a keyboard who has gained access (usually remote) to the system being attacked.

The packaging together of an access mechanism, a method for taking advantage of a vulnerability, and a payload that does what the attacker wants done yields what might be called an offensive cyber weapon—a technological artifact that can be used, perhaps with human intervention, to compromise the confidentiality, integrity, and/or availability of information. Note that describing this package as an offensive cyber weapon is *not* a statement about the intent behind using it—nearly all weapons can be used for defensive as well as offensive purposes. The term "offensive" is used here to indicate the damaging or compromising *effect* that the weapon can inflict, rather than the intent with which it is used.

It is also important to note that it is *people* who interact with information technology, and sometimes trusted insiders go rogue. Two examples are the leaks of classified information associated with Edward Snowden and Chelsea Manning. Both Snowden and Manning circumvented the cybersecurity measures intended to protect such information by abusing their access privileges, thereby obtaining classified information that they subsequently released to the public.[11] In some cases, it may be easier to trick, bribe, blackmail, or otherwise persuade an insider into doing the bidding of a hostile party than it is to develop an entirely technology-based attack. Such operations are often referred to as "social engineering." For example, close access to a system may be obtained by bribing a janitor to insert a USB flash drive into a computer. A vulnerability may be installed by blackmailing a programmer into writing defective code. In such cases, technical tools and people-based techniques can be combined.

In one social-engineering experiment, a hacker team scattered USB drives in parking lots, smoking areas, and other areas of high traffic. If one of these drives was inserted into a computer, a harmless "report-back" program on the USB drive would run, notifying the hacker team. The result was that 75 percent of the USB drives distributed did in fact report back, and the program might not, of course, have been harmless.[12]

Security and reliability issues for cyber-physical systems are considerably different and may be more complex than for the ordinary information technologies with which most lay people are familiar. Cyber-physical systems (which include but are not limited to devices on the so-called Internet of Things) are networked systems with sensors, processors, and actuators that sense and interact with the physical world and with human users. These systems operate in real time, which means their operations are tied to external events in the physical world. In automobiles, cyber-physical systems control engine, braking, and steering functions. In airplanes, they control engine thrust, control surfaces such as rudders and wing flaps, and weapons systems. In satellites, they control orientation and position in orbit, using thrusters. In radar systems, they control beam direction and process the return signal. Computing, control, sensing, and communications are integrated into every component of a system, and into every system that is part of a larger system of systems.

Some of the most important characteristics that distinguish cyber-physical systems from ordinary technologies include the following:

- Higher requirements for availability. Whereas most business information technologies may go down from time to time, and rebooting is generally a minor inconvenience, a cyber-physical system controlling important physical processes must be always available when needed; for example, rebooting a flight-control computer during an aerial maneuver is generally not a safe procedure. Thus, outages may have to be planned with significant lead times to ensure that unavailability does not compromise mission performance.
- Time-criticality of the responses of cyber-physical systems. Not only must their responses be the correct ones, they must also occur on the right timetable; this process is made more complex because cyber-physical systems often involve multiple devices demanding attention at the same time.
- Major risk impact of failures. For business information technology, the major risk is the failure of business operations; the risk impact for cyber-physical systems can be major system failure with physical consequences resulting in death and destruction of property.
- Security focus. Security for business information technologies focuses on the protection of the computing and communications technology assets and the information stored on or transmitted among these assets. The security focus of cyber-physical systems is the protection of the systems within which they are embedded.

- Available computing resources. Business information technology as
  deployed in practice generally has enough resources to support the
  addition of third-party security solutions, whereas cyber-physical systems are often deployed with just enough resources to perform their
  assigned tasks and generally do not have the capacity for activities such
  as anomaly detection or virus scanning.

One illustration of a cyber attack on the cyber-physical systems in a car
was related by a *WIRED* reporter in 2015.[13] The reporter volunteered to
be the driver of a Jeep Cherokee that two hackers knew how to manipulate
without a physical connection to the car. While he was driving, the air
conditioning came on at the maximum setting. The radio started playing at full volume, and failed to respond to attempts to turn it off. The
windshield wipers turned on and wiper fluid sprayed onto the windshield.
Then the hackers manipulated the transmission, causing the car to slow
to a crawl. Later, they were able to disable the brakes. Hackers can kill a
car's engine, abruptly engage the brakes, or disable them altogether. Under
some circumstances, they can control the steering.

What defenses are available against the threats described above?
"Defense" implies a protection against a problem caused by a malicious
party. Thus, a precondition for thinking about defense at all is determining whether a problem actually exists—that is, whether something "bad"
has happened to a computer system or network or cyber-physical system. "Badness" involves the computer or system behaving in a way that
it should not do. Examples abound: the computer freezes; commands
given to the computer do not have the expected result; the printer spews
out paper with gibberish. More serious examples of badness include: a
fly-by-wire airplane does not turn when the pilot turns the joystick; a
computer-controlled missile misses a target it should have hit; a radar
system fails to detect a target that the operator knows is present.

After recognizing bad behavior on the part of the system, the next step
is to determine its cause. It may be that the bad behavior was the result of
bad inputs into the system. If the missile misses its target or the airplane
does not turn when the pilot turns the joystick, it is possible that a human

operator aimed the missile at a shadow or the pilot turned the stick the wrong way, thinking he had turned it correctly. It is also possible that the bad behavior was the result of a flaw in the program introduced by accident rather than intentionally, so that even given the correct inputs, the computer generated the wrong result.

Security concerns arise when the bad behavior has been determined not to be the result of operator error and also not the result of an accidentally introduced flaw—ruling out those possibilities leaves only foul play as a possible explanation. A variety of technological tools and people-based techniques can be used to mitigate foul play in cyberspace (i.e., cyber threats). Some tools (e.g., firewalls) close off routes of access before an adversary can use them—often such routes are inadvertently left open. Other tools identify programming errors (vulnerabilities) that can be fixed before a hostile party can use them. For example, some relatively small software programs can be proven mathematically to conform to their requirements; if the requirements are correct (a big if!), such programs are known to be free of vulnerabilities. (On the other hand, large systems are not yet similarly verifiable.) Still others serve to prevent a hostile party from doing bad things with any given payload (e.g., a confidential file may be encrypted so that even if a copy is removed from the system, it is useless to the hostile party).

Defensive people-based techniques essentially involve inducing people not to behave in ways that compromise security—a part of which is commonly known as practicing good cyber hygiene. Good cyber hygiene includes practices such as an appropriate policy regarding the composition of passwords, installing software updates regularly, backing up data consistently and frequently, and limiting user privileges to the minimum necessary for doing the job. Education teaches (some) people not to fall for scams that are intended to obtain log-in names and passwords. Audits of activity persuade (some) people not to use computers in ways that are suspicious or not authorized. Rewards for reporting persuade (some) people to report questionable or suspicious activity to the proper authorities.

The effectiveness of the defensive tools and techniques described above is drastically reduced when access paths and vulnerabilities are unknown to the defender. Also, modern computer systems are so complex that it is essentially impossible for a defender to know every possible access path and/or vulnerability. It is for these reasons that given the time and resources to attack and the luxury of setting the timetable for attack, the cyber attacker generally has the advantage over the cyber defender, at least as the defender sees the situation.

Absent evidence to the contrary, the cyber defender must presume that the attacker has been able to realize all of the attacker's possible advantages. A defender cannot be justifiably confident that an attacker will not try X even though the attacker may be unsure that X will work. Indeed, a defender who was confident that an attacker will not try X (and let the world know about its confidence) would in effect be inviting the attacker to try X. The cyber defender has to succeed 100 percent of the time in warding off attacks, whereas an attacker can try many times unsuccessfully and need succeed only once in penetrating the system of interest. Defenders must thus assume that their systems have been penetrated for a long time, that the adversary has identified important vulnerabilities, and that the adversary may use offensive cyber capabilities to achieve goals known with certainty only to the adversary.

On the other hand, many of the advantages of the attacker are present only when the attacker can control the timing of the attack, and from the attacker's point of view, cyber attacks are often fraught with uncertainty.[14] An attacker with control over an attack's timetable (including deciding when, if at all, to launch an attack) has all the time necessary to obtain the information (especially intelligence information) needed to mount an attack that reliably serves his purposes. But if the timetable for a cyber attack is determined by external events (e.g., the cyber attack must disable the air defense radar *before* the bombers get within detection range), success is harder to achieve. If the cyber attack does not achieve its effects on time, it may effectively be useless.

Would-be cyber attackers must also cope with necessary intelligence that is inherently fragile and often ephemeral. Have the operators of the target system installed a system patch that renders a particular cyber weapon useless? Have they discovered an access path previously implanted by would-be attackers and taken measures to neutralize it, perhaps even denying the attacker the knowledge that it has been neutralized? Is the cyber attacker unknowingly caught in a decoy system that looks like the real thing but in fact is not connected to anything of consequence? How long will it take for the operators of the targeted system to recover from an attack? Having only limited time to answer these questions satisfactorily may mean the would-be cyber attacker will not attack in the first place.

Offensive operations in cyberspace also rely on operational preparation of the cyber battlefield. Operational preparation refers to actions not resulting in immediate harm and taken before hostilities actually start. An analogy in non-cyber conflict is the digging of a tunnel across a border. While no actual harm has been done until enemy forces come through the tunnel, the digging of the tunnel is a distinctly unfriendly act, and no one believes that the tunnel has been dug to enable a parade of children carrying flowers to emerge on the other side of the border.

Operational preparation of the cyber battlefield means that the attacker ensures access to the targeted computer or network is available before launching an attack. For example, before launching an attack, an attacker could penetrate the target computer to set up a new account with high-level privileges that would allow the attacker to do many hostile things on that computer, without actually doing any of those hostile things. At the time of the attack (which may be months later), the attacker then simply logs in to the target computer on the new account and strikes.

For a cyber attack to happen today against a given target, intelligence must usually have been gathered and access prepared in advance. And because access must be established and vulnerability discovered in advance of when a cyber target might be attacked, both access and vulnerabilities are often fragile, that is, easily lost when a password is changed or a system update installed. For example, during the several months after installation of the account, the defender may have noticed it and deleted it or changed the password or reset the privilege level, any of which could well stymie the attacker. In one instance known to me, the fragility is that two people in the targeted organization must not have a certain conversation with each other. If they were to have that conversation and then take action based on it, the cyber attack capability currently possessed by the attacker would vanish.

The requirement for high-quality intelligence also emerges from the difference between kinetic weapons and cyber weapons. Unlike kinetic weapons, whose lethality can be estimated on the basis of a few physical parameters of the target and the weapon, an offensive cyber capability can be negated by small changes in the target's software or configuration. In other words, intelligence about cyber target vulnerabilities is often much more fragile and perishable than for the kinetic weapons.

A particularly important question is how and to what extent the cyber attacker is able to assess the damage from a cyber attack. Whereas an air defense radar destroyed by an anti-radiation missile (i.e., a missile that homes in on a radar) is shown by a photograph of wreckage at the radar's last known location, a successful cyber attack turns off the radar, a state that is in certain important ways indistinguishable from the operator shutting the radar off for maintenance. The attacker must decide whether it is not emitting because (a) the attack was successful or (b) because the commander detected the cyber attack and shut down the radar to trick the attacker into believing the attack was successful, but can turn it back on at will.

Real-time control over a cyber weapon may well be difficult or impossible because of air gaps, as might be present in, for example, a submarine at sea. Thus, instead of a skilled cyber weapon operator being able to react to unanticipated conditions that the weapon may encounter in executing its cyber payload, the developers of the weapon must anticipate the conditions that the weapon will encounter and program the weapon accordingly. This requirement greatly increases the complexity of the weapon and increases the likelihood that it may fail or be detected before it is put into use.

Lastly, for national security purposes, it is usually important to be able to determine the party ultimately responsible for a cyber attack, and again defenders and attackers have different perspectives. Attribution is the process by which it is determined who or what is responsible for the intrusion.[15]

Attribution is in part technical—the association of an attack with a responsible party through technical means based on information made available by the fact of the cyber attack itself, namely, technical clues available at the scene (or scenes) of the attack. However, in practice, attribution is almost never an entirely technical affair. Intelligence analysts integrate information from all sources, not just technical sources monitoring the attacked system, to arrive at a judgment (rather than a definitive and certain proof) concerning the identity of the attacker. These other sources of information include intelligence (e.g., informants or monitored communications); technical information about other attacks or details of the scale and nature of the attack in question; and temporal proximity to other factors, such as ongoing hostilities.

In general, attribution is a complex process, and it may well take a long time to arrive at an actionable (if not definitive) judgment. Nevertheless, while attribution of cyber attacks cannot be assured in all cases, attribution is not as hopeless as often portrayed. The attacker cannot be certain of remaining anonymous, and the defender cannot be certain of being able to unmask the attacker.

On U.S. nuclear strategy, operations, and systems

This section reviews some of the basic elements of U.S. nuclear strategy, operations, and systems. As with the prior section, readers new to this terminology and thinking can draw on this section as a primer, while those already familiar with the field can take this section as a reminder of the concepts that will be used throughout the book.

The stated policy of the United States regarding the use of nuclear weapons is that it would use them only in extreme circumstances to defend its vital interests and those of its allies.[16] Nevertheless, the policy also stipulates that nuclear weapons play a critical role in deterring nuclear and nonnuclear attack against the United States, its allies, and its partners, and in limiting the damage that would ensue should deterrence fail by ending conflict at the lowest level of damage possible and on the best achievable terms.

Deterrence refers to the practice of dissuading an adversary from taking certain undesirable actions, the ultimate of which would be launching a nuclear attack.[17] Analysts typically distinguish between deterrence by denial and deterrence by punishment.

- Strategies for deterrence by denial focus on making an adversary believe it is too costly or uncertain to achieve whatever objectives it might have in mind, thus inducing the adversary to refrain from the undesirable adversarial action in the first place.
- Strategies for deterrence by punishment focus on making an adversary believe that the penalties that it will suffer outweigh any benefits it might reap, again inducing the adversary to refrain from taking action. Strategies for deterrence by punishment may fail if the adversary believes that the victim will not or cannot follow through on the threatened punishment.

To support the requirements of deterrence, the United States deploys its nuclear forces. Taken as a whole, U.S. policy as stated in the 2018 *Nuclear Posture Review* indicates that these forces must be:

- Survivable. A substantial portion of the nuclear force should be able to survive any potential adversary attack and endure throughout crises and conflict.
- Forward deployable. Some U.S. nuclear forces should be capable of operating on allied or partner territory, in large part to be able to demonstrate to allies and partners U.S. willingness to come to their defense.
- Flexibly usable. U.S. nuclear forces should be able to provide diverse and graduated options (e.g., with varying yields, weapon types, delivery methods, trajectories, and ranges) to effective tailoring of actions across a range of adversaries and contingencies.
- Accurate. U.S. nuclear forces should have the precision needed to hold adversary assets at risk while minimizing unintended effects.
- Penetrating. U.S. nuclear forces should be able to achieve military objectives with high confidence despite the presence and/or operation of adversary defenses.
- Responsive. U.S. nuclear forces should be deployable and employable as promptly as necessary to pose credible threats.

- Visible. U.S. nuclear forces should be able to display national will and capabilities as desired for signaling purposes throughout crisis and conflict.

- Retargetable. U.S. nuclear forces should be rapidly retargetable in a manner that supports adaptive planning and effective employment.

For a force with these overall characteristics, U.S. nuclear forces will for the foreseeable future maintain a triad of strategic nuclear forces— land-based ICBMs (intercontinental ballistic missiles), submarine-based SLBMs (submarine-launched ballistic missiles) carried by nuclear-powered submarines, and an airbreathing force of bombers armed with gravity bombs and cruise missiles—as well as dual-capable aircraft associated with NATO. (An "airbreathing" vehicle is the term of art for an airborne vehicle powered by one or more jet engines.) Weaving these capabilities together is an extensive system for nuclear command, control, and communications (NC3).

The ICBM force consists of 400 single-warhead Minuteman III ICBMs deployed in hardened underground silos in a number of states. These missiles can be launched within a few minutes of receiving a properly authorized order because they are connected to higher authority by a variety of both wired and wireless communications channels. In their silos, they are also highly survivable against any attack except a large-scale nuclear attack. But since they can be launched within a few minutes, it is also possible to launch them while adversary missiles are en route, thereby ensuring their survival (and use)—that is, they can be launched once U.S. command authorities receive warning of an attack on them.

The SLBM force consists of up to 240 Trident D-5 missiles deployed aboard fourteen Ohio-class submarines (SSBNs, nuclear-powered submarines carrying nuclear-armed ballistic missiles)—as of September 1, 2019, the number of deployed SLBMs was 220.[18] Each SSBN has twenty tubes capable of carrying a single SLBM, and two to four SSBNs are in dry dock at any given time.[19] Each SLBM is capable of carrying up to 8 nuclear warheads, although at present each carries an average of 4.2 warheads to conform to limits imposed by the New START agreement,[20] which limits deployments of ballistic missiles and bombers for the United States and Russia. Also, for at least one deployed SLBM, the warhead loading includes a low-yield nuclear weapon as of February 4, 2020.[21]

When SSBNs are on patrol at sea, they constitute the most survivable portion of U.S. nuclear forces, inasmuch as they are virtually undetectable at present. (When in port, they are highly vulnerable.) The performance characteristics (range, accuracy, speed, penetrativity) of Trident D-5 missiles are roughly similar to those of the Minuteman III missiles, but because they can be fired from SSBN patrol areas in the Atlantic and Pacific oceans, they can attack Eurasian targets from east and west. As for responsiveness, one public report indicates that SLBMs can be launched after receipt of a launch order nearly as fast as ICBMs—15 minutes for SLBMs, 5 for ICBMs.[22] A 1992 report from the General Accounting Office (GAO—now known as the Government Accountability Office) is consistent—based on an analysis of test and operational SSBN patrol data, the GAO concluded that "the speed and reliability of day-to-day communications to submerged, deployed SSBNs were far better than widely believed, and about the equal of speed and reliability of communications to ICBM silos. Contrary to conventional wisdom, SSBNs are in essentially constant communication with national command authorities and, depending on the scenario, SLBMs from SSBNs would be almost as prompt as ICBMs in hitting enemy targets."[23] Fourteen years later, a senior official at U.S. Strategic Command noted that a conventionally armed Trident missile launched from a submarine would "provide America the ability to defeat a diverse set of threats *on short notice* [emphasis added]."[24] Thirty years after the GAO conclusion, it is unlikely that the reliability of communications to the SSBNs has gone down, at least under peacetime conditions.

The airbreathing strategic nuclear force consists of 46 nuclear capable B-52H and 20 nuclear capable B-2A "stealth" strategic bombers. In addition, the United States fields a number of U.S. dual-capable F-15E fighter-bombers on behalf of NATO for the delivery of non-strategic nuclear weapons, with about 200 deployed.[25] Both are supported by a fleet of tankers for inflight refueling, and thus their range is limited only by crew performance and needs (and of course the availability of tankers). Strategic bombers on alert can survive pre-emptive attack through their ability to take off upon receipt of initial warning that a missile attack might be starting, but unlike missiles, they can be recalled after takeoff.

Bomber flight time from takeoff to target (or to cruise missile launch) is measured in hours rather than minutes. Bombers can also be redirected after takeoff to attack targets other than those on their target list on takeoff. Bombers can be targeted by adversary air defenses as they penetrate to their targets; if they carry cruise missiles instead, the bombers can stay out of range of adversary air defenses. Nuclear cruise missiles are not designed today to be retargeted after being launched, but they are more survivable than bombers against adversary air defenses.

To support nuclear decision-making and communicate those decisions to the nuclear forces in the field for operational execution, the United States also fields an extensive system for nuclear command and control. The uniformed military distinguishes between nuclear command and control and nuclear command, control, and communications (NC3). Nuclear command and control refers to "the exercise of authority and direction by the President to command and control United States (US) military nuclear weapons."[26] By contrast, NC3 provides the means through which such authority and direction are executed, and consists of an integrated system made up of facilities, equipment, communications, procedures, and personnel. This book uses the term "NC3 infrastructure" or "NC3 system" interchangeably.

The nuclear command, control, and communications (NC3) system is constructed to perform a variety of day-to-day or ongoing functions and, when necessary, a number of episodic functions. The day-to-day functions of NC3 are:

- Force management: monitoring the condition and availability of U.S. nuclear forces. Which nuclear weapons platforms are available for use today? Where are they located? How long would they take to strike designated targets? How long will it take to bring systems in maintenance to operational readiness?

- Nuclear planning: developing, modifying, and updating of new and pre-existing nuclear plans. What targets should be attacked? When should they be attacked? How should attacks be coordinated with other related military activities? What forces should be moved where?
- Situation monitoring: gathering and understanding information on the status of friendly forces, adversary forces and possible targets, emerging nuclear powers, and worldwide events of interest. Where are adversary forces located? What are they doing now? What does intelligence say about adversary intentions? What military or other actions by allies, adversaries, and third parties that might affect nuclear strike plans are under way?

Episodic functions become necessary only when circumstances warrant. The two basic episodic functions of NC3 are:

- Decision-making: assessing and reviewing available information and consulting with appropriate parties when the employment or movement of nuclear weapons may be contemplated.
- Force direction: directing U.S. forces and personnel to implement decisions regarding the use or movement of nuclear weapons.

These five functions are described in greater detail in chapter 3 ("The U.S. Nuclear Enterprise") below.

The NC3 infrastructure needed to support these functions consists of as many as 160 different systems: satellites, aircraft, command posts, communication networks, land stations, radio receivers, and so on,[27] for about 75 percent of which the U.S. Air Force has responsibility.[28] These elements include:

- Infrared satellites that look for the hot flare of missile launches, providing initial indications of missile launches and a rough idea of their ultimate flight profile. These satellites can also provide warning of many tactical ballistic missile launches all over the world.
- Ground-based early-warning radars that look northward for signs of ICBM warheads launched from the Eurasian land mass and towards the oceans east and west for signs of SLBM warheads.

- A much larger number of air surveillance radars constituting the Joint Surveillance System that scan for aircraft and cruise missiles. These radars are located on the periphery of the United States and are operated jointly by the Federal Aviation Administration and the Department of Defense.
- Nuclear detonation detection capabilities, space-based and possibly ground-based as well, that can identify and geo-locate above-ground nuclear explosions.
- Fixed command centers and facilities for data analysis to interpret sensor information include the National Military Command Center (NMCC) at the Pentagon, the Alternate NMCC at Raven Rock in Pennsylvania, the Global Operations Center of U.S. Strategic Command at Offutt Air Force Base (AFB) in Nebraska, the North American Aerospace Defense Command (NORAD) at Petersen AFB and Cheyenne Mountain in Colorado. Command centers also formulate and transmit operational orders to nuclear forces in the field.
- Mobile command centers include the E-4B National Airborne Operations Center (NAOC), and the E-6B TACAMO ("Take Charge and Move Out") Airborne Command Post. The latter also has a communications role and can transmit launch orders to the triad of U.S. nuclear forces. U.S. Northern Command also operates a semi-trailer-based Mobile Consolidated Command Center.
- Communications facilities, space-based and ground-based (both wireless and wired), that connect civilian leadership to U.S. military forces and others. Terrestrial wired systems include non-secure "plain old telephone services" that are commercially purchased; leased lines equipped for secure communications; and undersea cables.

Wireless systems include space-based systems on commercial and dedicated military satellites as well as land-based communications, both fixed and mobile. These systems operate over a wide range of frequencies in the electromagnetic spectrum. Although information can be carried over electromagnetic radiation of any frequency, nearly all wireless communications in use today occupy the radio and microwave portions of the spectrum. Each frequency has characteristics that make it more or less suitable for different physical environments. For example, some frequencies are better suited for use in a nuclear environment, that is, an atmosphere in which nuclear weapons have been detonated in various places. Some propagate over very long range (around the world). Some are better at penetrating water—a necessity for communicating with submarines. Some offer higher bandwidth. Over a number of decades, the U.S. armed forces (primarily the Navy and Air Force) have developed communications systems to take advantage of different frequencies for different purposes.[29] Mobile weapons platforms such as airplanes, cruise missiles, submarines, and land-mobile missiles (of which the United States has none) obviously require wireless communications to receive instructions from higher authority. Satellites also make use of wireless communications, both to transmit and receive information useful to users on the ground and to control their operation.

Wired systems have a much larger data-carrying capacity than wireless systems, and it is widely believed that they better ensure reliable connectivity, at least under some conditions short of ongoing nuclear war, notwithstanding the 1992 GAO report cited above. Wired systems also present greater difficulties for cyber attackers, since they must gain physical access to some part of the wired system to effect an attack (unlike when attacking a wireless system). On the other hand, wired systems are at fixed locations and so their endpoints are subject to physical attack, and the wires (cables, intermediate relay stations, and the like) can be disrupted or destroyed.

At the apex of the NC3 system is the president of the United States, who has the sole authority to direct the use of nuclear weapons. A substantial portion of the NC3 system is focused on presidential needs, such as the president's survival and the ability of the president to obtain advice and exercise command and control over the nuclear forces under the most adverse circumstances from wherever he or she might be.

A Roadmap to the Rest of This Book

Chapter 2 briefly identifies several important aspects of the cyber-nuclear connection. It begins by noting the high dependence of the U.S. nuclear enterprise on information technology. It then describes several prominent cyber incidents in the past decade or so that have drawn attention to cybersecurity as a national security issue, and discusses some of the most notable non-government reports on the cyber-nuclear connection. Most of these reports have focused on cyber risk to nuclear command and control, but as this book will demonstrate, cyber risk potentially affects all aspects of the nuclear enterprise.

Chapter 3 applies a cybersecurity lens to the various elements of the U.S. nuclear enterprise—the nuclear weapons complex that is responsible for various aspects of U.S. nuclear weapons; the nuclear delivery systems and platforms responsible for carrying weapons to targets; and the nuclear command, control, and communications system needed to operationalize orders from U.S. nuclear command authorities to the forces in the field. The next section of this chapter considers briefly the relevance of cyber considerations to other nuclear powers. Then, cyber risks to the U.S. nuclear modernization program are addressed. Chapter 3 concludes with a high-level accounting of DoD responses to cybersecurity challenges in the nuclear enterprise. The Department of Defense has not ignored these cybersecurity challenges, and it has a variety of cybersecurity activities under way.

Chapter 4 reviews certain critical aspects of cybersecurity that are often underappreciated outside (and even inside) the technical community but are particularly relevant to the nuclear enterprise. The first section notes that increasing functionality of a system generally leads to increased complexity, and increased system complexity generally leads to a weaker cybersecurity posture. A second section addresses the point that, all else being equal, attention paid to improving cybersecurity and resilience will have a negative impact on the schedule for project development, especially in an environment of changing performance requirements. The next section notes that cybersecurity measures almost always lead to lower ease of use and reduce operational efficiency. The last section characterizes

Table 1.1. Summary of Observations and Imperatives

Observation	Imperative(s)
Observation 1: Vulnerabilities of the U.S. nuclear enterprise to adversary cyber operations are not limited to technical attacks on NC3 components.	Efforts to enhance the cybersecurity posture of the U.S. nuclear enterprise must include all of its elements and address cybersecurity in both its acquisition and operational aspects.
Observation 2: Entanglement of conventional and nuclear functions in operational systems increases the risk of inadvertent nuclear escalation.	Designers of modernized computer-driven systems, whether NC3 or weapons platforms, should moderate their appetites for increased functionality in the face of strong and hard-to-resist temptations to add new functionality for users.
	The network infrastructure built to support conventional-nuclear integration should prioritize the needs of the nuclear enterprise first. A corollary of this imperative is that U.S. Strategic Command's hand in making NC3 acquisition decisions, and indeed in any decisions that relate to acquisition of dual-capable weapons systems and platforms, should be strengthened, preferably with the ability to allocate funding that supports its nuclear mission.
	Nuclear-armed nations should do what they can to minimize the possibility that attacks on conventional assets will be seen as attacks on nuclear assets.
Observation 3: Short timelines for decision-making increase cyber risk.	To reduce cyber risk, NC3 systems should be designed to give senior leaders more time to make decisions of high consequence.
Observation 4: The legacy NC3 system has not failed catastrophically since 1985.	System architects and designers should establish as a requirement for a modernized system that it should do what the legacy system would do if faced with the same operational scenarios.
Observation 5: The tension between keeping up with a rapidly changing threat environment and maintaining an adequate cybersecurity posture cannot be resolved—only managed.	Users (including those at the most senior levels with the authority to specify the requirements for functionality related to nuclear weapons and operations) and system architects and designers must be prepared to make trade-offs between measures to reduce cyber risk and performance requirements.
Observation 6: The cybersecurity posture across the U.S. nuclear enterprise is highly heterogeneous, with some elements having weaker cybersecurity than others.	Operators should be taking the precautions that would be necessary if they were operating on systems and networks known to be compromised by an adversary.

cybersecurity as a holistic, emergent property of a complex system, a point that is particularly relevant to an inevitably complex NC3 system.

To illustrate cyber risks more concretely, Chapter 5 presents a number of hypothetical scenarios describing how cyber risks might play out in a nuclear context. The last section of that chapter identifies a number of threads common to most of the scenarios.

Building on the discussions in Chapters 2–5, Chapter 6 presents six observations relevant to cyber risks and the nuclear enterprise and identifies a number of imperatives for overseers of the U.S. nuclear enterprise that follow from these observations. These are displayed in table 1.1.

Chapter 7 concludes with thoughts on moving forward relevant to a changing administration. It identifies inadvertent or accidental escalation resulting from differing interpretations of the intent behind cyber activities that are not intentionally conducted to adversely affect the nuclear enterprise as a cyber risk that must be mitigated in addition to the risks associated with deliberate cyber attacks on the nuclear enterprise. Additionally, the chapter points out that high-level policy attention to cybersecurity does not necessarily translate into improved cybersecurity practices on the ground. Paying attention to the observations and imperatives of chapter 6 would not ensure adequate cybersecurity for the nuclear enterprise, but ignoring them will guarantee its inadequacy.

It is also helpful to consider what this book does *not* cover. It does not delve very deeply into the question of whether U.S. cyber attacks on adversaries might have a similar impact on them. In other words, the question of whether U.S. offensive cyber operations before or during kinetic conflict would have an escalating or a de-escalating effect is beyond the scope of this book.[30]

In addition, the mere use of computers to increase the threat to U.S. nuclear capabilities is not generally regarded as a cyber attack per se, and therefore not of particular consideration for this book. For example, an adversary using computers to perform data analysis more rapidly or more comprehensively in ways that might damage U.S. nuclear capabilities is not a cyber attack, even though it might have a very negative effect.

Finally, this book does not address the impact of artificial intelligence on the nuclear enterprise in any but the most cursory of ways. This omission is conspicuous by its absence, but an extended discussion of that point is beyond the book's scope. However, because "AI" is such a broad label, it will help to mention more explicitly certain important topics that call for further examination in another document.

One such topic is the use of artificial intelligence in systems for information display and data analysis to support for presidential decision-making and senior leadership consultation. Here some of the important issues involve possibilities of overconfidence and over trust in AI-based systems and of extracting useful explanations from AI systems about the logic behind their inferences. A second topic is the possibility that some combination of AI and new sensor technology may shift today's advantage of "hiders" (strategic weapons platforms such as submarines and mobile missiles that are survivable because they are hard to find) over "finders" (intelligence, surveillance, and reconnaissance assets that can geo-locate adversary weapons platforms that are trying to hide) and thereby increase temptations for military planners to target strategic nuclear assets that were previously untargetable for all practical purposes.[31] A third topic is the idea that AI can contribute to solving problems related to scenarios with highly compressed timelines, including those in the nuclear environment.[32] Where AI goes regarding the nuclear enterprise, no one yet knows.

What we do know is that hackers pose a very real danger to the national security posture of the United States. Damage has already been done, sometimes on a vast scale, by canny adversaries penetrating critically important computer systems. An equivalent level of damage to the United States nuclear enterprise would be orders of magnitude more dangerous to our security. It is this book's intent to aid readers in anticipating and addressing cyber risks to the nuclear enterprise of the United States.

2
The Cyber-Nuclear Connection

Over the past three or four decades, information and communications technologies (aka digital technologies, computing and communications technologies, or cyber technologies—all terms used interchangeably in this book) have become increasingly important in every aspect of civilian and military life. While it is true that military forces have always used technology to communicate, information is increasingly the lifeblood of military organization and power, enabling commanders to direct appropriate amounts of force where and when needed. The effective use of information is also an optimizer for individual weapons systems, and thus these systems reach levels of performance that would otherwise be unattainable—faster, more accurate, more fuel-efficient, longer range, and so on. Logistics operations are greatly enhanced by the use of information and communications technologies, which enable just-in-time delivery of supplies, spare parts, and reserve equipment to reduce wasteful inventory in storage. Essential administrative functions from personnel management and payroll also depend on these technologies to operate efficiently.

At the same time, the very fact that the application of these technologies helps so much to improve the operation of U.S. military forces suggests that these technologies would be natural targets for adversaries who would seek to degrade the effectiveness of these forces. Increasing integration of these technologies in the civilian sector further enlarges the target set for adversaries bent on harming the United States, which in turn makes it easier for them to do so.

The U.S. nuclear enterprise—that is, the collection of its nuclear weapons, its nuclear delivery platforms and missiles, the nuclear command, control, and communications infrastructure that ties all of these components together in nuclear operations, and its operational plans and strategy for using nuclear weapons—is no exception to the trend of increasing dependence on information technology. In this book, the cyber-nuclear connection refers to the issues that arise when information technology is used in ways that affect nuclear operations, strategy, doctrine, and so on.

Cyber technology and the *Nuclear Posture Review*

In 1983, United Artists released *War Games*, a techno-thriller film whose protagonist David Lightman, a teenage hacker, discovers and accesses a top-secret military computer with the ability to run simulations of nuclear war between the Soviet Union and the United States and also to feed information from a simulation of a Soviet attack on the United States to the North American Air Defense Command (NORAD). NORAD interprets this information as real and begins preparation to retaliate against the Soviet Union. NORAD learns that the attack reports are false, and tries to cancel the retaliatory strike. However, the computer is further programmed to launch missiles by itself in the event of a confirmed attack, and it believes it has such confirmation. In the end, Armageddon is avoided when Lightman teaches the computer that nuclear war is like tic-tac-toe—it is a game with no winners, so the only way to win is not to start the game.

According to press accounts, President Ronald Reagan saw the film the day after it was released.[1] Shortly thereafter, he asked some of his national security staff if they had seen it; when they replied in the negative, he described the plot. He then asked John W. Vessey Jr., then chairman of the Joint Chiefs of Staff, "Could something like this really happen? Could someone break into our most sensitive computers?" A week later, Vessey told the president, "The problem is much worse than you think."

This 1983 encounter is the first widely known recognition in the U.S. government that adversarial cyber activities might have some impact on the nuclear domain. Fast forward thirty-five years to the 2018 Trump administration's *Nuclear Posture Review*, which stated that:

> The United States would only consider the employment of nuclear weapons in extreme circumstances to defend the vital interests of the United States, its allies, and partners. Extreme circumstances could include significant non-nuclear strategic attacks. Significant non-nuclear strategic attacks include, but are not limited to, attacks on the U.S., allied, or partner civilian population or infrastructure, and attacks on U.S. or allied nuclear forces, their command and control, or warning and attack assessment capabilities.[2]

The first sentence in the above paragraph was identical to that of the Obama *Nuclear Posture Review*, released in 2009.[3] The second sentence was new, and was widely interpreted to mean that cyber attacks could constitute significant nonnuclear strategic attacks. The third sentence suggested that attacks, including cyber attacks, on U.S. nuclear forces, nuclear command and control, or warning and attack assessment capabilities could be regarded as strategically significant.

Elaborating on this point, Christopher Ford, then-assistant secretary of state for international security and nonproliferation, wrote in October 2020:

> [I]t is possible that a future cyber attack could constitute a use of force or armed attack. So grave is the potential threat that is emerging, in fact, that in the name of deterring the worst such attacks, the U.S. Nuclear Posture Review of 2018 took pains to emphasize that we do not rule out even the possible use of *nuclear weapons* in response to a sufficiently "significant non-nuclear strategic attack"—a term that includes, but is not limited to, "attacks on the U.S., allied, or partner civilian

population or infrastructure, and attacks on U.S. or allied nuclear forces, their command and control, or warning and attack assessment capabilities." This is a critical new element in U.S. nuclear declaratory policy, and lest there be any confusion about whether a cyber attack could potentially constitute a "significant non-nuclear strategic attack," I can say with confidence that *it most certainly could* if it caused kinetic effects comparable to a significant attack through traditional means.[4]

Ford did not take note of the 2004 National Military Strategy from the Joint Chiefs of Staff, which stated explicitly that U.S. nuclear capabilities play an important role in deterring the use of "weapons of mass destruction or effect," including "cyber attacks on US commercial information systems or attacks against transportation networks" that have a "greater economic or psychological effect than a relatively small release of a lethal agent."[5] Thus, the proposal for possible first use of nuclear weapons in response to a devastating cyber attack is likely less of a departure from previous policy than it might seem.[6]

Nevertheless, the 2018 *Nuclear Posture Review* prompted a number of news reports in the mainstream media and defense trade press.[7] At bottom, the reason for such attention is simple—taken together, the three sentences above from the *Nuclear Posture Review* were apparently intended to indicate that the United States might contemplate a nuclear response to certain kinds of cyber attack, such as a cyber attack on U.S. nuclear command and control or early-warning/attack assessment capabilities.

That implication was understandably controversial (and is not addressed in this book), but lost in the noise was the key idea, now made explicit, that cyber attacks on U.S. nuclear forces and capabilities were, in fact, strategically significant. To underscore the point—it is critical to consider how cyber attacks of various kinds might affect the U.S. nuclear enterprise: its nuclear weapons, its nuclear delivery platforms and missiles, the nuclear command, control, and communications infrastructure that ties all of these components together in nuclear operations, and its operational plans and strategy for using nuclear weapons. Much of today's nuclear enterprise was designed and deployed decades ago, but issues related to cyber risk are likely to become increasingly important to all aspects of the U.S. nuclear enterprise.

Hacking National Security

A series of cyber incidents involving U.S. information technology systems have compromised U.S. national security interests to a considerable degree. These events demonstrate how widespread cyber vulnerabilities are, even in organizations that most people would expect to take cybersecurity very seriously. Extrapolating from the totality of these incidents how similar attacks on the U.S. nuclear enterprise might play out is sobering. This series includes:

Buckshot Yankee

In 2008, an intelligence agency of an undisclosed foreign country (suspected to be Russia) placed malicious computer code onto a flash drive that was inserted into a U.S. military laptop on a base in the Middle East. William L. Lynn III, then deputy secretary of defense, described what happened as a result as "the most significant breach of U.S. military computers ever." Writing in *Foreign Affairs*, Lynn described how the flash drive's malware "uploaded itself onto a network operated by the U.S. Central Command. That code spread undetected on both classified and unclassified systems, establishing what amounted to a digital beachhead, from which data could be transferred to servers under foreign control."[8] In response to this breach, the Pentagon launched Operation Buckshot Yankee, an operation to counter the attack and shore up the military's cyber defenses. One of the primary impacts of Buckshot Yankee was increased recognition among senior military and civilian officials of the need to bolster American cyber defenses. Within months, in June 2009, Secretary of Defense Robert Gates ordered the consolidation of the Pentagon's various cyber task forces into the new U.S. Cyber Command.[9]

The North Korea hack of Sony Pictures Entertainment

Sony Pictures Entertainment had scheduled the release of its film *The Interview* on Christmas Day 2014 in movie theaters across the United States. The film stars Seth Rogan and James Franco as journalists who plan to travel to North Korea to interview North Korean leader Kim Jong-un but then are recruited by the Central Intelligence Agency to assassinate Kim. Ahead of the film's release, the North Korean foreign ministry called it "the most blatant act of terrorism and war."[10] On November 24, 2014, hackers calling themselves "Guardians of Peace" (later publicly identified by the Federal Bureau of Investigation as agents of North Korea) hacked Sony Pictures, crippling many of its information systems, destroying data, and leaking many confidential communications, including embarrassing e-mails by studio executives. President Obama called the incident "cyber-vandalism" and said that the United States would "respond proportionally . . . in a place, time and manner of our choosing."[11] The Sony Pictures hack illustrated both how cyber operations could cause irreversible destruction to computer systems and was the first high-profile instance of a "hack and leak" operation by a foreign adversary, in which harm to the victim comes as much from the subsequent disclosure of hacked material as from the intrusion and destruction of information systems themselves.

The China hack of the Office of Personnel Management

In June 2014, the U.S. Office of Personnel Management (OPM) reported that it had fallen victim to two separate cyber incidents that resulted in the compromise and likely exfiltration of confidential personal information about, in the first instance, 4.2 million current and former federal employees, and in the second, 21.5 million individuals. Among the compromised data were fingerprint records and sensitive personal information gathered in the course of background investigations for security clearances. Many experts have attributed the OPM breach to China and believe it was conducted for espionage rather than identity theft or other criminal purposes. The Chinese government may be using the data for a database on U.S. government employees. Of possibly gravest concern was the potential for the hacked data to be used to identify U.S. clandestine intelligence officers, as well as to provide Chinese intelligence services with sensitive personal information that could be used to help them recruit Americans with access to government secrets to spy for China.[12]

Russian Interference in the 2016 and 2020 U.S. Elections

Starting about 2014 and continuing through the 2016 U.S. presidential election, various elements of the Russian state, including its military intelligence service (GRU) and Internet Research Agency (IRA), conducted operations to interfere with the U.S. elections. Perhaps most consequentially, the GRU hacked the e-mail accounts of prominent Democrats linked to the Democratic presidential nominee Hillary Clinton, including her campaign chairman John Podesta. In the several months before the election, the Russians used intermediaries such as Wikileaks to leak sensitive hacked information, some of which proved to be quite damaging to Clinton's campaign, especially as it was amplified by the press and on social media. There has been a great deal of reporting and analysis on the Russian interference in the 2016 election and its impacts on U.S. national security and democratic processes.[13]

Fewer details are publicly known regarding Russian interference in the 2020 election. In a report dated March 10, 2021,[14] the U.S. intelligence community expressed high confidence in its judgment that "Russian President Putin authorized, and a range of Russian government organizations conducted, influence operations aimed at denigrating President Biden's candidacy and the Democratic Party, supporting former President Trump, undermining public confidence in the electoral process, and exacerbating sociopolitical divisions in the US." In addition, "[a] key element of Moscow's strategy this election cycle was its use of proxies linked to Russian intelligence to push influence narratives-including misleading or unsubstantiated allegations against President Biden-to US media organizations, US officials, and prominent US individuals, including some close to former President Trump and his administration." A prime example of such narratives was one "alleging corrupt ties between President Biden, his family, and other US officials and Ukraine."

The Russian hack of SolarWinds

In 2020, a group suspected to be the hacking group "Cozy Bear" backed by Russia's foreign intelligence service (SVR) launched a campaign that breached thousands of computer systems globally by exploiting a vulnerability in the Orion platform of the U.S. software company SolarWinds, which provides network monitoring and management services. Users of Orion include Microsoft as well as U.S. government departments, including the Department of Treasury and the National Telecommunications and Information Administration within the Department of Commerce. SolarWinds has stated it believes 18,000 of their customers were susceptible to this attack.[15] Note that victims were not attacked individually by an adversary; instead, they all downloaded allegedly trustworthy software from their common supplier, SolarWinds, thus making this hack an example of a supply chain attack. In response the U.S. Cybersecurity and Infrastructure Security Agency ordered federal agencies to "remove SolarWinds products from agency networks."[16] While preliminary reporting indicates another significant breach of U.S. commercial and government computer systems by Russian intelligence services, the full scope and impact of the SolarWinds incident, and its long-term significance for U.S. national security, has yet to be determined. In April 2021, the Biden White House attributed the SolarWinds attack to Russia.[17]

Incidents such as those described above have understandably and reasonably given rise to concerns that U.S. defensive capabilities against adversary offensive capabilities in cyberspace are inadequate—and that these inadequacies may well reach into the nation's most important military systems, namely, those that carry the nuclear burden.

In addition to these incidents, in 2013 and in 2017, the Defense Science Board (DSB) issued two important reports specifically calling attention to the connection between adversary cyber operations and nuclear forces. In 2013, it pointed to the need to ensure the survivability of U.S. nuclear forces and their associated command and control against an all-out cyber attack from a technically sophisticated nation-state.[18] (On pages 22–23, the report defined an "all-out" cyber attack as one involving "state actors who create vulnerabilities through an active program to 'influence' commercial products and services during design, development or manufacturing, or with the ability to impact products while in the supply chain to enable exploitation of networks and systems of interest," and who in addition use "all of their military and intelligence capabilities . . . to achieve a specific outcome in political, military, economic, etc. domains.")

The report further stated that "the traditional U.S. nuclear deterrent incorporates survivability as a basic precept; now the U.S. must add survivability in the event of a catastrophic cyber attack on the country as a basic precept." It also noted that at that point in time, most elements of U.S. nuclear systems had not been assessed end-to-end against such an attack to understand possible weak spots.

Regarding conventional forces, the 2013 DSB report stated that "the accomplishment of U.S. military missions is critically dependent on networks and information systems. [Cyber] threats . . . may impose severe consequences for U.S. forces engaged in combat [such as]:

- Degradation or severing of communication links critical to the operation of U.S. forces, thereby denying the receipt of command directions and sensor data;
- Data manipulation or corruption may cause misdirected U.S. operations and lead to lack of trust of all information;
- Weapons and weapon systems may fail to operate as intended, to include operating in ways harmful to U.S. forces;
- Potential destruction of U.S. systems (e.g., crashing a plane, satellite, unmanned aerial vehicles, etc.)."

In 2017, the DSB repeated the point with greater emphasis, arguing that the cyber security and resilience of U.S. nuclear forces (especially nuclear command, control, and communications) is of comparable importance to that of the reliability and performance of U.S. nuclear weapons themselves as reflected in the annual nuclear stockpile assessment for the president and Congress.[19] Regarding cyber incidents of the sort described above, the 2017 DSB report noted that such incidents "do not represent the 'high end' threats that could be conducted by U.S. adversaries today," noting that "major powers (e.g., Russia and China) have . . . an increasing potential to also use cyber to thwart U.S. military responses to . . . attacks [on U.S. critical infrastructure]" and that they are both "able to cause disruptive attacks against the United States without resorting to highly advanced cyber tools." In short, "the United States will not be able to prevent large-scale and potentially catastrophic cyber attacks by Russia or China."

Cassandra Revisited: Previous Reports on the Cyber-Nuclear Connection

In Greek mythology, Cassandra was able to foretell the future but was doomed never to be believed. Beginning in 2017, a number of reports, papers, and books have sought to illuminate some of the connections between cyber technologies and nuclear weapons. What stands out in most of them is a concern about cyber vulnerabilities in nuclear command and control whose exploitation could unintentionally lead to nuclear war.

In 2017, the British-American Security Information Council released a report *Hacking UK Trident: A Growing Threat* pointing to the inadequacy of "air-gapping" as a prevention for penetrating the various computer systems on which Trident submarines of the United Kingdom rely for propulsion, navigation, weapons control, and so on.[20] ("Air-gapping" refers to the lack of a physical connection, whether wired or wireless, to the Internet or to other external networks.) This report accurately pointed out that a network that is air-gapped from other networks significantly reduces the threat of real-time external access by remote hackers. However, it does not prevent attacks originating from inside the submarine or the on-shore implantation of hostile software or hardware during manufacture, construction, and on-shore maintenance. In addition, the report notes that because ballistic missile submarines (SSBNs) do receive some radio communications from higher authority (how else would they know whether they should fire their missiles?), the implants already pre-positioned on board by an adversary could be triggered by some message received while at sea. A cyber attack could result in a disruption of submarine operations and the possibility that such disruption could interfere with the proper launch of missiles.

A book published in 2018 by Andrew Futter took note of the tension between civilian officials, who are in general more concerned about preventing unauthorized use of nuclear weapons and accidents and mistakes involving nuclear weapons, and military officers who are more concerned with threats that might prevent their use of nuclear weapons when they are properly ordered to use them.[21] Futter also raised the question of the circumstances, if any, under which a large-scale cyber attack by Nation A on Nation B's nuclear weapons arsenal would be regarded as equivalent to a surprise, decapitating nuclear first strike by A on B's weapons? (A "decapitating" attack is one that strikes at adversary leaders, usually in the hope that with their leaders dead or unable to communicate, adversary responses would be degraded, uncoordinated, and haphazard, and therefore less effective than they would otherwise be.) If so, such a conclusion could prompt the same kind of response as would an attack with nuclear weapons. Finally, Futter makes the point that modernization of weapons systems, nuclear or not, almost inevitably calls for the addition and integration of cyber technology (information and communications technology) into the basic weapons system—indeed, in some cases, it is only the integration of such technology that justifies modernization at all. New weapons systems may well be more vulnerable to cyber attack than older systems.

A 2018 report by the Nuclear Threat Initiative (NTI)[22] noted the possibility that the level of digitization of U.S. systems and the pace of the evolving cyber threat could lead to the compromise of nuclear weapons systems, and that such a compromise could have catastrophic consequences. Such consequences could increase the risk of use as a result of false warnings or miscalculation or the risk of unauthorized use of a nuclear weapon; they could also undermine confidence in the nuclear deterrent, affecting strategic stability. Most importantly, the NTI report noted that mitigation of cyber threats to U.S. nuclear forces could not rely solely on technical cybersecurity measures, but would also entail changes in U.S. nuclear policies and posture.

In 2019, Michael Klare took note of the reliance of U.S. NC3 systems on computers for virtually every aspect of their operations (e.g., early-warning radars, launch facilities, communications with the chain of command) and argued that attempts to penetrate and infiltrate NC3 presented new and potentially dangerous pathways to escalation.[23] Klare argues that both sides have incentives to use cyber weapons early in a great power crisis to achieve advantages, but cyber attacks on an adversary's NC3 could generate a "fog of war" in which the target state would fear the loss of its own arsenal and launch its weapons sooner rather than later. Penetration of NC3 could furthermore cause the target/victim to misconstrue the nature of an enemy attack: its leaders might not trust the information provided by computer systems in a crisis and overreact. Yet another escalation pathway could arise from a cascading series of cyber attacks and counterstrikes against national infrastructure (e.g., economic and financial systems, power grids, transportation networks) rather than military targets, which might provoke unintended or accidental escalation.

Another 2019 report, this time by Jon Lindsay, also focused on an increasingly digitized nuclear command, control, and communication (NC3) network that links warheads, delivery platforms, and early-warning satellites to political leaders and military commanders.[24] Lindsay argued that adversaries have incentives to penetrate NC3 for intelligence in peacetime and for counterforce in wartime, and further that most nuclear weapon states also have some technical ability to take advantage of vulnerabilities in NC3 systems. At the same time, he notes that the challenges associated with exploiting those vulnerabilities under actual operational and political conditions are nontrivial; not all nuclear rivalries will be destabilized to the same degree by cyber operations given asymmetric NC3 vulnerabilities, cyber capabilities, and expected consequences; and finally, that not all pathways to escalation are equally plausible or dangerous. His conclusion is more measured than Klare's—he concludes that cyber-NC3 interactions marginally raise the risk of nuclear war, thereby making highly unlikely events slightly more likely.

Also in 2019, David C. Gompert and Martin Libicki argued that advanced information technology has "arguably enhanced stability by making NC3 more resilient."[25] On the other hand, they point out, "conducting cyber operations against the NC3 of a major nuclear state, particularly one already concerned about a disarming nuclear or nonnuclear first strike, might cause it to adopt a hair-trigger launch policy, and could lead to nuclear war." They believe that it is incumbent on the United States to "take the lead in reconfiguring nuclear deterrence to withstand cyber war," arguing that the United States should propose understandings with Russia and China that NC3 is categorically off-limits for cyber operations against one another.

A 2020 paper by James Acton argues that cyber warfare exacerbates the risk of inadvertent nuclear escalation in a conventional conflict by adding three different and qualitatively new mechanisms that might induce a state to conclude mistakenly that its nuclear forces were under attack.[26] First, he argues that cyber espionage could be mistaken for a cyber attack. Second, he is concerned that malware (i.e., software designed to serve an adversary's interests) accidentally spreads from systems that support nonnuclear operations to nuclear-related systems. Finally, he notes that a cyber operation carried out by a third party could be misattributed by one state in a bilateral confrontation with its opponent.

Various components of the U.S. nuclear enterprise have been incrementally upgraded since the mid-1980s, and many of these upgrades have called for the use of cyber technologies to improve functionality, reliability, maintainability or some other important attribute of the components they were replacing. But the basic architecture of the nuclear enterprise and some of its components have not undergone significant change. However, in early 2021, the United States is embarking upon an ambitious nuclear modernization program for nearly all aspects of the nuclear enterprise—and nearly every aspect of the modernization effort will involve cyber technologies to a far greater degree than in the past.

3

The U.S. Nuclear Enterprise

Connected to even a single nuclear weapon is a vast array of people, things, policies, procedures, and plans, each of which are vulnerable in its own ways cyber to attack—from the top of the command chain down to the most seemingly insignificant bit of hardware. All of these elements must be considered if to understand what is potentially at stake if we fail to manage cyber risk properly.

This book uses the term "nuclear enterprise" to refer to the entire array of activities and operations that have some significant connection to any aspect of nuclear explosive devices (usually known as nuclear weapons), whether in production, acquisition, operations, organization, or strategy. The term is uncomfortably similar to the term "nuclear weapons enterprise," which many analysts use to refer to activities and operations associated specifically with the life cycle of the explosive devices themselves, as opposed to the platforms that carry them, or how they might be used, but no better term is available as of yet. Other analysts use the term "nuclear weapons complex" to mean the same thing, and this book adopts that term (nuclear weapons complex).

The nuclear weapons complex

Although the Department of Defense deploys and operates the nuclear arsenal and the NC3 infrastructure, the National Nuclear Security Administration (NNSA) of the Department of Energy (DoE) is responsible for the nuclear weapons themselves. Within NNSA, the Office of Defense Programs maintains and modernizes the nuclear stockpile through the Stockpile Stewardship and Management Program (SSMP).[1] This program is intended "to ensure the safety, security, and effectiveness of the U.S. nuclear weapons stockpile and to maintain the scientific and engineering tools, capabilities, and infrastructure that underpin the nuclear security enterprise," and according to the DoE, the nuclear security enterprise is "at its busiest since the demands of the Cold War era."[2]

Although the United States has not produced an entirely new nuclear explosive device for decades, the Fiscal Year (FY) 2020 SSMP includes many activities to maintain and improve the U.S. nuclear weapons stockpile, seeking to ensure that nuclear weapons in the arsenal are capable of fulfilling evolving requirements. The 2020 plan calls for the production of at least 80 plutonium pits per year by 2030; achieving the first production unit of the W80-4 warhead by FY 2025; delivering the first production unit of the B61-12 gravity bomb by 2022; and completing delivery of the W88 Alteration 370 warhead by 2024. Under the auspices of the FY 2019 plan, the DoE completed production of the W76-1 Life Extension Program, began work on the W76-2 low yield ballistic missile warhead, and restarted design activities for the W78 replacement warhead (the W87-1).[3]

Nuclear weapons are complex manufactured devices. As with other manufactured devices, the components of a nuclear weapon can degrade simply with the passage of time—anyone who has seen pipes rust understands that aging can render a manufactured artifact useless. A manufactured device may also include components of limited life that must be replaced every now and then if the device is to operate properly—an obvious component of a thermonuclear weapon is tritium, with a half-life of 12.3 years. Batteries also have limited lifetimes. Aging in nuclear weapons involves the additional complication of the radioactivity found in some of its components—over time, such radiation often has degrading and damaging effects on materials or components in the weapon. Periodic testing and analysis of the test results is the most common way to ensure continuing reliability of old devices. A test determines what has caused a failure, and corrective action can be taken to remediate that failure. But the United States has not tested nuclear weapons since 1992 (more precisely, it has conducted only subcritical tests that have resulted in zero nuclear yield).

A variety of laboratories do conduct nonnuclear testing and flight testing of nuclear weapons components as part of the SSMP. In addition, the basic physics underlying nuclear explosions is explored in facilities such as the National Ignition Facility and the Dual-Axis Radiographic Hydrodynamic Test facility. Computer simulations of nuclear explosive phenomena, combined with basic physics and data from past nuclear tests and data collected from nonnuclear testing today, are used to generate the scientific basis on which judgments and assessments about the existing nuclear stockpile can be made. Through this process, each nuclear weapon in the U.S. nuclear arsenal is assessed to determine its reliability and to detect and anticipate any potential issues that may result from aging.[4]

From time to time, problems are found that require remediation, such as the replacement or remanufacture of some component of equivalent function. Also, a new requirement may emerge, such as a safety requirement, that did not exist when the weapon was first manufactured. In such cases, modifications to the original design are necessary, and the modifications implemented physically. Regardless of the reason for a change in the weapon's physical construction, the effects of any such change must be ascertained, a process that also relies heavily on computer-based simulation.

Computer-based simulation is the process through which scientists seek to model accurately the performance of nuclear weapons of whatever age and their underlying physics and whatever changes have been made to their makeup since they were originally constructed. Given the extreme dependence of the SSMP on simulation, maintaining the security of the computer programs involved is an obvious requirement. Such security has always been necessary, but because of the inability to conduct nuclear testing, the relative importance of simulation has grown.

"Maintaining security" in this context mostly refers to two problems. First is the problem of maintaining the secrecy of the sensitive program codes and databases that underlie nuclear simulations. Since these computer programs and databases embed much of the technical expertise of the U.S. nuclear weapons community, such expertise in the hands of adversaries could lead to the emergence of a significant nuclear threat to the United States.

A second important problem is ensuring that no unauthorized or improper changes are made in the program codes or databases. Such changes could compromise the performance of simulations, rendering their output unreliable. But because the United States is also not conducting nuclear testing, the information derived from subtly corrupted computer simulations may give the scientists using that information a false sense of confidence in their judgments. On the other hand, if it became known that such changes had been improperly introduced (and that the changes could not be reversed with certainty), many scientists would be likely to have less confidence in their judgments about the nuclear weapons stockpile and might undertake remediation to solve problems that do not actually exist.

The aspect of maintaining the confidentiality and integrity of programs and databases most difficult to address is the insider threat—the concern that a trusted insider with all of the necessary clearances might go rogue and exfiltrate sensitive data or make unauthorized changes to them. Many safeguards are in place to defend against the insider threat, as well as other cybersecurity threats, which the laboratories take very seriously.

For example, imagine a specific code base that needs to be protected against unauthorized alteration but still needs to be updated from time to time with authorized changes. To ensure that all changes are authorized, one could establish a procedure in which a team of responsible scientists and engineers would vet proposed changes thoroughly. Once they were satisfied that a certain set of changes should be made, there would remain the problem of how to make those changes to the actual code base. One way to ensure that no unauthorized changes are made to the code base would be to charge several people with making approved changes to it and have each of them work separately and independently on their own copies of the code. Upon completion, the modified code bases would then be compared, and finding them identical would increase confidence that only the approved changes had been made. If they were not identical, all of the modified copies would be discarded and the procedure restarted. Whether this specific technique is used within the laboratories to help ensure the integrity of the code base is not publicly known—I have provided it as an illustration of a security measure that could be taken to this end.[5]

As noted earlier, concern about cybersecurity in the nuclear weapons complex was raised the SolarWinds incident, one of whose victims was the Department of Energy.[6] What the adversaries did after they gained such access is unknown at the time of this writing. However, the fact that NNSA is a component of the DoE raises the possibility that the compromised software might have enabled adversaries to access classified NNSA networks, including those that contain nuclear weapons information.

Responding to this concern, the DoE acknowledged the incident on December 18, 2020, but said that up to that point, the malware "has been isolated to business networks only, and has not impacted the mission essential national security functions of the Department, including the National Nuclear Security Administration (NNSA). When DoE identified vulnerable software, immediate action was taken to mitigate the risk, and all software identified as being vulnerable to this attack was disconnected."[7] Whether these reassurances should be taken at face value is unclear at this time, but it should be noted that hackers seeking to gain access to classified information have two distinct problems: penetrating the networks to gain access, and exfiltrating the desired information *out* of the penetrated networks. Conceptually, these are separate problems, and hackers have to solve both of them.

In December 2020, the online political magazine *Politico* reported that DoE had discovered an issue within the Office of Secure Transportation (OST), which is responsible for the secure transportation of nuclear weapons and materials.[8] Penetration of OST's classified networks could reveal sensitive information about the transportation of nuclear weapons or materials and provide valuable intelligence information that could assist parties wishing to hijack them or otherwise interfere with their transportation.

Another dependency of the SSMP on computing is that computer-controlled fabrication machinery is used to shape various components of nuclear weapons. For example, an essential component of plutonium-based nuclear weapons is the controlled detonation of nonnuclear explosives to compress plutonium to a critical mass that will lead to a nuclear explosion. However, in a nuclear weapons accident, conventional high explosives could detonate in an uncontrolled manner, scattering radioactive plutonium into the environment. Thus, to improve nuclear weapons safety, one SSMP activity examines the feasibility of using "insensitive" high explosives (IHE) in nuclear weapons that were originally fabricated using conventional high explosives. IHE is much harder to detonate than conventional high explosives, and the use of IHE would decrease the likelihood of an unwanted detonation in an accident.

But IHE has different properties than conventional high explosives (for example, how fast it burns, how much energy it contains, and so on). A basic element of controlled detonation is the shaping of the explosive, and new shapes must be determined and fabricated if IHE is to replace conventional explosives in a weapon. Determining the proper shapes is dependent on simulation. But the shapes must also be precisely machined to very tight tolerances, and so computer-controlled equipment must be used to form the IHE into the appropriate shapes.

Such equipment would not be connected directly to the Internet, but it must be possible to program them appropriately (by trusted employees), and the computers must access data from appropriate databases to fabricate components. Compromising these programs and/or data could cause the components to be fabricated in ways that are slightly out of specification. Such imperfections would likely be caught in subsequent inspection, but their deliberate introduction into the fabrication process would be a definite minus for quality control.

A last vector discussed in this book for cyber threats to nuclear weapons is the electronics they contain. For example, the triggering of a nuclear explosion requires a number of events to occur in a precisely timed sequence, and electronic mechanisms play a key role in orchestrating that sequence. The integrity of the supply chain—from the initial fabrication of these components to assembly and integration into the final weapon that enters the arsenal, along with any necessary programming—must thus be assured, because a vulnerability might be introduced at any point in this chain. Inspection and testing of the hardware and software could catch some such problems, but as compared to inspections that seek physical defects, finding flaws that an adversary could exploit is generally more problematic.

Nuclear delivery systems and platforms

Nuclear deterrence relies on the credibility of the threat to use nuclear weapons when they are called upon, and that credibility is grounded in the operational capability of delivery systems to place weapons on target. At present, airplanes and missiles (both ballistic and cruise missiles today, perhaps hypersonic boost-glide vehicles or airbreathing missiles in the future) are the delivery systems used for nuclear weapons. Moreover, missiles themselves may be carried on platforms such as submarines or bombers.

Airplanes, submarines, and missiles all rely on embedded computer systems to operate properly, and embedded computing is found in targeting and weapons control systems; radars; identification friend-or-foe systems; flight control software for propulsion, steering, and attitude control; navigation systems; communication systems; platform area networks; and target identification databases and maps. As one example, it is known that the F-35 fighter will require at least eight million lines of software code.[9] The survivability of these platforms and delivery systems in the face of attack and their effectiveness in combat may also depend on computer systems (and networks) that are a part of the combat and logistical support infrastructure with which they operate.

Nuclear delivery systems and platforms are cyber-physical systems, and cyber threats to the integrity and availability of information and computing resources involved in the operation of a weapons system are of critical importance to its performance. An airplane carrying a nuclear gravity bomb might not be able to release it at the appropriate time should

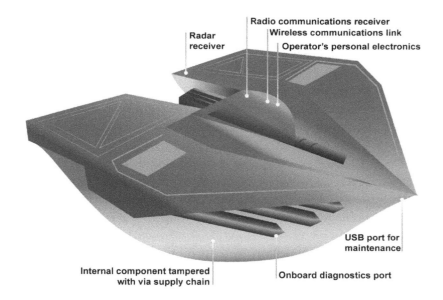

Figure 3.1. Possible Interfaces for Cyber Attack Access. SOURCE: U.S. Government Accountability Office, *Weapon Systems Cybersecurity: DOD Just Beginning to Grapple with Scale of Vulnerabilities.* GAO 19-128. October 9, 2018. www.gao.gov/products/GAO-19-128.

the computers controlling the weapons' release be rendered unavailable then. An airplane carrying a nuclear weapon might not be able to take off because the onboard computer systems are constantly rebooting.[10]

Cyberattacks could also compromise the survivability of weapons platforms. Warplanes carry warning receivers that automatically indicate when the planes are being illuminated by radar or lasers. Stealth aircraft almost certainly achieve some of their undetectability to radar due to active measures that are controlled by computer; the same may be true of ballistic missile submarines trying to evade being detected by active sonar. A small unauthorized change to a computer program could make a stealth aircraft more visible to radar[11] or a submarine noisier in the ocean.

In short, exploitation of cyber vulnerabilities in nuclear delivery systems could prevent or impede proper delivery of a weapon to its target. Figure 3.1 shows possible access paths into a weapons system. Some paths—radar receivers, radio communications systems for both voice and data, and Wi-Fi maintenance links—are wireless. Others, such as maintenance and diagnostic ports, require physical contact with the system. Personal electronics (e.g., cell phone, escape radio) are an indirect method of access to the system. Lastly, the airplane, submarine, or missile uses a variety of electronic components from myriad suppliers, making them vulnerable in principle to cyber attacks against elements of the supply chain.

Figure 3.2 shows possible points of vulnerability that an attacker can exploit once access has been gained. Computers control key systems in nuclear platforms such as those for propulsion, collision avoidance, navigation, life support, targeting and weapons release, and weapons system status. Modern airplanes are fly-by-wire vehicles; the metal cables and hydraulic systems in planes of old have been replaced by controls linked to movable surfaces by wires carrying information from computers controlling the movement of those surfaces. Communications—once limited to simple voice communications—now carry voice and data in large volume bidirectionally. Onboard electronic systems (including those that control physical components) are tied together with a weapons-system-wide network. Onboard logistics management systems tie into base and depot maintenance systems, flagging maintenance and repair needs even before the airplane lands.

Figure 3.3 depicts how weapons systems are tied together through battlefield networks that provide awareness of adversary and friendly forces and enable weapons systems to coordinate their activities for greater effect. For example, forward unarmed sensor platforms pass information on targets through such networks to shooting platforms that are themselves too far away to see those targets on their own. Appropriate coordination of air assets penetrating enemy airspace increases their survivability and thus their ability to deliver weapons on target. Many platforms and delivery vehicles also depend on global positioning satellites (GPS) for position and speed information. Other satellites provide important information through imagery, collect and analyze electronic signals and communications of adversaries, and enable U.S. forces to communicate with each other.

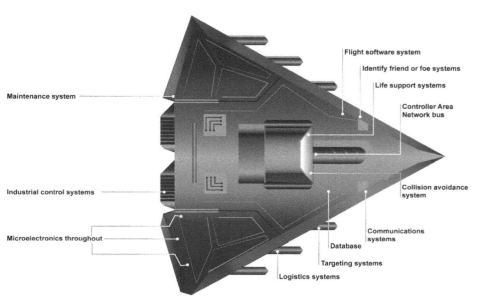

Figure 3.2. Possible Points of Vulnerability to Cyber Attack. SOURCE: U.S. Government Accountability Office, *Weapon Systems Cybersecurity: DOD Just Beginning to Grapple with Scale of Vulnerabilities.* GAO 19-128. October 9, 2018. www.gao.gov/products/GAO-19-128.

Similar considerations apply to networked platforms as to individual platforms. For example, a significant amount of coordination is needed to perform the mission of suppressing enemy air defenses—surface-to-air missile sites and radars need to be destroyed or disabled before they can engage. So timing is an essential aspect of coordination, and a cyber-induced delay in transmitting information that disrupts the timing of the suppression mission may be just as consequentially harmful as an actual failure to destroy those sites themselves.

Taken together, Figures 3.2 and 3.3 suggest that the infrastructure on which weapons platforms depend also provide lucrative targets for the cyber attacker. Whether that infrastructure involves sensor systems or maintenance and repair, compromising it may significantly degrade the performance of the weapons platforms themselves.

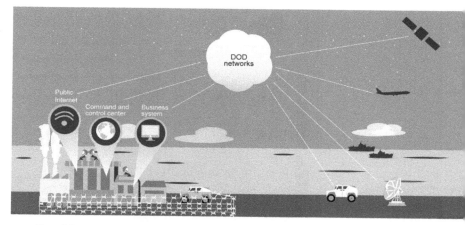

Figure 3.3. Computer-based Networks Tie Weapons Systems Together. SOURCE: U.S. Government Accountability Office, *Weapon Systems Cybersecurity: DOD Just Beginning to Grapple with Scale of Vulnerabilities.* GAO 19-128. October 9, 2018. www.gao.gov/products/GAO-19-128.

U.S. weapons systems rely on components and/or services that DoD does not fully control. As noted earlier, airplanes, submarines, and missiles are potentially vulnerable to supply-chain attacks. DoD also engages in a large volume of electronic commerce with a variety of private-sector commercial entities to supply its substantial logistical needs. Connections to these other entities may well provide an access pathway to attack DoD networks, much as the 2014 data breach at the Target Corporation was effected through an initial penetration of the company that provided heating, ventilation, and air conditioning services to some of its stores.[12] The integrity and availability of internal DoD systems and those of commercial providers are thus essential aspects of DoD operations, and compromising those functions could impact readiness.

As shown in figure 3.3, operational military networks also connect to internal DoD business systems (e.g., for payroll, food, and office supplies) and to the broader Internet. Internal DoD systems help to manage department-wide operations. DoD also does a very large volume of business with private-sector commercial entities, a substantial fraction of which contributes to military logistics. The integrity and availability of internal DoD systems and those of commercial providers are thus essential aspects of DoD operations, and compromising the functions of those systems could impact operational effectiveness. Lastly, the connections between DoD networks and the broader Internet provide multiple access paths through which weapons systems and C3 networks can potentially be compromised. Disconnecting weapons systems from U.S. military systems and networks sometimes helps limit adversary access but is no guarantee that adversaries cannot reach them, because adversaries may gain physical access to the systems.

Perhaps the best-known attack on an air-gapped nuclear system is the Stuxnet attack on Iranian centrifuges in 2010 or thereabouts. A nation-state hacker team, widely believed to be American and Israeli, was able to compromise a nuclear enrichment facility in Natanz, Iran, by uploading malware to USB drives that were eventually physically connected to the computers controlling enrichment centrifuges in the Natanz facility.[13]

A 2018 report from the U.S. Government Accountability Office (GAO) probed cyber vulnerabilities in U.S. weapons systems and arrived at some worrisome conclusions,[14] not just for what it showed about the vulnerabilities, but for what it showed about officials' mistaken confidence in their systems. The *New York Times* indicated that in interviews with the GAO, officials confirmed that the acquisition programs under review included the Columbia-class ballistic missile submarine (SSBN) and the Ground Based Strategic Deterrent (GBSD—the new ICBM proposed for replacing the Minuteman III), neither of which have yet been deployed or even tested in prototype form.[15]

As shown in box 3.1, DoD has found mission-critical cyber vulnerabilities during operational testing of weapons systems under development, stating that "[U]sing relatively simple tools and techniques, testers were able to take control of systems and largely operate undetected." Even worse, GAO said, the discovered vulnerabilities represented only a fraction of total vulnerabilities, since not all weapons systems were tested; DoD testing did not reflect the full range of cyber threats that a sophisticated adversary might deploy against the weapons systems being tested;

Box 3.1. Cyber Vulnerabilities in U.S. Weapons Systems

The U.S. Government Accountability Office (GAO) concluded that nearly all major defense acquisition programs operationally tested between 2012 and 2017 had mission-critical vulnerabilities. GAO found widespread examples of weaknesses in protecting against cyberattacks, detecting and responding to cyberattacks, and recovering from cyberattacks.[1] For example:

- Testers took one hour to gain initial access to a system, one day to gain full control.
- Security measures prevented access by remote users, but not insiders and near-siders.
- Testers took control of the operators' terminals, and saw, in real time, what the operators were seeing on their screens; manipulated the system; and were able to disrupt the system and observe how the operators responded.
- Testers caused a pop-up message to appear on users' terminals instructing them to insert two quarters to continue operating.
- Testers were able to copy, change, or delete system data, including one team that downloaded 100 gigabytes of data.
- Testers successfully used default passwords for open-source software to achieve access.
- Testers found one system using access controls but also unencrypted communications that allowed them to capture credentials in transit.
- Testers were sometimes detected but no action was taken.
- Testers rebooted a system in operation.

1. U.S. Government Accountability Office, *Weapon Systems Cybersecurity: DOD Just Beginning to Grapple with Scale of Vulnerabilities.* GAO 19-128. October 9, 2018. www.gao.gov/products/GAO-19-128.

thorough review was sometimes impossible because DoD was denied access to review proprietary software; and certain tests were not performed because cybersecurity testing would interfere with operations.

Although the problems were thus likely to be worse than GAO reported, DoD program officials seemed to believe their systems were secure and discounted some test results as unrealistic. This reaction is not unusual, because, from the user's standpoint, perfect cybersecurity for a system is demonstrated when a user can proceed without caring about an adversary's security-penetrating activities. Moreover, this demonstration is entirely indistinguishable from the state in which the user is simply unaware of such activities—as the DoD program officials were.

Adversaries may gain access to nuclear delivery systems and platforms in a variety of ways with a number of different purposes in mind. For example, adversaries have demonstrated their ability to exfiltrate unclassified data on weapons systems. In 2007, before the F-35 was deployed, suspected Chinese hackers exfiltrated information on the Pentagon's Joint Strike Fighter project (i.e., the F-35, an aircraft designed to be capable of carrying conventional and nuclear ordnance) by exploiting vulnerabilities in the networks of several contractors helping to build the plane.[16] Obtaining information on the inner workings of U.S. weapons systems, even if such information is not classified, can help adversaries find vulnerabilities in the delivery systems, increasing the likelihood of their developing successful defenses against them. Classified information has been exfiltrated from supposedly secure networks as well, as in the Buckshot Yankee incident, thus proving that cyber-enabled exfiltration of classified data can indeed happen.

The production stage of weapons systems depends on a complicated international, and at times insecure, supply chain. Insecurity in the supply chain can introduce vulnerabilities into weapons systems, and counterfeit parts that are often of lower quality than legitimate products can lead to unexpected malfunctions in weapons systems.

Although countering the threats of corrupted and counterfeit parts often entails different measures, both are supply-chain problems. Furthermore, corruption (in the form of increased risk of "backdoors" that allow unauthorized access or implantation of maliciously manipulated circuits) can be more likely in counterfeit parts.[17] As one example, in 2007, when Israeli jets bombed a suspected Syrian nuclear facility, Syrian radar systems did not detect the incoming jets, leading some to suspect tampering in the microprocessors embedded in the Syrian radar system.[18] In particular, according to an anonymous U.S. contractor, a European chip maker had built a "kill-switch" into its microprocessors that could be accessed remotely. Thus, it is not unreasonable to be concerned that weapons systems relying on parts fabricated by untrustworthy manufacturers might contain purposefully introduced cyber vulnerabilities.

Of course, European chip makers have never raised particular security concerns for the U.S. military establishment. Today and for the foreseeable future, the hardware supply chain actor of concern is first and foremost China, which supplies or is in a position to influence a large fraction of the semiconductors on which U.S. military systems rely. In 2012, a Senate Armed Services Committee report called attention to the problem of counterfeit electronic parts in the DoD supply chain, uncovering "overwhelming evidence of large numbers of counterfeit parts making their way into critical defense systems" and noting that companies in China were the primary source of such parts.[19] If anything, the problem of counterfeit parts from China has grown since this report was issued.

Military contractors often use commercial off-the-shelf (COTS) hardware and software, because these products are much cheaper and more rapidly available than custom-designed ones. Moreover, since COTS products are widely used, the probability is higher that a flaw will be discovered and can thus be fixed. In 2019, it was estimated that 70 to 80 percent of the components in DoD systems were COTS-sourced.[20]

Nevertheless, COTS products, just like custom-designed ones, also contain flaws from time to time, and introducing COTS technology into critical weapons systems carries a number of security risks. First, COTS products are well-known and publicly available, making them easily available to the hacker community for examination. Hackers can use locally available versions of a COTS product, perhaps with legitimate access, to conduct experiments, do reverse engineering, and test attacks.[21]

In addition, maintaining COTS products integrated into weapons systems may allow third-party service providers and manufacturers to have "physical or logical access to sensitive Government information systems, software code, or intellectual property." Often these third parties are unable to "to protect data and mitigate vulnerabilities on systems and networks that store and transmit sensitive information"[22] and constitute a weak link, leaving systems using COTS products vulnerable to attack.

COTS products also suffer from software obsolescence. Weapons systems typically take many years to develop and are used for decades. COTS products tend to have much shorter life-spans, with companies releasing updated products on a time scale of months and even abandoning them in just a few years. Thus, products that were on the cutting edge when a defense system was developed quickly become outdated and many suffer from software obsolescence when the original vendor stops support, updates, upgrades, and fixes for known bugs.[23]

Finally, COTS products often serve as the base on which other software is built (for example, an operating system is often the base on which applications software is built). It is very difficult—many would argue impossible—to build secure systems using resources provided by an insecure base. An apparent exception to this general rule is the use of virtual private networks (VPNs) on the open Internet that provide relatively high levels of security for their users. Alas, the exception is indeed only apparent—though data confidentiality and integrity can be assured with high confidence, availability cannot be similarly assured even with the use of VPNs. It is also noteworthy that the Department of Defense will not rely on VPNs running on the open Internet to carry data classified at levels of classification above SECRET, using instead its own dedicated networks for such purposes.

Despite these security concerns about COTS technology, the cost and schedule advantages of using such technology are usually too great to forego them entirely, and DoD has some history of buying COTS products with known vulnerabilities.[24] Such products may be integrated into military systems—including nuclear delivery systems. For example, before it was abandoned, the automated logistics information system (ALIS) for the dual-capable F-35 ran on Windows 10.[25] ALIS was intended to reduce and streamline the logistics workload for the F-35, relying on automated transfer of status data from the airplane to the ground-based logistics system. From time to time, ALIS would sense a problem with an aircraft, even if the problem did not exist. Under these circumstances, it would disallow a pilot from taking control of the aircraft,[26] designate it as out of service, and create extra work for engineering teams.[27] In principle, such flaws could be exploited by an adversary to ground functional airplanes or at least to reduce the confidence that pilots had in flying them.

Nevertheless, in the case of the F-35, cybersecurity testers were sometimes not allowed to conduct tests on the airplanes themselves "due to safety concerns and the risk of losing the use of a test aircraft before testing is complete"[28] if testing malware was injected into the systems. Cybersecurity deficiencies may remain unfixed for years: in 2019, DoD found that the F-35 program "continued to demonstrate that deficiencies and vulnerabilities identified during earlier testing periods have not been remedied."[29]

Missiles that rely on GPS, whether nuclear or conventional, are subject to jamming, which results in a denial of GPS service to delivery systems that depend on it for velocity and position information. For example, a military exercise involving South Korea and the United States was partially disrupted through North Korean jamming targeted against GPS-guided missiles.[30] The F-35 uses GPS for navigation,[31] so jamming or other counter-GPS technologies could be disruptive in a nuclear conflict. Jamming involves overwhelming the legitimate GPS radio signals with radio frequency noise and is thus not carried out by the same technical means as Internet denial-of-service attacks, but it does result in the same effect—a denial of service to the target of interest.

In 2015, a German magazine reported that a German-owned conventional Patriot missile on the Syrian-Turkish border was hacked and that hackers remotely executed "unexplained" commands to it.[32] The report speculated that there were two possible vulnerabilities to exploit, one in the Sensor Shooter Interoperability system that "connects the physical missile launcher and the missile's control system" and a second "on the computer chip responsible for guiding missiles to the target." (The German government said there was "no evidence" that their missiles were hacked, which may be true—the unexplained execution of commands could be the result of an accidental glitch in the software rather than of hacker activity. On the other hand, absence of evidence for X does not mean that X did not happen—it may only mean that the perpetrators of X successfully concealed their activities.)

Ballistic missile defense systems have not been entirely cybersecure either. At a number of DoD installations that handled ballistic missile defense system (BMDS) technical information, a report from the DoD Inspector General found that network administrators and data center managers did not routinely and consistently require the use of multifactor authentication to access BMDS technical information; identify or mitigate known network vulnerabilities; secure server racks; protect or monitor data on removable media; implement intrusion detection software on their networks; or require justification for access to sensitive information.[33]

The audit was focused on protecting the confidentiality of classified technical information regarding U.S. BMD systems. Exfiltration of such information could enable an adversary to identify BMD system weaknesses and shortcomings and thereby compromise the performance of U.S. BMD systems in operation. Even worse, the access needed to enable exfiltration of information could also be used by adversary hackers to alter information on the system, and at least the declassified portions of the audit do not indicate that measures were taken to ensure the integrity of that information. It is possible that an adversary agent could use access to modify existing software or insert software or change data that would compromise the performance of the BMD system in operation, e.g., to reprogram a radar system to ignore certain types of radar signatures.[34]

Lastly, platform crews and support personnel are vulnerable to cyber attacks. (The same comments apply to those staffing command centers and the like.) At the onset of a crisis, it will generally be necessary for commanders to recall personnel on leave, off duty, and so on. For example, U.S. Strategic Command has established procedures to issue "alert/

recall notification of all personnel and organizations assigned in a primary or support capacity" in an emergency. These procedures call for the use of telephones as "the most effective means of relaying instructions and confirming contact of large numbers of personnel during emergency situations."[35]

Such a procedure makes good practical sense given that cell phones are ubiquitous today among civilian and military personnel. But it also has at least two operational weaknesses if the computer-based telephone switching systems can be hacked by an adversary. First, an adversary could track the geographical location of specific cell-phone-carrying individuals, a fact that might enable physical attacks on key personnel. Second and perhaps more significantly, an adversary monitoring traffic on the relevant telephone switching system could detect in real time the operation of a phone-based recall mechanism, thereby possibly obtaining early warning of a change in alert status.

The nuclear command, control, and communications system

As noted in chapter 1, the NC3 infrastructure provides the means by which nuclear command and control functions can be carried out.[36] Three of these functions operate regularly on a day-to-day basis: force management, nuclear planning, and situation monitoring, whereas two operate episodically as circumstances warrant: decision-making and force direction.

Day-to-day functions of the nuclear command and control system

NUCLEAR PLANNING

Certain aspects of nuclear planning require day-to-day or at least ongoing attention. The U.S. strategic nuclear war plan promulgated in 2012, OPLAN 8010–12, *Strategic Deterrence and Force Employment*, contains various options for the use of strategic nuclear weapons.[37] Whether the guidance and/or targeting options in this plan have been updated since 2012 is not publicly known.

Some options are preplanned. At the most basic level, a given preplanned attack option calls for allocating weapons to targets, taking into account target characteristics (e.g., location, resistance to blast) and determining the most appropriate weapon(s) for attacking that target, taking into account weapons characteristics such as yield, height of burst, reliability, and so on. But weapons must also be delivered to their targets, and coordinating weapons delivery is also a complex planning task, especially since not all U.S. nuclear forces may be available when the particular attack option is selected for use.

Illustratively, some of the considerations that nuclear planners must take into account are the following:

- Tankers must be coordinated with bombers so that they can be refueled in the air.[38] In 2020, every inflight refueling conducted by the U.S. Air Force was planned using an automated tool.[39] This capability is particularly important for bombers that must penetrate enemy airspace.

- Weapons detonations must be "deconflicted" (i.e., timed), so that one explosion does not negatively affect a second weapon heading for the same target.

- The use of defense-suppression weapons must be coordinated with the arrival of incoming weapons or platforms.

- Designated ground zeros for hard targets—that is, the three-dimensional coordinates for weapons detonations—must be specified very precisely. (Hard targets are targets that can be destroyed only by very high overpressures, such as those generated when a weapon explodes very close to the target.) Less precision is necessary for softer targets, but excessive imprecision would result in targets being missed entirely.

- Damage expectancies for various targets must be calculated as a function of several variables:[40] the pre-launch survivability of the weapons system used to deliver the weapon, the reliability of the weapons system, the probability that the weapons system will reach the target, the yield of the weapon, where in three-dimensional space it is expected to detonate, and target characteristics. Lower damage expectancies against critical targets may require more weapons directed against them.

- Routes to targets must be planned in detail. Airplanes, submarines, cruise missiles, and ballistic missiles depend on knowledge of their physical environment to adjust their courses appropriately. Information on relevant environmental features such as mountains (which exert gravitational forces that could affect the accuracy of ballistic missile warheads), strong winds, and terrain profiles over land and underwater are stored in databases that are accessed in route planning—maintaining such databases is generally the responsibility of the National Geospatial Agency.

All of these missions depend on automated databases whose currency must be assured. Much of the information in these databases is relatively stable and does not change frequently. For example, an enemy missile silo's location or the location of a mountain does not change. On the other hand, other elements of adversary forces, such as locations and types of air defense systems (missiles, radars) may well change, and at least some preplanned options must be updated continually to account for such changes.

Ad hoc missions to address unforeseen contingencies (also known as adaptively planned options) may be necessary as well. Planning such missions has all of the complications of pre-planned options with the additional burden of adding real-time intelligence feeds on target location and disposition and information about the status of friendly forces, which will almost certainly involve matters such as ad hoc planning for flight paths to deliver weapons to targets, some of which may well be identified in near real time and/or mobile. It is also possible that an ad hoc mission may consist of portions of several pre-planned options that must then be integrated into a more coherent whole.

Planning is highly dependent on databases that provide the information that planners need to assemble and coordinate. Corruption in these databases will inevitably lead to suboptimal outcomes in nuclear operations. Bad data on tanker and bomber flight paths and timing might result in a bomber failing to meet its tanker at the appropriate time and place, leaving it without enough fuel to complete its mission. Bad data on the time and place of nuclear detonations might cause the flight path of a cruise missile or a bomber to lead to an area where a nuclear explosion of another U.S. weapon could damage it. Bad data about flight speed might lead to the suppression of an air-defense radar after the bombers should be flying past it. Bad data about a target's location might lead to its being only lightly damaged rather than destroyed.

FORCE MANAGEMENT

Force management is a day-to-day process that is the set of "Command, Control, and Communications (C3) activities relating to the assignment, training, deployment, maintenance, and logistic support of nuclear forces and weapons, before, during, and after any crisis."[41] Especially in the context of the nuclear forces, force management is the function responsible for ensuring the safety, surety, security, and reliability of these weapons and their associated support systems.

One important example of a force management task is keeping track of the readiness status of the various nuclear forces—which B-52H bombers at Minot Air Force Base (AFB) and Barksdale AFB are in the shop for repairs and which are ready to fly today, which ICBM silos are inoperable today due to scheduled maintenance, the locations and disposition of all deployed nuclear weapons in the U.S. arsenal, and so on. A second force management task is to be able to identify the status and disposition of all parts and components related to nuclear weapons that are in the inventory. A third is the conduct of inspections to evaluate a nuclear unit's compliance with nuclear surety requirements and its readiness for the operational mission.

From time to time, nuclear force management also involves the transportation of nuclear weapons from one location to another. For obvious reasons, the security of such transport is of paramount importance. In August 2007, six nuclear-armed cruise missiles were mistakenly and improperly loaded onto a B-52H heavy bomber at Minot AFB in North Dakota and transported to Barksdale AFB in Louisiana.[42] The crew of the B-52H in question, as well as those loading the missiles onto the airplane, believed that the cruise missiles were inert, armed only with dummy warheads. The nuclear warheads in the cruise missiles should have been removed before the missiles were loaded.

The result was that for a period of thirty-six hours, senior leadership in the Air Force and the U.S. Defense Department would have reported those particular warheads as properly stored in a bunker at Minot AFB, when in fact they were mounted on the missile launch pylons of a B-52H either in the air or on the ground at either Minot or Barksdale AFBs. In addition, at no time during this period were the "missing" warheads guarded with the appropriate security personnel. Perhaps more seriously, a flight incident with that particular B-52H (e.g., an onboard engine fire) would have led the crew to invoke the safety protocols and procedures for nonnuclear aircraft, which are very different from those required when nuclear weapons are involved. A 2008 report by the Secretary of Defense Task Force on DoD Nuclear Weapons Management found that this incident was due to "a breakdown in procedures in the accounting, issuing, loading, and verification processes" associated with nuclear weapons management, the crew failing to follow proper procedure that called for tracking the status of the missiles while they are disarmed, loaded, moved and so on.[43]

SITUATION MONITORING

Situation monitoring is the set of NC3 activities relating to "the collection, maintenance, assessment, and dissemination of information on friendly forces; adversary forces and possible targets; emerging nuclear powers; and military, political, environmental, and other events."[44] An essential element of situation monitoring is tactical warning (TW) and attack assessment (AA)—the ability to detect an attack that has been launched against the U.S. homeland and to characterize the nature of that attack.

Attack assessment starts by determining the likely targets of missile or airbreathing threats against the homeland; it would continue through space-based capabilities for the detection of nuclear explosions. In general, attack assessment tries to answer questions of critical importance to policymakers. For example:

• Who is attacking? If the hot flares indicating missile launch are coming from the land mass of a given nation, it is pretty clear who is attacking.

But if they come from the middle of the ocean, it is less clear. An additional source of information may come from a comparison between the details of the hot plume (e.g., temperature, brightness) against a database of known signatures of adversary missiles.

- How big is the attack and what specific targets are at risk? Early-warning satellites provide preliminary assessment of the general geographical region that might be targeted, and the footprint of possible detonation points shrinks with the passage of time. When the boost phase of the missile launch ends, the actual trajectory of the launched missiles cannot be further refined through data from early-warning satellites. Radars begin to track missiles after they clear the radar horizon and refine the trajectory for further localization.

- When will targets be hit? Some decisions related to U.S. nuclear forces depend on the time available before nuclear weapons detonate on U.S. soil. For example, bombers that may be on alert could be ordered to take off so as to avoid being destroyed on the ground. Ground-based radars looking for ballistic missiles, cruise missiles, and bombers sense the position and velocity of incoming missile warheads or airbreathing vehicles to calculate time-to-impact and pass such information on to decision-makers.

- Where have nuclear weapons exploded? A variety of sensors, particularly space-based ones, provide real-time information that a nuclear explosion has occurred at such and such a location. Assuming they work properly, these sensors provide the only unambiguous indication that the United States has in fact been struck by nuclear weapons.

The NC3 system provides information such as that described above to U.S. decision-makers so that their decisions may be better informed. However, Ashton Carter has noted that because the NC3 system includes multiple sensors to warn of attack, it is possible that sensor readings will conflict (e.g., some indicating attack, others not).[45] In practice, it is not only possible—it happens frequently rather than rarely—and a significant role for senior commanders responsible for tactical warning and attack assessment (TW/AA) is to disambiguate conflicting sensor readings and to form judgments about the nature of sensor events based on their knowledge and experience (e.g., what set of sensor readings would probably not reflect an actual attack), understanding of the overall NC3 system (e.g., which sensors tended to be more reliable under what set of circumstances), and understanding of the geopolitical situation extant at that time (e.g., is the United States presently in a crisis with the indicated attacker).

Over past decades, the United States has experienced a number of computer-related faults in its NC3 system that have falsely signaled an attack in progress (i.e., a false positive).

- In 1960, U.S. early-warning radars indicated a large-scale Soviet missile attack; actions preparatory for nuclear response were initiated. Cause: Early-warning radars misidentified the moon rising over the horizon as a missile attack.[46]
- In 1961, communications with a U.S. early-warning radar in Greenland and with NORAD were lost; foul play was assumed due to the simultaneous loss of communications. Cause: failure of an AT&T switch in Colorado; backups required by contract were installed but physically routed through the same relay station, which had experienced an overheating motor that caused the failure of all circuits therein, including the backup.[47]
- In 1962, a radar located in New Jersey reported a missile launch from Cuba towards Florida right after Cuban Missile Crisis. Cause(s): a satellite appeared in the same orbit and trajectory that a Cuba-launched missile would use. Redundant radar systems that would have otherwise detected the false alarm were offline. A test tape simulating a Cuban missile launch was also running on the system.[48]
- Also in 1962, U.S. nuclear-armed fighters scrambled on warning at Volk Field in Wisconsin. Cause: A guard at a military base in Minnesota shot a bear climbing a protective fence, mistaking it for a saboteur, thus triggering a sabotage alarm that set off warnings at all nearby military bases. Volk field had an incorrectly wired alarm that ordered nuclear-armed fighters to take off rather than sound a warning.[49] The fighter launch was prevented when a car driven by

an officer from the command post to the tarmac signaled the fighters to abort.

- In 1979, NORAD displays indicated a large Soviet missile attack on the United States, and pre-planned defensive and precautionary measures were set into motion immediately. Cause: Data associated with a test scenario were inadvertently fed into operational displays which generated false alerts.[50]

- On two occasions in 1980, NORAD mistakenly signaled to the Strategic Air Command and the National Military Command Center at the Pentagon that a large Soviet missile attack on the United States was under way, and pre-planned defensive and precautionary measures were set into motion immediately in both cases. Cause: The link between NORAD and other command centers had been constructed in such a way to continuously indicate that "the number of incoming missiles is 0000," so that the link could be tested all the time in operation. However, a faulty chip apparently caused one or more of the zeroes to be randomly filled in with the numeral "2," so that the message indicated "the number of incoming missiles is 0002" and then "200" and so on.[51]

None of these incidents were caused by a cyber attack, but the fact that their root causes could be traced to computer-related problems suggests that every one of them could have resulted from a cyber attack intended to cause such outcomes. (It is true that human error has been implicated in a number of such incidents, but cybersecurity is a holistic property of a system, and people often constitute security vulnerabilities that decision-makers must take into account in the architecture and design of a system. I address this point further in chapter 4, "Cybersecurity Lessons for Nuclear Modernization.")

Of course, it would not have been in Soviet interests to interfere with U.S. TW/AA systems for nuclear attack—why would the Soviet Union want the United States to believe it was under Soviet nuclear attack if this was untrue? But it could conceivably have been in the interests of a third party such as a transnational terrorist organization seeking to provoke the United States and the Soviet Union into using nuclear weapons against each other.[52] In that case, all of the difficulties of prompt attribution of cyber incidents described in chapter 1 would apply.

As for false negatives, the world has fortunately not seen an incident in which a TW/AA system has failed to warn of an actual nuclear attack. But history is replete with instances in which tactical warning systems have failed to provide decision-makers with warning of an actual non-nuclear attack in progress.

An instructive case is the false negative provided by the World War II radar-based tactical warning system intended to detect aircraft that might be attacking U.S. military installations in Hawaii, especially at Pearl Harbor. A newly installed radar surveillance system detected inbound Japanese aircraft about fifty minutes before they struck on the morning of December 7, 1941.[53] The radar operator reported a large contact, but the party receiving the report believed that the contact referred to an incoming group of U.S. bombers that was due to arrive from the mainland and told the radar operator not to worry about the contact.

Any one of a number of changes might have led to a proper identification of the contact as attacking Japanese airplanes—the availability of an identification friend-or-foe capability on the radar system; more widespread knowledge about the much-discussed possibility of a Japanese attack on Pearl Harbor; a round-the-clock operational center for fusing intelligence, and so on. A cyber-induced failure that caused information of a missile launch to not reach its intended destination could have catastrophic effects, since the detonation of a nuclear weapon (or even of many weapons) with zero warning time would catch U.S. forces entirely flat-footed and unprepared.

Episodic functions

NUCLEAR DECISION-MAKING

Decision-making is the set of nuclear command and control activities relating to "the assessment, review, and consultation regarding consideration for use or movement of nuclear weapons or the execution of other nuclear control orders."[54] Nuclear decision-making may consider a host of actions short of decisions regarding actual use of nuclear weapons. For example, dispersing U.S. nuclear forces from their bases or raising their state-of-alert (DEFCON, or "defense condition") level can be aspects of nuclear decision-making. The lowest and least severe state is DEFCON 5 (normal peacetime). DEFCON 1 is the highest and most severe state of alert and corresponds to a state in which war is imminent. President Richard Nixon in 1973 placed all U.S. military forces on DEFCON 3, including U.S. nuclear forces, to send a signal to the Soviet Union regarding its impending intervention in the Arab-Israeli war.

Pre-planned options for using nuclear weapons span a wide range of possibilities. One option for nuclear use might grow out of conventional conflict in Europe or a pre-emptive strike against a nuclear-armed adversary such as North Korea or an adversary that is on the verge of going nuclear, such as Iran in the future. Still other options might entail very limited use as a demonstration of U.S. resolve but without causing much physical damage, or conversely inflict severe damage on a large fraction of adversary military power. In principle though unlikely in practice, a president could order the use of nuclear weapons in a way that entailed a combination of part of several different pre-planned options, or the creation of an entirely new option—such options would have to be generated on the fly and would take more time to implement than one that was pre-planned in its entirely.

Proper orders to use nuclear weapons can only be given by the president of the United States, subject to one possible exception—pre-delegation—described below. In support of this condition is the requirement that command authority for nuclear weapons must be human rather than automated. Within the NC3 system, humans are involved and must act affirmatively at various key steps before any launch can happen.

An important element of nuclear decision-making involves consultations between the president and others. Decision-making activities for all non-time-critical scenarios may require a robust and secure capability to conference and share information (bidirectionally) with foreign leaders in allied nations, domestic leaders (e.g., Congress, state, or local officials), trusted civilian advisors (including some perhaps with no official role in the U.S. government, senior military leaders in the United States, and social as well as traditional media outlets.

In addition, although it is not usually included in descriptions of the U.S. NC3 system, the ability to communicate with adversary leadership may also be an important aspect of nuclear decision-making during crisis or even during actual conflict. For example, during the Cuban missile crisis, communications between President Kennedy and Premier Khrushchev were less than prompt—President Kennedy had not yet had time to formulate a response to an initial communication from Khrushchev when a second communication arrived, this time with stronger demands than were made in the first one. Kennedy made the decision to respond to the first communication and ignore the second—and considering the timing involved, it may be the case that Khrushchev sent the second message because of a lack of U.S. response to the first. The Washington-Moscow hotline was created in the aftermath of the 1962 Cuban missile crisis, which demonstrated an inadequacy of communications so severe that Khrushchev chose to broadcast his response on Radio Moscow rather than to trust the existing communications infrastructure.[55]

A second example is associated with the terrorist attack on the World Trade Center and the Pentagon on September 11, 2001. In less than an hour of the second impact on the World Trade Center (South Tower), Secretary of Defense Donald Rumsfeld had raised the Pentagon's alert status to DEFCON 3, a level that called for heightened security at U.S. military bases but also for nuclear forces to raise their level of readiness. Russia noticed this increase, and President Vladimir Putin tried to call President Bush to discuss the change in DEFCON. NBC News reports that after trying for thirty minutes, the White House communications office was unable to establish communications with Air Force One, which was carrying President Bush.[56] Eventually, Putin gave up trying to reach Bush, and spoke instead to National Security Advisor Condoleezza Rice, who was in the White House at the time. (The stakes were heightened immeasurably by the fact that both the United States and Russia were independently conducting their own nuclear exercises—and raising the alert level of U.S. nuclear forces could have been dangerously escalatory.

However, Putin's conversation with Rice resulted in a stand-down of nuclear forces on both sides.)

In an actual conflict, of course, and especially if that conflict is nuclear, it will be particularly important to be able to maintain the ability for one side's national leaders to communicate expeditiously with the other side. Though no such dedicated mechanism to perform this function is publicly known to exist today, one example of a proposal to provide just such functionality is Catalink, a dedicated communications system capable of supporting leadership communications internationally during a nuclear crisis or other high-stakes events.[57]

Catalink is intended to be operable when the conditions of communication are degraded by the effects of nuclear weapons on the atmosphere, cyber attacks, electromagnetic jamming, and biological attacks. The Catalink system involves end-user devices based on open-source technology in the hands of leaders connecting to a global mesh network using multiple networks and channels/wavelengths to ensure reliable communications of text messages, images, and voice calls or messages. The endpoint devices used by national leaders to communicate on the network would be designed for "durability, availability, and ease of use, enabling parties to immediately connect with confidence amid crises." These devices would also be secure, meeting world-class requirements for security. The network would take advantage of "redundant transmission capabilities to ensure that multiple parties could connect under extreme conditions, including loss of power and the absence of cellular and/or internet connectivity."

The possible loss of confidentiality regarding deliberations and decisions is a severe cyber threat. Most political leaders prefer to keep their options open as they make momentous decisions, and revealing to the public the substance of their deliberations—especially in real time and especially with adversary leaders—is likely to increase pressure from one or another source to take a particular course of action. These leaders would generally regard cyber-enabled leaks of information mentioned in these deliberations as quite negative.

Force Direction

Force direction is the set of C3 activities relating to the implementation (preparation, dissemination, and authentication) of decisions regarding the execution, termination, destruction, and disablement of nuclear weapons.[58]

As noted earlier, only the president of the United States can order the use of U.S. nuclear weapons: how, when, and on what targets.[59] Thus, authentication of the president's identity is a critical and essential aspect of nuclear command and control, and only after the president's identity has been confirmed can U.S. military forces take the next steps towards nuclear use.

There is also the possibility that the president may choose to delegate his or her authority to order the use of nuclear weapons. For example, in the period from 1965 to 1992, the commander of the North American Air Defense Command (NORAD) had the authority to use nuclear missiles to defeat incoming Soviet bombers, although only "under severe restrictions and specific conditions of attack" on the continent.[60] However, although most analysts believe that a president would not do so, every president has the authority to delegate as he or she sees fit. The particulars of any such arrangements, and even their very existence, are likely to be highly classified.

From a logical perspective, pre-delegation often comes up in the context of a zero- or near-zero-warning-time nuclear attack on Washington, DC, when the president is in town. A nuclear weapon smuggled into Washington, DC, or a nuclear cruise missile launched from a Russian submarine near the East Coast could decapitate the U.S. NC3 structure at its apex; if it were followed closely by an attack on U.S. ICBMs, it might well be that a substantial number of ICBMs would be destroyed in their silos.[61]

A variety of security measures are in place to protect the president's life, including guards, underground shelters, and evacuation helicopters at the White House to extensive security forces deployed whenever the president travels. In addition, the Constitution specifies the order of presidential succession. During the annual State of the Union message, a cabinet member eligible to be president is designated to be away from

Box 3.2. Emergency Action Messages

An essential construct of the nuclear communications system is the emergency action message. EAMs are used for many purposes— in general, an EAM has a short preamble that indicates its general purpose, which could include (illustratively) movement of forces, execution of a war plan option, or a change in DEFCON, and also provides information on message formatting (e.g., message length).[1] If the purpose is to communicate an order to use nuclear weapons, an EAM would be long enough (perhaps a few to several tens of alphanumeric characters) to include these items of information:

- A code indicating what preplanned option to execute. All nuclear forces have a library of all preplanned options, but any individual force element knows only what it is supposed to do under any specific option.
- A reference time indicating when the plan is to be put into effect.
- Information that can be used with other information already in the force element's possession to unlock the PALs (or to access the safe in the case of the SSBNs).
- Authentication to indicate that message has been properly authorized.
- Information to ensure that the message has not been corrupted in transmission or is otherwise properly formatted.
- The time at which the EAM is sent, to ensure that the receiving force element can act on the most current information available.
- A single EAM is disseminated to all forces, thus simplifying the communications task. But because it can only specify which of a number of preplanned options to execute, it is limited in its flexibility.
- When crews receive a message appearing to be an EAM, their first action is to authenticate it as a valid message, checking it against their own reference materials (generally stored in safes that they unlock then and only then) for proper formatting, consistency, and proper authority. Once the message is authenticated as a valid EAM, crews are trained to follow a predetermined set of steps to carry out the order contained in the EAM.

1. Much of this information is taken from Ashton Carter, "Communications Technologies," in *Managing Nuclear Operations*, ed. John Steinbruner, Ashton Carter, and Charles Zraket (Washington DC: Brookings Institution, 1987), 223.

Washington, DC, to ensure presidential continuity. Nevertheless, there is no technical solution to the zero-warning-time attack problem apart from one in which the decision to launch nuclear weapons is made entirely by computer on the basis of various automated inputs. Other solutions are necessarily procedural—the authority to issue orders to use nuclear weapons can be delegated, almost certainly to a senior military commander, to prevent a decapitating attack from imperiling the ability to launch its nuclear weapons.

In any event, a presidential decision to use nuclear weapons must then be communicated to military subordinates to convert that decision into an emergency action message (EAM; see box 3.2) that is sent to U.S. nuclear forces through the various NC3 channels set up for such use. To ensure that it is indeed the president giving an order to use nuclear weapons, the president must authenticate his or her identity to parties at the National Military Command Center (NMCC) or alternate command centers.

The information for authenticating the president's identity is changed daily and kept both by the president (or the relevant aide) and the NMCC. Public reports indicate that at least for the president, the relevant information is printed on a card, often called "the biscuit," which is not machine-readable (it is not publicly known how these cards are generated for printing, nor how and where computer technology is used to generate them). The card with the relevant information is supposed to be immediately available to the president at all times, including scenarios in which the president decides to authorize immediate nuclear use in the event of an incoming attack.

Authentication of the president's identity is one aspect of what is sometimes called the always/never dilemma for U.S. decision-makers: nuclear weapons must *always* be used when they are properly authorized for use and must *never* be used when they are not so authorized.[62] These two principles are in tension—the NC3 system should always do the right thing, and the right thing is different depending on whether proper orders have been given or not. It is fundamentally impossible for the system to *always* do the right thing, but the system is intended to do the best possible job in balancing the requirements of these two principles. In other words, the tension between these two conflicting goals can only be managed—never resolved—and thus increases the vulnerability of these nuclear weapons systems to cyber attacks.

As a rule, civilian authorities are highly invested in upholding the "never" part of the requirement, and military authorities highly invested in upholding the "always" part of the requirement. Although in the United States, both are committed to the principle of civilian control over the military, the military has the operational responsibility for carrying out orders for use—hence, they place a very high priority on always being able to use the weapons once they receive orders to do so. On the other hand, since civilian authorities deal much more with peacetime rather than wartime circumstances, they place a very high priority on making sure nuclear weapons are never used without proper authority and direction.

A successful cyber attack on the "always" requirement would prevent the delivery of a properly authorized launch order or otherwise interfere with it (e.g., by garbling or delaying it). This outcome could be achieved in several ways:[63]

- Communications channels between command authorities and forces in the field could be severed through cyber attacks or have increased latency through denial-of-service attacks. The same is true for the channels supporting presidential conference capabilities, thus delaying the decision-making process. U.S. Strategic Command acknowledges the possibility that crews will not receive a valid emergency action message and may not perform all necessary actions to commit a nuclear weapon when directed.[64]
- Authentication procedures of key individuals may be compromised or made cumbersome. The precise methods used to authenticate individuals other than the president are not known, but circumstances under which communications links to key individuals cannot be established promptly, thus delaying the decision-making process, can be imagined.
- Cyber attacks (or threat of cyber attacks) may degrade leadership confidence in the usability of nuclear forces, thereby increasing decision times.
- The information streams received by key individuals (e.g., social media feeds) may create doubts in their minds about the validity of orders.

For example, ICBM launch control officers have access to the Internet through a system known as Launch Control Center Netlink.[65] This system is not connected to any other computer systems to which they have access while on duty, but it is routed through NIPRNET, which for practical purposes is the network used by the Department of Defense to handle unclassified information and provides selective access to the open Internet. Unit commanders decide the scope of access to the open Internet that is possible through NIPRNET, and under many circumstances, launch control officers in the capsules will have access to personal e-mail (e.g., Gmail, Yahoo mail, and so on), most news sites, and Facebook. As Americans get more of their news from online sources, including websites, apps, and social media, the content of these information feeds could lead launch control officers to be more hesitant to act on launch orders that appear to be inconsistent with their understanding of the state of the world, even if they are skeptical of news delivered through social media.[66] Not incidentally, launch control officers in their launch control centers can also access the outside world by telephone and receive cable television.[67]

- Information provided to the arming mechanisms of a nuclear weapon may be invisibly corrupted, causing a weapons failure upon arrival at the target. (The Stuxnet attack on Iranian centrifuges provides an example of invisible corruption—while one portion of the malware was manipulating the spin cycles of the enrichment centrifuges, another portion was feeding operators "all-is-well" signals that appeared on their consoles.)

- Data from early-warning sensors might be corrupted in a way that interferes with their warning function during an actual attack, leading to a U.S. failure to respond promptly and the destruction of a significant portion of U.S. nuclear forces.

Cyber attacks on the "always" requirement would most likely originate with parties who might engage in nuclear conflict with the United States and who thus would have something to gain by preventing or interfering with the authorized use of U.S. nuclear weapons—parties such as Russia or China. Of all possible adversaries, these are also the nations that have the most cyber expertise and knowledge of the U.S. NC3 system and thus are likely to pose the greatest threat to the "always" requirement.

A cyber attack on the "never" requirement would enable or lead to the improper issuance of a launch order that appears valid, perhaps resulting in the use of nuclear weapons when no one in authority wanted such use to occur. This too could be achieved in a number of ways:

- If the "biscuit" card is compromised, it is possible that someone else might find the card and be able to impersonate the president. Henry Hugh Shelton, chairman of the Joint Chiefs of Staff from October 1997 to September 2001, notes that for a multi-month period during the Clinton administration, the biscuit had apparently been misplaced and would not have been immediately available to the president, thus precluding any prompt response involving U.S. nuclear weapons.[68] But even if someone else found it and tried to succeed in impersonating the president, this other person would need a considerable amount of information about how to interpret and use the card, how to specify a given option, and how to access the appropriate communications channels to access the National Military Command Center, which is where presidential orders are turned into operational orders for U.S. military forces. This other person would have to behave in such a way as not to arouse suspicion, and furthermore the geopolitical situation would have to be such that nuclear use orders would not be surprising.

- U.S. land-based ICBMs can be launched through two mechanisms— ground-based Launch Control Centers (LCCs) and Airborne Launch Control Centers (ALCCs) housed in E-6B TACAMO aircraft. At presidential direction, these control centers receive orders to launch and activate circuits to launch the ICBMs. Communications with ground-based LCCs are regarded as more secure and reliable than those with ALCCs in large part because the former are wired, whereas the latter are wireless. These launch-control arrangements are structured so that the LCCs are the primary mechanism, with the ALCCs being the backup—if the LCCs are destroyed, the ALCCs can still launch the

Box 3.3. First Hostilities of World War I Follow a Communications Failure

The importance of effective command and control regarding war termination messages was on vivid display in 1914.[1] Faced with the possibility of a two-front war with France in the west and Russia in the east, German war plans at the time had called for the rapid conquest of France (during which time Russia—needing time to mobilize—would not pose much of a threat to Germany. After eliminating the French threat to the west, Germany would then be able to concentrate on the Eastern front.

On August 1, 1914, Kaiser Wilhelm II declared war on Russia, but had reconsidered the wisdom of attacking in the west. The offensive to the west had been scheduled to begin at 7:00 p.m., with German troops invading Luxembourg. Minutes before 7:00 p.m., however, the Kaiser cancelled the Luxembourg invasion. The orders revoking the attack arrived at 7:30 p.m., with an explanation that "a mistake had been made" in the original orders. However, in the intervening half-hour, news of the attack on Luxembourg had arrived in London, Paris, and Brussels. The wheels of the German war plan were set into motion, and World War I ensued. History might have been very different had the German movement into Luxembourg been scheduled for 8:00 p.m. rather than 7:00 p.m.

1. Barbara Tuchman, *The Guns of August* (New York: Macmillan, 1962), chap. 6.

ICBMs. On the other hand, if the LCCs are intact, ALCC commands should be inhibited. If a cyber attack disrupts the LCCs in a way that they appear to be offline, the ICBMs would accept ALCC commands, in which case an adversary could inject a wireless signal mimicking the ALCC to launch ICBMs, just as though it were coming from a legitimate airborne launch control center. Again, such an intervention would require quite detailed technical knowledge about the precise nature of the signal that would trigger a launch.

- A cyber attack on NC3 communications channels at an inappropriate time could result in a failure to withdraw an order or authority to use nuclear weapons; to stop an unauthorized use; to reverse orders to escalate; to halt a particular ongoing nuclear operation; or to cease nuclear hostilities.[69] Sending such termination messages would also require presidential authority. Box 3.3 provides a historical example of the importance of such messages.

- Data from early-warning sensors might be spoofed in a way that provides false indications of an actual attack, leading to a prompt U.S. launch of its ICBMs in response to what amounts to a false alarm.

Another way to compromise the "never" requirement would involve a cyber attack that would enable military personnel to bypass safeguards intended to ensure positive control over nuclear weapons. For example, permissive action links (PALs) are devices that inhibit the explosion of nuclear weapons if a certain code has not been inserted into the device. PALs are used on all U.S. nuclear weapons except for those carried by SLBMs. An EAM to use nuclear weapons contains the information needed by human crews to reconstruct the PAL codes for the specific nuclear weapons to be used. However, if the PAL code is easily guessed, the EAM is not needed to arm the weapon. In the 1970s, the PAL code for Minuteman ICBMs was reportedly set to all zeros by the Strategic Air Command, to ensure that the inability to obtain a PAL code would not inhibit a U.S. response.[70]

Another example is that U.S. SSBNs carry the information needed to unlock their nuclear weapons in highly secured safes. Although these safes could be physically breached with blowtorches and the like, an EAM to the submarine contains the information needed to unlock the safes without a physical breach.[71] A scenario to trick an SSBN into firing its weapons would necessarily involve an attack combining technical means and social engineering that would fool the relevant officers on the boat into breaching the safes. (Such an attack would make a "Mission Impossible" plot look like child's play!)

Cyber attacks on the "never" requirement would most likely originate with parties who believed they had something to gain by the unauthorized use of U.S. nuclear weapons—terrorist groups or rogue nations that wished to provoke nuclear war. Such parties are much more likely to want this outcome than Russia or China (which in fact both have strong incentives *not* to compromise the "never" requirement for the United States), but since they are also likely to have inferior cyber expertise and poorer insights into the U.S. NC3 system, they are also much less able to affect it.

Observations about today's NC3 system

The description of the NC3 system above leads to a number of important observations.

First, the overall system has undergone substantial evolution over the past thirty years, with new communications systems being added frequently. Because a common underlying architecture has not existed to support the overall system, each new system has been pursued as a stand-alone, and their integration into the then-existing system necessitated new hardware, new software, and new operating procedures and practices. Admiral Cecil Haney, a former commander of U.S. Strategic Command, characterized the existing system as being composed largely of "point-to-point hardwired systems."[72] General John Hyten, another former commander of U.S. Strategic Command, has testified to Congress that he could not explain the functionality of today's nuclear command and control system because it was built several decades ago using a variety of different kind of pathways and structures.[73]

Second, although U.S. nuclear command and control is exercised primarily through the communications systems and channels described above, it can also be exercised through other systems intended primarily for exercising nonnuclear command and control. Since all U.S. nuclear forces have the latter types of communications capabilities, such redundancy increases the likelihood that emergency action messages will in fact be able to reach the forces. Indeed, in principle, there is no reason that EAMs cannot be broadcast over insecure channels or even open commercial channels, such as television, Gmail, or Twitter. What counts in directing actions taken by the crews of nuclear forces is that the message be valid and authentic.

The reverse is true as well—according to the GAO, while some NC3 systems are specific to the nuclear mission, most NC3 systems support both strategic and conventional missions.[74] Long-distance communication assets are dual-use and support both nuclear and conventional missions, nuclear detonation detectors are placed on GPS satellites, which also guide both nuclear and conventional weapons systems.

Third, in the opinion of many senior military leaders, the cyber threat to today's NC3 system is "fairly minimal,"[75] a fortuitous outcome due to the age of the system and the consequent fact that the system is largely disconnected from the rest of the military and civilian world—that is, today's system is more cyber-secure because it is not connected to other parts of the world, from which various cyber threats could emanate. The minimal nature of the cyber threat against today's U.S. NC3 system arise, not so much because of the age of its components (many of which have been individually modernized), as because even newly modernized components have been constrained by the need to plug into the old point-to-point hardwired architecture.

That said, even today's NC3 system has not been entirely immune to cyber threat. For example, NC3 for U.S. ICBMs has displayed cyber or cyber-related vulnerabilities. In 2010, U.S. ICBM launch crews in ground-based LCCs lost contact with fifty nuclear-armed missiles for an hour in Wyoming because of an improperly installed circuit card.[76] About this incident, Bruce Blair expressed a concern that the LCCs had lost "their ability to detect and cancel any unauthorized launch attempts" that might have come from the ALCC backup or unauthorized signals pretending to come from the ALCCs.[77] This incident also prompted the Obama administration to investigate the cybersecurity of ICBM silos, resulting in a highly classified report known as "Red Domino."[78] Blair has also written that another cyber vulnerability discovered in that investigation could have "allowed hackers to cause the [Minuteman] missiles' flight guidance systems to shut down, putting them out of commission and requiring days or weeks to repair."[79]

Blair earlier reported on security vulnerabilities in communications to U.S. SSBNs that could have been exploited to transmit unauthorized missile-launch orders. Specifically, he has written about a Pentagon-led investigation in the 1990s indicating such a vulnerability: "unauthorized

Table 3.1. Selected Soviet/Russian NC3 Incidents

1962	During the Cuban Missile Crisis, some Soviet submarines had nuclear torpedoes and were authorized to use them without further orders from the Kremlin. One submarine came close to using such a torpedo in response to U.S. anti-submarine warfare (ASW) efforts intended to force the submarine to the surface rather than to seriously damage it (the ASW efforts involved the use of hand grenades thrown overboard rather than real depth charges). The grenade explosions rattled the Soviet submarine in question, and led to the possibility of launching a nuclear torpedo in response. The United States had informed the Soviet Union of the ASW activity, but the information failed to reach the Soviet submarines. Moreover, one Soviet submarine was unable to communicate with higher authority.[1]
1983	A Soviet early-warning satellite indicated that five U.S. nuclear missiles had been launched at the Soviet Union. Satellites misidentified sunlight reflecting off the tops of clouds as missile launches—the autumn equinox, satellites, sun, and U.S. missile fields were aligned, maximizing the sun's reflection.[2]
1995	The launching off the coast of Norway of a U.S.-Norwegian scientific rocket whose flight characteristics were similar to those of a U.S. submarine-launched ballistic missile (SLBM) was detected by Russian early-warning radar and misidentified as an SLBM launch. Norway had notified Russia in advance of the launch, but the notification didn't contain enough information to raise Russian concerns.[3]

1. "The Submarines of October: U.S. and Soviet Naval Encounters during the Cuban Missile Crisis," in *National Security Archive Electronic Briefing Book No. 75*, ed. William Burr and Thomas S. Blanton, October 31, 2002, nsarchive2.gwu.edu/NSAEBB/NSAEBB75.

2. David Hoffman, "I Had a Funny Feeling in My Gut," *Washington Post*, February 10, 1999, www.washingtonpost.com/wp-srv/inatl/longterm/coldwar/shatter021099b.htm, and Eryn Macdonald, "The Man Who Saved the World," in Union of Concerned Scientists, *All Things Nuclear* (blog), February 3, 2015, allthingsnuclear.org/emacdonald/the-man-who-saved-the-world.

3. Eric Schlosser, *Command and Control: Nuclear Weapons, the Damascus Accident, and the Illusion of Safety* (New York: Penguin Books, 2014), 478.

persons, including terrorist hackers, might be able to slip electronically inside the network, seize control over the radio transmitters, and illicitly send fake orders to the boats. The deficiency was deemed so serious that the sub launch crews had to be given elaborate new instructions for validating launch orders in order to ensure that they would not fire upon receipt of phony orders."[80] In a 2017 op-ed,[81] Blair revealed further details—the radio transmitters were in Maine and would be used to communicate with SSBNs patrolling in the Atlantic, and the new launch instructions required submarine crews to reject a launch order that came out of the blue unless it could be verified through a second source.

The fourth and final observation about today's NC3 system is that its fixed elements depend on civilian critical infrastructure such as the electric grid.[82] Although these elements (e.g., command posts) have the capability to operate on their own for some period of time, they cannot do so indefinitely—diesel fuel tanks for backup generators, for example, eventually need to be refilled. Thus, cyber attacks on civilian infrastructure have some capacity to disrupt the operation of these elements, depending on how long various cyber-attack-induced outages last. To a lesser degree, the same is true of mobile assets: airborne command posts must land eventually; even the E-4B National Airborne Operations Center, used by the president, can only stay airborne for less than a week.[83] On the other hand, a cyber attack on the infrastructure supporting the hosting base or airport is much more problematic than one attacking a fixed command post. Since the airborne command post could land at any suitable base or airport, the scale of a cyber attack able to affect airborne command posts by targeting infrastructure would have to be national or even international in scope. In sum, the ability of the NC3 system to support wartime operations depends to some extent on the ability of the relevant civilian critical infrastructure to resist cyber attacks.

What about other nuclear powers?

So far, this book has focused on the U.S. nuclear enterprise, but the United States is not the only nuclear power in the world. An important question thus arises—how and to what extent, if any, do the issues and concerns addressed here apply to the nuclear enterprises of other powers. Far less is known in the open literature about this. Some Soviet/Russian NC3 failures are known, and are shown in table 3.1.

The following high-level considerations apply in this respect:

- The weapons systems of all nations are increasingly dependent on computers, whether they are imported or domestically produced.
- Computers will almost certainly be an important part of nuclear weap-

ons design and sometimes production. The World War II Manhattan Project produced nuclear weapons without the benefit of numerically controlled machining or digital computing as we know them today, and a nation today could likely produce nuclear weapons the same way. However, the Manhattan Project cost $20 billion in 1940's dollars, which would be around $280 billion today, and its present-day equivalent would be very expensive and difficult. Access to advanced computing would greatly ease the task.

- Force structures involving nuclear weapons systems of other nations may be significantly different than those of the United States. A most notable difference is that whereas the United States relies heavily on submarines (SSBNs) for its secure second-strike capability (the United Kingdom and France almost entirely so), Russia and China put greater emphasis on mobile land-based missiles. Given the physics of their respective operating environments, the vulnerabilities to cyber attack of the NC3 infrastructures of land-mobile missiles and SSBNs differ considerably.

- Command and control protocols for nuclear weapons in other nations vary,[84] but all will require an extensive information technology infrastructure to support those arrangements.

- To the extent that the budgets of other nations are more limited than those of the United States, it may be that other nations will be more likely to economize by sharing conventional and nuclear functionality in NC3 and weapons systems to a higher degree than the United States would. For similar reasons, they may also be more dependent on commercial off-the-shelf technologies for the computing base on which to build their NC3 and weapons systems applications.

If these considerations are valid, it is likely that the nuclear enterprises of other nations are also subject to cyber risk that is comparable in scope and nature to the risk faced by the U.S. nuclear enterprise. Given historical U.S. advantages over other nations in information technology, those risks may be even greater than those faced by the United States.

The Growing Complexity of Nuclear Modernization

The 2018 *Nuclear Posture Review* specifically called attention to the need for a modernization of U.S. NC3 systems.[85] In March 2019, General John Hyten, then-commander of U.S. Strategic Command, said that the NC3 system was resilient, reliable, and effective, but that its functionality would be questionable in about a decade.[86]

According to the 2018 *Nuclear Posture Review,* the need for U.S. NC3 modernization is driven by two issues. First, space as a domain of military operations is much less of a sanctuary than it was in the mid-1980s, when the U.S. NC3 system last underwent significant modernization and change, and is "increasingly congested, competitive, and contested." Since nations like Russia and China have developed the means to disrupt, disable, degrade, and destroy U.S. space assets, space-based elements of the U.S. NC3 system must become more survivable, defendable, and resilient.

Second, the *Nuclear Posture Review* states that because potential adversaries are emphasizing the employment of limited nuclear options, the U.S. NC3 system must be resilient in the context of limited nuclear strikes by an adversary. Such strikes could even include nuclear strikes that did not directly harm individuals on earth—high-altitude nuclear electromagnetic pulse (EMP) attacks and space use of nuclear weapons, could significantly degrade NC3 capabilities even if they did not harm a single person themselves.[87]

In these scenarios, nuclear weapon effects could potentially impair the theater elements of U.S. and allied NC3 systems, inhibiting early-warning sensors, multinational leadership conferencing, and prospective orders to theater-based nuclear forces.[88] Such effects could force the United States to exercise nuclear command and control for further nuclear operations, should they become necessary, in that degraded environment (e.g., ionospheric disturbances, nuclear-induced electromagnetic pulses).[89] Although much of the NC3 infrastructure is (and will be in the future) designed to mitigate the effects of such an environment, it is likely and expected that such an environment will nonetheless degrade or disrupt the operation of some NC3 elements.

The *Nuclear Posture Review* thus calls for U.S. leadership, including

Box 3.4. Joint All-Domain Command and Control

Joint All-Domain Command and Control (JADC2) is the Department of Defense's concept for connecting sensors from all military services into a single network that can seamlessly, easily, and rapidly pass data to commanders so that they—possibly assisted by AI-based decision support systems—can recommend the most appropriate weapons, regardless of service ownership, to engage targets that reflected in the data.[1] The intent underlying the JADC2 concept is to allow operations that integrate military capabilities across all domains simultaneously. Successful implementation of JADC2 would enable targets to be identified, data to be processed, and weapons to be allocated in hours or minutes (and potentially seconds) compared to the multiday timeline in which such operations currently sometimes occur.

1. U.S. Congressional Research Service, "Joint All-Domain Command and Control (JADC2)," *In Focus*, IF11493, Version 13, March 18, 2021, fas.org/sgp/crs/natsec/IF11493.pdf

combatant commanders, to be able to communicate and share information across their command and control systems, and to integrate nuclear and nonnuclear military planning and operations in the context of adversary nuclear employment. Indeed, a number of senior DoD officials even before the Trump administration have spoken of the need for conventional-nuclear integration.[90] In September 2016, Secretary of Defense Ashton Carter said: "[W]e're refreshing NATO's nuclear playbook to better integrate conventional and nuclear deterrence to ensure we plan and train like we'd fight and to deter Russia from thinking it can benefit from nuclear use in a conflict with NATO."[91] Assistant Secretary of Defense for Strategy, Plans, And Capabilities Robert Scher stated that in conventional-nuclear integration, "nuclear planning needs to account for the possibility of ongoing U.S. and allied conventional operations," and that integration means "being prepared to restore deterrence following adversary nuclear use, so that failure to deter first use does not translate into failure to deter subsequent nuclear use."[92] Comments such as these suggest a much greater degree of conventional-nuclear integration in the future NC3 system as compared to that of today's NC3, even if the U.S. NC3 system is also used today both for nuclear and nonnuclear purposes (though primarily intended for nuclear purposes).[93]

The 2018 *Nuclear Posture Review* reinforces this conclusion, stating that "U.S. forces will ensure their ability to integrate nuclear and non-nuclear military planning and operations. Combatant Commands and Service components will be organized and resourced for this mission, and will plan, train, and exercise to integrate U.S. nuclear and nonnuclear forces and operate in the face of adversary nuclear threats and attacks."[94] Further elaborating on this point, General Hyten stated in February 2020 that NC3 and Joint All-Domain Command and Control (JADC2), DoD's strategy for connecting sensors and shooters of all U.S. military services into a single seamless network (Box 3.4), are intertwined. NC3 will operate in elements of JADC2, and each must inform the other.[95] With today's NC3, the information flows are largely protected and separate from conventional military data flows. That will change with JADC2 and the new NC3, Hyten said.

Separately, the *Nuclear Posture Review* also identifies adversary offensive cyber capabilities as creating new challenges and potential vulnerabilities for U.S. NC3. The U.S. NC3 system today remains assured and effective, it claims, but additional steps will be needed to "address [future] challenges to network defense, authentication, data integrity, and secure, assured, and reliable information flow across a resilient NC3 network."

Not much is known publicly about the design of the modernized NC3 system. Admiral Haney testified that it would likely involve "a networked IP-based national C3 architecture" that is at "the core of a broader, national command and control system."[96] (IP stands for "Internet Protocol," a set of rules and requirements for moving data on the Internet. Even networks that are not connected to the Internet can use IP for moving data.) General Hyten asserted: "[W]e [will] transition to a modern threat-based NC3 enterprise architecture and address the growing cyber, asymmetric, and kinetic challenges."[97]

One important potential benefit of a successful modernization program for NC3 is that the new design can help to rationalize the underlying architecture. In light of General Hyten's comments above that he could not explain the workings of today's NC3 system, this benefit is particularly significant. But in large part because the system must be in continuous operation throughout the modernization process, the future "to-be" system will necessarily evolve from today's "as-is" system—it is neither desirable nor practical to build an entirely new system and then one day transfer all operational responsibilities from old system to new system. Thus, the future modernized NC3 system may well be simpler from the standpoint of the underlying technologies (e.g., with fewer point-to-point hard-wired systems and more interoperable systems running on a common network infrastructure), but its complexity will also be driven by its functional requirements—what users want the system to do. The operative question is thus whether the security gains afforded by simplification, mostly of the underlying hardware, will be offset by security losses incurred as the result of added software complexity driven by new demands for functionality. (The relationship between functionality, complexity, and security is addressed further in chapter 4, "Cybersecurity Lessons for Nuclear Modernization.")

Nuclear platforms and delivery systems also included in the overall nuclear modernization program—the B-21 bomber, the Long Range Stand-Off (LRSO) cruise missile, the GBSD, and Columbia-class submarines—will need to be integrated with the architecture of the modernized NC3 system.[98] These platforms will be "much more like all systems today, network connected. They'll be cyber enabled" and will have "some level of connectivity to the rest of the warfighting system," according to Werner J. A. Dahm, chair of the Air Force Scientific Advisory Board.[99] The shift to "cyber-enabled" connectivity will mean a higher degree of interoperability among NC3 systems, which will no longer be as constrained by hardware restrictions.

The TW/AA portion of the NC3 system will also have to be modernized to address previously uncontemplated technologies.[100] For example, maneuverable hypersonic weapons will necessitate new capabilities for launch detection and tracking of flight trajectories. Surveillance to identify anti-satellite attacks in progress will also become necessary, as such attacks may signal the onset of a strategic attack.

Satellites are also subject to cyber attacks, either on the ground stations controlling their operation or by a direct transmission to the satellite that enters its control channels. For example, in 2002, the U.S. Government Accountability Office found that some commercial satellites do not employ encrypted control links, which means that an adversary could take direct control of these satellites.[101] There is no particular reason to believe that no military satellites suffer from this same security vulnerability—indeed, I know of one military satellite for which this was true in the 1980's. One might expect military satellites to employ encrypted command links as a matter of course, but such expectations are from time to time not borne out in practice.

It is likely that the bandwidth supplied by the modernized system will be significantly greater than that of the current NC3 system. Leaders engaged in consultation with senior advisors, allies, and perhaps even adversaries will require high-fidelity voice, video, and data connections that will require orders of magnitude more bandwidth than an NC3 system designed primarily to transmit EAMs consisting of a few to several tens of alphanumeric characters. In practice, these high-bandwidth channels will be less able to operate and operate securely in a nuclear environment and also be less available because of the varying physical location of the relevant human actors.[102]

Finally, General Hyten has provisionally articulated one particular technical design principle for NC3 modernization: the ability to support a sufficiently large number of pathways for messages to be transmitted such that "nobody can ever figure out exactly where it is or deny the ability for that message to get through."[103]

Given the needed characteristics of the modernized NC3 system, in October 2018, then-Secretary of Defense James N. Mattis designated the commander of U.S. Strategic Command as the NC3 Enterprise Lead responsible for NC3 enterprise operations, requirements, and systems engineering and integration.[104] To fulfill this responsibility, U.S. Strategic Command established the NC3 Enterprise Center (NEC) in 2019, which works with the NC3 capability portfolio manager in the Office of the Undersecretary of Defense for Acquisition and Sustainment. In turn, the NC3 capability portfolio manager is responsible for missile warning, presidential decision-making, and communications links to the bomber, submarine, and missile legs of the nuclear triad, developing NC3 policy, guidance, and plans; providing programmatic risk assessments and analyses of current and future enterprise capabilities; and developing and advocating for NC3 investments within DoD's annual budget process.[105]

These institutional responses speak to the necessity of complex systems design to have a single architectural team in charge of the overall design who can maintain its conceptual integrity, an important aspect of design for secure systems. On the other hand, the DoD acquisition system is service-oriented, and U.S. Strategic Command does not have any acquisition authority of its own for NC3,[106] but will rather rely on that of the services, at least for now. (Acquisition authority for nuclear weapons as such resides primarily with the Department of Energy,[107] and for weapons platforms with the individual services.)

DoD Responses to Cybersecurity Challenges to the U.S. Nuclear Enterprise

Senior DoD representatives have expressed awareness of cyber risks associated with nuclear modernization, at least rhetorically, and have noted the importance of mitigating these risks. "Our NC2 hardware infrastructure fails if the NC3 fails due to a cyber-attack. . ... Cyber defense is not a 'trade space' discussion; it is an additive necessity in today's technology-centric world," Admiral Charles A. Richard, commander of U.S. Strategic Command, testified to Congress in 2020.[108]

In a similar vein, the 2020 version of the DoD *Nuclear Matters Handbook,* issued by the Office of the Deputy Assistant Secretary of Defense for Nuclear Matters, states:

> Cyber risks will accelerate as nuclear modernization proceeds and systems are migrated to internet protocols. The new generation of nuclear forces, the Columbia-class SSBNs, ground-based strategic deterrent (GBSD), ICBMs, B-21, long-range standoff (LRSO) cruise missiles, and F-35 will be designed to modern cyber standards. It will be critical for designers of future NC3 to adopt cyber defense to mitigate threats from

adversary offensive cyber action against these systems. Cyber threat mitigation will address the network vulnerabilities to ensure U.S. NC3 remains an assured, effective, and resilient network.[109]

Has such awareness translated into adequate action? It is useful to recall a bit of history along these lines.

In 2017, the Defense Science Board recommended that U.S. Strategic Command conduct an annual assessment of the cyber resilience of the U.S. nuclear deterrent, including all essential nuclear "Thin Line" components (e.g., NC3, platforms, delivery systems, and warheads),[110] and that the Nuclear Weapons Council—the U.S. government body that serves to coordinate the acquisition of DoD-provided delivery systems with DoE-provided nuclear weapons—establish a program of action with milestones to support cyber certification of U.S. nuclear forces and NC3 in the face of "concerted adversary attack against nuclear systems based on extensive preparation (e.g., including supply chain, insider threats, and physical sabotage or attack in addition to remote cyberattacks)."[111]

Possibly in response to the 2017 DSB report, the U.S. Congress directed the Department of Defense in Section 1640 of the FY 2018 National Defense Authorization Act (NDAA) to establish a Strategic Cybersecurity Program (SCP) to help improve the cybersecurity of certain U.S. government systems, including "nuclear deterrent systems."[112] Specifically, the program is given the responsibility for conducting "reviews of existing systems and infrastructure and acquisition plans for proposed systems and infrastructure" before a DoD decision to enter the relevant program into system development and demonstration ("Milestone B" in DoD acquisition parlance,[113] a point usually regarded as the official start of a program). The conference report on the FY 2018 NDAA stated congressional expectations that the SCP would "organize and focus efforts, and improve our understanding of where gaps may exist in terms of people, resources, focus and authorities" and noted that much of the capability needed to execute the program already existed in DoD combat support agencies such as the National Security Agency (NSA) and the Defense Information Systems Agency.[114]

Congress took further action to address cybersecurity for NC3. Subtitle D of the FY 2018 NDAA required the secretary of defense to provide an annual assessment of the cyber resiliency of the nuclear command and control system (Section 1651), to prohibit the use of telecommunications equipment from China or Russia in any system substantially involved in either the nuclear deterrence or homeland missile defense missions (Section 1656); and to evaluate the supply chain security aspects of nuclear NC3 (Section 1659).[115] Possibly as the result of the Section 1651 requirement, the director of operational testing and evaluation (DOT&E) undertook a number of classified cybersecurity assessments in FY 2019 to characterize the status and identify options for improving the mission assurance and cyber-related aspects of NC3 capability.

The outcome of these directives has not been entirely satisfactory. One data point is that a year after the passage of the FY 2018 NDAA, the director of the Strategic Cybersecurity Program said: "There's no way that I can do an assessment of that many systems and I don't even know what that term [strategic cybersecurity] means yet," noting that he would be responsible for over 4,500 systems and had only nine certified NSA red teams across the various combatant commands.[116] (A red team is a group of cyber personnel skilled in attack methods [one might call them "ethical hackers"] that is given the task of penetrating a target system and reporting up the chain of command the security weaknesses identified so that the weaknesses can be remediated.) A second data point is provided by the DOT&E cybersecurity assessment, which noted that its assessment had been briefed at senior levels of DoD leadership, and had "resulted in a significant increase in focus in this vital area,"[117] thus implying that the prior focus on NC3 cybersecurity had been inadequate.

Nor has the Congress been satisfied with DoD progress on these matters. Section 1747 of the FY 2021 NDAA required the secretary of defense to submit to it a comprehensive plan for implementing the findings and recommendations of the assessment required by the 2018 NDAA, including a concept of operations to defend the NC3 system from cyberattacks and develop an oversight mechanism to ensure implementation.[118] Had the Congress (or at least the relevant members and/or their staffs) been satisfied with progress to date, this additional requirement would not have been necessary.

In addition, Section 1712 of the FY 2021 NDAA completely revamped the SCP. In addition to being much more prescriptive about its organization and structure, this section called for the SCP to include "all of the systems, critical infrastructure, kill chains, and processes, including systems and components in development" that comprise a number of military missions, including but not limited to nuclear deterrence and strike. Again, such radical change in a program's legislative charter indicates clear dissatisfaction with how the program has been operating to date.

4 Cybersecurity Lessons for Nuclear Modernization

Human beings set foot on the moon in 1969, and electronic computers were critical to the success of the Apollo mission. And yet, an iPhone in 2020 is a hundred million times faster than the Apollo computers.[1] We have become accustomed to remarkable advances in computing occurring frequently, and we expect our computers to be faster and easier to use, to do familiar things faster, and to help us do tasks we had not previously imagined.

But this sophisticated functionality has come at a cost. Though often hidden from view, the underlying technology is also ever more complex, and more complexity inevitably means more insecurity.

Functionality, complexity, and insecurity

Information technologies have spread throughout global society like wildfire (or Covid) because people everywhere find them useful for processing and managing information to improve their lives. However, all else being equal, greater functionality of an information technology system entails increased complexity of design and implementation of that system. That is, for a given level of technological sophistication, more functionality means more complexity. An increase in the technological sophistication of software can break this link in the short term—compilers that translated high-level languages into machine code enabled the development of programs that were much less complex (at the human-readable source code level) for a given level of functionality (as defined by what the computer actually did at the machine code level). But in the absence of regular and frequent increases in sophistication of software-building technology, more functionality is sure to mean more complexity.

In his 1980 Turing Award lecture (in computer science, the equivalent of the Nobel Prize lecture), C.A.R. Hoare noted that "there are two ways of constructing a software design: One way is to make it so simple that there are obviously no deficiencies, and the other way is to make it so complicated that there are no obvious deficiencies."[2] These lessons have been taken to heart by cybersecurity analysts, who are virtually unanimous in their contention that system complexity is the enemy of cybersecurity. Greater system complexity means a larger attack surface (i.e., more places where flaws can be found), which an adversary can exploit (i.e., vulnerabilities). Evaluating the security of a system thus becomes more difficult as the system grows in complexity—more interfaces, more options, more specifications and requirements, more modules, more code, more interactions with external entities, more users, more human errors.[3] System developers work hard to eliminate vulnerabilities, but they don't find every one, and as the system becomes more complex, the harder it is to identify them.

And yet, in all domains of life, including the domain of military operations, the evidence to date is that the appetite for increased functionality afforded by information technology is unlimited. Users want more functional information technology systems—they want them to operate faster and more accurately, to offer more options, to be more easily used, to be interoperable with one another, to process more and different kinds of data, and so on. This phenomenon is a manifestation of what software engineers often describe as the "second system" effect.[4] Later versions of a system are inevitably more complex than earlier versions, in large part because engineers attempt to remedy perceived and real inadequacies in the functionality of those earlier versions.

Security, however, is in a category by itself. Security is not desirable in and of itself—it is only desirable as a means to an end and to the extent that it enables users to have the functionality they really do want when they are subject to cyberattack. Good security is demonstrated by bad things that do not happen. Thus, by not moderating their appetites for functionality, users are implicitly asking for—indeed, demanding—systems that will inevitably be more insecure.

The current NC3 system is complex. But one particular aspect of the modernized NC3 system raises concerns about the security and reliability that can be expected from the modernization, namely, the scope and nature of how it connects to conventional-nuclear integration. A system that supports the integration of both nuclear and nonnuclear functions for warfighting will entail more functionality (and thus will be more complex) than one that supports mostly nuclear functions for deterrence purposes. That additional complexity will almost certainly be at least as much of a driver of increased cyber vulnerability as the fact that NC3 will have some connections to the outside world through a networked IP-based national C3 architecture at the core of a broader, national command and control system.

These comments put Admiral Richard's comments about cyber defense not being a "trade space" discussion in a somewhat different light. In his testimony, he was trying to emphasize the importance of cybersecurity when he called it an "additive necessity." In other words, he was saying that cybersecurity had to have equal and not lesser status compared to other characteristics of the infrastructure. On the other hand, his testimony did not address the possibility that other system functionality might have to be given up to achieve adequate levels of cybersecurity.

Building complex systems when requirements change rapidly—what could possibly go wrong?

Concerns about security flaws become even more salient in light of public comments from senior DoD officials that a modernized NC3 system must be flexible and adaptive in an environment of rapidly changing requirements. For example, in November 2018, U.S. Strategic Command noted in an announcement regarding a U.S. government contracting opportunity that the future NC3 system would have to "enable delivery of a flexible, continuously evolving, threat-driven set of capabilities."[5] In June 2019, Elizabeth Durham-Ruiz, director of U.S. Strategic Command's Nuclear Command, Control, and Communications Enterprise Center, said that "we must design an architecture that is flexible, resilient, and adaptive and can evolve with the threat and advances in technology."[6]

In 2020, Admiral Richard stated that U.S. Strategic Command "will continue to develop the [nuclear] enterprise's future requirements and ensure a safe, secure, and reliable architecture for the future. As we move towards the next generation of NC3, we must work with industry to rapidly prototype new technologies and experiment with them to determine their effectiveness. In addition, we will continue cooperation on NATO NC3 systems that require modernization to enable appropriate consultations and effective nuclear operations, improve survivability, resilience, and flexibility. We need to move rapidly and if a new technology appears promising, acquire and field it quickly—and if our experiment shows it is not feasible, to 'fail fast,' and move on."[7]

Cybersecurity is inherently a drag on development schedules, however, which does not add to the system's utility for the end user. Cybersecurity is a desirable property of a system, just as usability, interoperability, functionality, and so on are desirable, but security is different because its effect is to ensure that nothing happens when an adversary tries to compromise a system. As noted earlier, good cybersecurity for a system is demonstrated when the system performs as though nothing is wrong and attackers don't exist. Resources spent to improve cybersecurity are thus at first glance apparently superfluous—and it is easy to divert these resources to fund other aspects of the development effort or to reduce the overall cost of the effort. In this environment, it will always be faster and cheaper to develop a less secure system of a given functionality than a more secure one of equal functionality, or for equal cost to develop a less secure system of greater functionality or a more secure one of lesser functionality.

The preceding argument ignores the fact that military systems should always be designed with an adversary's response in mind. In principle, cyber threats could be just one more aspect of that response against which defenses must be erected, and cybersecurity just one more aspect of the defensive functionality for those systems. For past systems, one could argue that cyber threats were new and therefore underappreciated—but with all of the attention given to such threats today, shouldn't systems designers and operators be more cognizant of cybersecurity issues?

Yes. But the empirical evidence suggests that whatever awareness these individuals have about the problem simply does not translate into adequate action. One piece of evidence is the 2018 GAO report that showed not only that many cyber vulnerabilities existed in U.S. weapons systems, but that they were routinely discounted.[8] Another data point comes from field exercises that do not accurately portray the cyber threat. I once had the opportunity to observe an Army brigade combat exercise involving an opposing force that was supposed to be operating under free-play conditions—that is, the opposing force was free to innovate tactics against the brigade in training as it saw fit.[9] However, conversations with the personnel running the exercise revealed that the opposing force was highly constrained in the cyber dimension—and the reason offered was that giving them full free rein would shut down the exercise prematurely and prevent the brigade from achieving its other training objectives.

The logic of this rationale is understandable—given the multi-million dollar cost of the exercise, it made more sense not to shut down the exercise prematurely. But one result of conducting the exercise under the conditions described is that the brigade's personnel will experience an unrealistically attenuated cyber threat, and will thus be severely handicapped if and when they deal with real-world adversaries that do have significant cyber capabilities. Perhaps allowing expensive exercises to collapse because of inadequate attention to cyber issues would promote greater awareness of and motivate greater action on cybersecurity matters.

An environment of rapidly changing requirements exacerbates the tension between functionality and security. As a variety of senior military leaders have indicated, the new environment for nuclear operations is one in which threats and threat actors will emerge rapidly and with little warning, and they have called for an NC3 architecture that can evolve just or nearly as rapidly. Looking at today's NC3 architecture, developed in the 1980s without the benefit of either the Internet or modern software engineering techniques, the expectation seems to be that the techniques of today will facilitate such an evolvable architecture.

As Silicon Valley has demonstrated, these techniques do produce software that is flexible, adaptive, and responsive to rapid changes in the market. On the other hand, such software is neither resilient nor secure. Software engineering techniques that work well for low-stakes Uber and Doordash applications are not necessarily well suited for high-stakes applications such as NC3. Even large information technology-based organizations such as Google and Amazon suffered from hours-long world-wide service outages in 2020 when their business models call for 24/7/365 availability.[10] Such failures would not be consistent with Durham-Ruiz's inclusion of resilience in her architectural requirements—imagine the significance of a hours-long system-wide outage that resulted in a loss of connectivity between the president and U.S. nuclear forces. (It is true that submarines on patrol are not in constant communications with higher authority under normal circumstances. But they do maintain connectivity and are *capable* of receiving messages at any time.)

How is Silicon Valley able to deliver software as rapidly as it does? One significant factor is the availability of large bodies of source code segments in repositories such as GitHub that are publicly available for incorporation into products. Code segments that are not precisely suitable can be modified for use, thus reducing development time significantly.

More important is a philosophy that emphasizes close communications between system designers, developers, operators, and users. This makes possible the deployment of useful working software in small increments on short time scales—days or weeks rather than months or (as was often the case with the software engineering of the 1980s) years. Rapid cycles greatly increase the likelihood that the developer will deliver functionality that the user wants and will actually use. This is the actual idea behind "failing fast": a wrong turn by the developer can be identified quickly based on user feedback that the interface is too awkward to use or the user needs to import data from a different system. And so, the next iteration, available in a week or two, has a streamlined interface or a new data import capability.

With this philosophy in mind (one Silicon Valley buzzword for which is "agile DevOps"), system development is not deferred until a complete set of system requirements is in hand. Because the time needed to generate a complete set of requirements may be long, the system may well be at least partially obsolete by the time it is deployed. Instead, it is acceptable—indeed, expected—that the requirements will evolve as users become more confident about what they want based on actual use of earlier iterations of the system, and they will get their hands on usable capabilities much more rapidly. In principle, the only truly fixed requirement of this software development philosophy is that the user should get what the user wants and get it fast.

For Silicon Valley, the users of a system are the customers who are willing to pay (either in time or exposure to advertisements) for using a given product or service. Such willingness is a good metric through which developers can measure success. Rapid iteration brings product or service into greater alignment with user desires, and thus increases such willingness.

But who are the users of the NC3 system? The operators of the weapons systems at the receiving end of the nuclear command and control apparatus? Senior decision-makers, such as the commander of U.S. Strategic Command? The U.S. president? One could make a plausible argument for any of these, but in fact the answer is—all of them. They all have different requirements for NC3. Unlike the Silicon Valley environment, the military environment—and especially the nuclear weapons environment—is much more driven from the top down rather than from the bottom up.

To wit—it is entirely appropriate for the pilot of a dual-capable bomber carrying nuclear weapons to provide input and feedback on what appears on a display screen. Perhaps the screen is too cluttered or the colors lack sufficient contrast, and developers working with pilots should have the flexibility to change those requirements. But it may also be a requirement that the pilot must obtain approval from a senior commander for using a nuclear weapon to strike a target of opportunity. A pilot may complain that seeking such approval will introduce delay into such a strike, but that is not a requirement that should be changed or eliminated only by pilots working with coding teams.

Moreover, a fail-fast mindset is unacceptable in nuclear operations. To his credit, Admiral Richard's comment about "failing fast" applied to experiments with technology proposed for incorporation into a modernized NC3 system, and not to its ongoing operation, where he and most other people would agree that failing fast is highly undesirable. Yet how precisely to draw the line between requirements that should be changed, can be changed, or should never be changed will be an ongoing challenge in applying a Silicon Valley mindset to NC3 modernization. One possible strawman guideline could be that when a portion of the system focuses only on a single user's needs, an agile DevOps approach may make sense. On the other hand, if a portion of the system focuses on the needs of many users separated by significantly different levels in a command hierarchy, agile DevOps should be avoided at all costs.

Being secure or getting work done

When users turn off or bypass or disable or fail to deploy available security features, they serve no protective function. Management may promulgate practices or procedures to improve security, but if they not followed in practice, they too serve no protective function. Consider an experience reported by Donald Norman that is directly on point. In his telling:[11]

> I recently attended two conferences on Usability, Security, and Privacy. The first, SOUPS (Symposium on Usable Privacy and Security), was held on the Google campus in Mountain View, California, the second at the National Academies building in Washington, DC. Google is a semi-restricted campus. People can freely wander about the campus, but most buildings are locked and openable only with the proper badge. Security guards were visibly present: polite and helpful, but always watching. Our

meetings were held in a public auditorium that did not require authorization for entrance. But the room was in a secure building, and the
toilets were within the secure space. *How did the world's security experts
handle the situation? With a brick. The side door of the auditorium that
led to the secure part of the building and the toilets was propped open with
a brick.* So much for key access, badges, and security guards. (Emphasis
added.)

Let me emphasize again: This event was a meeting for *security experts*!
And we know about similar examples—passwords on yellow Post-It notes
stuck to monitors or hidden under the keyboard, door keys under door-
mats or inside fake rocks.

Experience demonstrates that even when cyberthreats are ubiquitous,
users often turn off security features and fail to follow security practices.
For example, passwords present an innate tension between usability
(which is aided by having short, easily memorizable passwords and re-
using them across multiple systems) and security (which dictates longer,
more diverse passwords that are difficult to crack, as well as distinct passwords for each system). Left to their own devices, users almost inevitably
opt for usability and convenience.

Another example: personnel in different locations often need to share
files with each other, but the approved methods for sharing files are often
a hassle to use. If they have not worked together before, these people
may be required to go through a complex multistep process to designate files that they want to share with one another—identifying specific
files, entering ID information for the permitted recipients, and so on. If
deadlines are pressing, they may well choose to circumvent this process
by e-mailing their files to one another on their personal accounts. If the
files are password-protected, they may even transmit the passwords by e-
mail. This alternative process eliminates the hassle factor of the approved
procedure, but makes their files vulnerable to all of the security issues
associated with the open Internet.[12]

A similar issue arises for system administrators who are required to
specify privileges for what specific users are allowed to do—read files,

copy files, and so on. Good security practice calls for individuals to have the fewest privileges they need to do their work; having more privileges than necessary can facilitate abuse. But in the real world, an individual's role is often not as well-defined as in a formal job description. An individual might be asked by a supervisor to take on a task that is not within that person's usual responsibilities, and that task might require a different set of privileges. The system administrator must now change the individual's privileges (and of course must also verify with the individual's supervisor that the new task requires those new privileges). This is a recipe for delay. If it is common practice to assign tasks to individuals based on their talents rather than their roles, a system administrator may for entirely good reasons assign a broad rather than narrow set of privileges to all users simply to improve work flow—at the cost of better security.

With few exceptions, security features are clumsy and awkward to use; some are hard for everyone except security engineers to understand (and even some security engineers are confused); and some get in the way of doing real work. Especially important in the context of an unfolding crisis, they also slow down work processes. Users circumvent cybersecurity measures, not because they are lazy, but because they are trying to do their jobs well. When security gets in the way, users switch it off and work around it, designers avoid strong security, and administrators make mistakes in using it.

The design of any computer system entails trade-offs among various system characteristics: trustworthiness or security, better or less costly administration, ease of use, and so on. Because the aim of security is to make a system completely unusable to an unauthorized party but completely usable to an authorized one, system designers must make trade-offs between security and the ease of getting work done. More secure systems are generally harder to use and have fewer features that are helpful for users.

Butler Lampson, another Turing Award recipient, has written that "users, administrators, organizations, and vendors respond to the incentives they perceive. Users just want to get their work done; they don't have good reasons to value security, and view it as a burden. If it's hard or opaque, they will ignore it or work around it. . . If you force them, less useful work will get done."[13] This is a reality on the ground that NC3 system architects and designers will have to face, and accounts for practices such as setting permissive action link (PAL) codes to all zeros.[14] Put differently, security mechanisms for NC3 inevitably impede fulfillment of the "always" requirement.

Cybersecurity as a holistic, emergent property

Systems built around computer and communications technologies have many places where operationally exploitable vulnerabilities can be found.[15] This is especially true of large, complex systems, and as the discussion of Chapter 3 indicates, the nuclear enterprise is particularly complex.

Elaborating on the earlier discussion of cyber vulnerabilities, one set of vulnerabilities is found in the software running in those systems. In such software, exploitable vulnerabilities may be present as the result of faulty program design or implementation, usually accidentally but occasionally deliberately. Should the system or network come into electronic contact with a hostile source, malware can be introduced by way of such vulnerabilities.

Software vulnerabilities can be introduced through more subtle paths as well. For example, compilers are used to generate object code (i.e., the 1's and 0's that actually direct the operation of computers) from source code (i.e., the human-readable lines of programming code that are the medium in which people formulate programs). The compiler itself must be secure, for it could otherwise introduce object code that subversively and subtly modifies the functionality represented in the source code.[16] A particular sequence of instructions could exploit an obscure and poorly known characteristic of hardware functioning, which means that programmers well versed in small details of the machine on which the code will be running could introduce functionality that would go undetected in any review of the source code.

Hardware vulnerabilities may also be present. Hardware includes microprocessors, microcontrollers, firmware, circuit boards, power supplies, peripherals such as printers or scanners, displays, storage devices, and communications equipment such as network cards. Hardware is physical, so tampering with these components requires physical access at some point in the hardware's life cycle, which may be difficult to obtain. However, hardware is difficult to inspect, so hardware compromises are hard to detect. An auxiliary graphics display card usually has an onboard processor and memory that can support the execution of a program that is entirely separate from that running on a system's "main" processor. Peripheral devices such as external disk drives in bidirectional communications with their hosts, providing possible access for an adversary to introduce malware to them.

The communications channels between the system or network and the "outside" world present another set of vulnerabilities. A system that does not communicate with the outside world is generally secure, but it is also largely useless. Thus, communications of some sort must be established, and those channels can be compromised—for example, by spoofing (an adversary pretends to be the "authorized" system), by jamming (an adversary denies access to anyone else), or by eavesdropping (an adversary obtains information intended to be confidential). Communications channels that lead to other systems also provide routes that adversaries can use; penetrating System A (of secondary interest to the adversary) may well afford the adversary the opportunity to penetrate System B (of primary interest to the adversary).

Another important category of "communications channel" vulnerabilities involves the physical channels over which components are delivered to system integrators and finished systems are delivered to customers. Components and systems are put into boxes, loaded onto trucks and boats and planes, and delivered to their destination, usually unattended for long periods of time. Every one of these periods is an opportunity to introduce a vulnerability. A set of CD-ROMs may be intercepted and a different set introduced in its place; extra functionality might be introduced during chip fabrication or motherboard assembly; a default security configuration might be set in an insecure state—and so on.

Collectively, the above set of vulnerabilities provides some detail on supply chain vulnerabilities, and they speak to the fundamental point that

Box 4.1. Difficulties of Defending against Supply-Chain Attacks

Supply-chain attacks render a computational artifact vulnerable before it is put into use.[1] If that artifact is a component that is subsequently integrated into a system, the entire system may become vulnerable. Defense against supply-chain attacks seeks to ensure that components supplied are themselves secure. But that is easier said than done. On what basis should the system integrator decide that a component that comes from some other party is secure? For example, does the fact that the component comes from a large, well-known company mean that it should be trusted? What if the system integrator performs extensive testing on the component before integrating it and the component passes all of the tests?

Alas, neither of these approaches is fully adequate. A large, well-known company could be under the control (either overt or covert) of the government to which the company is accountable by law, and might introduce compromises in the products it delivers due to government compulsion. Passing tests is a necessary but not sufficient condition to declare a component secure. Testing generally cannot demonstrate the presence of unwanted (and hostile) functionality in a component, although it may be able to provide evidence that the component does in fact perform as it is supposed to perform. For example, a component may always perform as it should except when one of the inputs is a particular sequence of digits; upon receiving that sequence, the component can (deliberately) perform some unexpected and hostile action.

Perhaps one could inspect the inner mechanisms of a supplied component (e.g., reading the human-understandable software source code supplied) before integrating it into a finished system. But that would require access to source code, which a supplier may well resist for fear of divulging valuable intellectual property. Moreover, inspection and review can take substantial amounts of time, and waiting for inspection to be completed can unduly affect a schedule. Also, what if the component is a fix to a security problem? In that case, a delay can leave a system more vulnerable.

Many methods have been developed (and some deployed) to mitigate the effects of possible supply-chain attacks. Nevertheless, cyber risk associated with such attacks cannot be avoided entirely.

1. Sources: Fred Schneider and Justin Sherman, "Bases for Trust in a Supply Chain," *Lawfare*, February 1, 2021, www.lawfareblog.com/bases-trust-supply-chain; National Research Council (NRC), *Toward a Safer and More Secure Cyberspace*, ed. Seymour Goodman and Herbert Lin (Washington, DC: National Academies Press, 2007), 103–4, doi.org/10.17226/11925; NRC, *At the Nexus of Cybersecurity and Public Policy: Some Basic Concepts and Issues*, ed. David Clark, Thomas Berson, and Herbert Lin (Washington, DC: National Academies Press, 2014), 112–13, doi.org/10.17226/18749.

it is essentially impossible for an organization to create a working system from scratch. Others supply the end-user organization with products and services, and those others are themselves supplied by still others. And to the extent that "others" may be influenced by adversaries, they are all potential threat vectors. Box 4.1 provides some additional commentary on how it is hard to address supply chain attacks, which remain a serious threat.

In addition, operators and users can be compromised through blackmail or extortion. Untrustworthy operators and users can be planted as spies. Users can be tricked into actions that compromise security, thus becoming unwitting "insiders." For example, phishing is the practice of an adversary's sending emails appearing to originate with trustworthy sources such as a friend or a reputable company but containing information intended to induce recipients to open file attachments, click on links, or visit websites that will grant unauthorized access to the user's machine or invite the recipient to provide personal or confidential information such as passwords or credit card numbers. With the authorized user's credentials in hand, an adversary can impersonate that user and has permission to do anything that the authorized user can do.

Authorized parties are also not always careful in protecting sensitive or classified information. In a classified working environment, multiple safeguards are often used to protect information. But the mere existence of multiple safeguards can tempt those working within that environment to ignore certain safeguards in the name of convenience because other safeguards are in place. Instead of storing classified information in a safe at the end of the workday, a person puts a classified document in a desk drawer and covers it with a manila folder—and feels OK about it because he is late for an appointment and besides, the office is protected by armed guards anyway. Passwords may be written on Post-it notes and hidden under a calendar. Furthermore, even the most well-intentioned people sometimes make security mistakes in the course of their day-to-day work.

The organizational environment in which people use these systems are a final source of vulnerability, though it is affects security indirectly. Policies, regulations, laws, budgets, operational business demands, and institutional culture shape how and to what extent users observe appropriate security practices, and often they induce users to make choices that result in greater insecurity. For example, organizations that place higher premiums on employee productivity may well incentivize users to bypass inconvenient security measures. Pressures to lower "time-to-market" may reduce the ability of a vendor to attend to security issues. Would-be users of a product or a service may demand functionality that has a negative impact on security.

Given the dependence of system security on all of the elements described above, security should be considered an emergent, holistic property of a system. The point has two implications. First, a system can be attacked at any point in its supply chain or life cycle: systems (and their components) can be attacked in design, development, testing, production, distribution, installation, configuration, maintenance, and operation. Second, the security of a system should be broadly rather than narrowly construed to include local factors such as people who fail to practice good cyber hygiene or are "insider" threat actors, as well as technical factors such as formal proofs of software correctness. In practice, the actual vulnerabilities that a system must resist are specific to that particular system embedded in its particular context.

5

Cyber Risks in Selected Nuclear Scenarios

This chapter discusses several nuclear scenarios in which the use of offensive cyber capabilities by one side might have an operational effect on the outcome. These scenarios are intended as illustrative, and not exhaustive in any sense of the term. Any individual scenario below may be unlikely (thus making that scenario more difficult to foresee and avoid), but taken together they do suggest a broad range of possibilities for how cyber risks might play out in exacerbating crises involving nuclear weapons, and they should thus be viewed in that light.[1]

Scenario 1: Differing perceptions of cyber penetration of NC3 prior to or during a nuclear crisis

During the 1962 Cuban Missile Crisis, a U-2 reconnaissance aircraft on a routine intelligence gathering mission (collecting air samples over the Soviet Union as part of the monitoring of Soviet nuclear tests) in the Arctic went off course and flew into Soviet airspace. The Soviet Union launched fighters to intercept the airplane, and the United States launched its own nuclear-armed fighters to protect the U-2. Upon hearing this news, Secretary of Defense Robert McNamara expressed grave concerns that the U-2 flight could have been interpreted as the prelude to a U.S. nuclear strike on the Soviet Union.[2]

Although this event had nothing to do with the exercise of cyber capabilities on either side (in 1962, the Internet and personal computers were nothing more than a gleam in the eyes of certain technologists), it has everything to do with the different meanings that each side could assign to the same event. Adapting this scenario for the cyber age, it is further noteworthy that as discussed above, cyber attack and cyber espionage/intelligence gathering employ the same penetration techniques and use the same access pathways; they differ only in the payloads they carry. If a party detects a cyber intrusion before anything untoward has happened, it is often impossible to tell whether the intrusion is intended to cause damage or to exfiltrate information.[3] It would be as if U-2 airplanes were sometimes sent on their missions armed with nuclear weapons and the adversary knew that—under those circumstances, how would they have reacted to the knowledge that a U-2 was over Soviet airspace during the Cuban missile crisis?

A cyber intrusion from nation A detected in B's NC3 system could be part of a relatively benign attempt to gather intelligence or the start of a serious cyber attack by A—and it is impossible for B to know what A intends to do before the payloads are executed. A worst-case judgment could well regard A's intrusion as the start of an attack on B's NC3 system, and could indeed precipitate a major crisis when a lesser one existed before.

To make this discussion more concrete, consider a case in which Nation B announces that it is conducting nuclear exercises that simulate preparation for execution of a strategic nuclear attack. B may in fact be preparing to launch a nuclear attack against A, but under the cover of a nuclear exercise. For example, B may hope that A will not go on full alert because it believes that B is "merely" conducting an exercise.

As part of the exercise, B sends a number of its normally-in-port ballistic missile submarines to sea, an action that could be taken as either an exercise or as the prelude to a real attack. Nation A needs to know what B is intending to do given the dispersal of B's submarines, and A begins a variety of cyber-enabled intelligence-gathering operations in B's NC3 system, hoping to learn something of value in ascertaining B's intentions. (In this context, it is likely that "beginning" means the activation of implants in B's NC3 system placed there long ago, rather than the inserting of new implants at the start of B's suspect activities.)

Now, because of the increased level of A's cyber activities, B detects some of them. What happens next?

A is concerned that B is about to launch an attack and does not trust B's statements that these activities are "only" an exercise. A understandably needs its own intelligence—collected surreptitiously without B's knowledge—to ascertain B's true intentions. One of the most effective ways of collecting that intelligence is to gather communications and to examine documents found inside B's NC3 systems. A wants this information because in its absence, it may overreact to an activity that is indeed just an exercise.

B has a very different perspective. Raising the readiness of military command and control networks would (or should) be a standard part of any exercise. Thus, in the initial phases of the B's exercise, B intensifies cyber scans of its own NC3 system to ensure its security and integrity. This intensification of defensive efforts increases the likelihood of detecting A's cyber activities.

If B finds evidence of A's cyber activities, that evidence is likely to indicate the fact of penetration, but not necessarily the purpose or the capability of the penetration. Thus, B must consider all of the possibilities that a successful penetration might entail—including the possibility that the penetration could be part of or prelude to a cyber attack on B's NC3 system. An additional exacerbating factor would be the tendency to assume that a recent discovery of a penetration corresponds to a recent and successful penetration attempt—and of course, if the penetration happened recently (as opposed to long ago), it may well indicate the recent emergence of hostile intentions on the part of A. Under these circumstances, a reasonable conclusion might well be A is planning an imminent attack on B's NC3 systems, prompting B to take further action to raise the readiness of its nuclear forces.

Consequently, the situation is one in which A knows its intentions are benign, and when it observes B taking further nuclear actions, it does not operate under the assumption that B has a good reason for doing so, and thus believes B is acting more provocatively. Under these circumstances, both A and B have incentives to take more aggressive action, though for different reasons. A is incentivized by the observation that B appears to be mobilizing for more aggressive action without good cause (because A's actions are benign and B should realize that). B is incentivized by the valid observation that it cannot rule out the possibility that A's penetration of B's NC3 infrastructure will compromise B's NC3 capabilities.

Scenario 2—Mistaking attacks on conventional command, control, and communications as attacks on NC3

Command and control is an essential aspect of warfare—indeed, many military doctrines assert that command and control is the single most important activity in war, because no other warfighting activity (e.g., target destruction, logistics resupply, movement of forces) is possible without effective command and control. For example, a U.S. Marine Corps publication asserts:

> "No single activity in war is more important than command and control. Without command and control, campaigns, battles, and organized engagements are impossible, military units degenerate into mobs, and the subordination of military force to policy is replaced by random violence. In short, command and control is essential to all military operations and activities.
>
> With command and control, the countless activities a military force must perform gain purpose and direction. Done well, command and control adds to our strength. Done poorly, it invites disaster, even against a weaker enemy."[4]

Given the importance of command and control, it is entirely understandable that a nation involved in armed conflict might wish to attack its adversary's command and control capabilities and thereby degrading its combat power. Thus, during the initial stages of a kinetic conflict, nation

A may well target the facilities of nation B's military infrastructure used for command and control of conventional forces.[5]

On the other hand, B may have chosen to integrate its conventional and nuclear command and control functions on the same physical technology platforms and taking advantage of the same military information technology and communications infrastructure, much as the United States is planning to do as described earlier. Such integration is possible because from a technology perspective, command and control systems for nuclear forces and for conventional forces have a great deal in common, and the benefits of financial economy and operational simplicity may well prove to be compelling advantages.

But if the technological infrastructure for both conventional and nuclear command and control is the same, such attacks could have two untoward effects. First, A's attacks could actually degrade B's nuclear command and control capabilities, though perhaps as an undesirable side effect of its attack on B's conventional capabilities. Second and just as likely, they could cause concerns on B's part that A is deliberately trying to degrade B's nuclear capabilities pre-emptively.[6]

A couple of vignettes set in the context of the early stages of conventional kinetic conflict will make these concerns more concrete. A first vignette involves a cyber attack on military communications networks used for passing orders and status reports between commanders and subordinates. Depending on how communications paths are arranged between forces and commanders, some portions of the network for conventional forces may be shared with portions used for nuclear forces—this may well be more likely when the conventional forces in question are in fact dual-capable (designed to carry either conventional or nuclear ordnance). A cyber attack that affects the performance of network links common to both conventional and nuclear C2 will, by definition, have effects on nuclear C2.

A second vignette involves early-warning satellites that identify the launch points of ballistic missiles. Nominally designed to monitor the globe for signs of strategic ballistic missile launches (ICBMs and SLBMs), U.S. early-warning satellites are also capable of identifying launches of ballistic missiles with shorter range.[7] Using launch information, theater and tactical ballistic missile defenses can react more quickly and thereby increase the probability of intercepting incoming missiles. Thus, in a conventional conflict, an adversary might be able to increase the effectiveness of its own short-range ballistic missiles by interfering with the operation of U.S. early-warning satellites—and one means of such interference would be cyber attacks on these satellites (or their ground links). But conducting such an attack might lead the United States to conclude that its strategic ballistic missile warning capabilities were under attack, and prompt concerns about the survivability of these capabilities. Similar concerns attach to a cyber attack on an advanced extremely high-frequency communications satellite to degrade tactical communications—such an attack could also degrade nuclear communications provided by that same satellite.[8]

Scenario 3: Cyber attack as a secret nuclear counterforce weapon in large-scale conflict

Conflict between two nations may well result if the two nations find themselves in a confrontation with each other and neither is willing to back down. Stalemate may occur, but if the confrontation escalates, a game of chicken is likely to ensue, with each side tempted to escalate to force the other side to back down. Many factors influence a nation's willingness to back down in a confrontation, such as its perceptions of its own and the adversary's capabilities and willingness to follow through on commitments made not to back down.

A nation's military capabilities are often well known to its adversaries, especially if they are strong. By advertising its capabilities (e.g., by conducting visible exercises), it can build in potential adversaries an impression of strong military power. However, offensive cyber capabilities are an important exception to this rule, since they are usually concealed out of a concern that revealing the capabilities may enable an adversary to negate them technologically. For example, if a particular access path to an adversary's system depends on knowing a secret password, the adversary can deny access simply by changing the password. If the attacker demonstrates the ability to access that system, forensic investigation may well reveal that it was a compromised password that was responsible for the security breach.

Secret capabilities may have value in warfighting, but they are not valuable before war breaks out, because the adversary does not know about them. Under peacetime conditions, adversarial states are more likely to reveal otherwise secret capabilities when those capabilities are not unique, and when their adversaries are less able to develop countermeasures to them.[9]

In the film *Dr. Strangelove or: How I Learned to Stop Worrying and Love the Bomb,* directed by Stanley Kubrick, the Soviet Union is said to have a "Doomsday Machine" that will destroy all life on earth if the United States launches a nuclear attack on it. General Jack D. Ripper does launch such an attack, thereby causing an international crisis during which the Soviet ambassador reveals the machine's existence and purpose to the United States. Dr. Strangelove then says to the ambassador, "The whole point of the Doomsday Machine is lost—if you keep it a secret! Why didn't you tell the world, eh?" The ambassador lamely responds: "It was to be announced at the Party Congress on Monday. As you know, the Premier loves surprises."[10] The Doomsday Machine is thus a secret weapon easy to make operationally effective but which also fails at deterring U.S. nuclear attack, simply because its existence is kept secret from the United States.

Thus, consider a scenario in which Nation A is able to penetrate Nation B's NC3 using clandestine cyber means.[11] Nation A gains an advantage over B because with access to B's NC3 networks, it is able to transmit false orders, delay the transmission of messages, alter important information needed by decision-makers, and so on. But B does not know any of this, because A has been successful in conducting the penetration clandestinely.

In a crisis, A knows it has the upper hand over B, and feels less need to back down or to refrain from escalation. However, because B does not know about the penetration, B believes itself to be as strong as it ever was and thus overestimates its actual capabilities. B does not see the operational weakness that would, if revealed, lead it to refrain from escalation, and thus it too does not back down. Each side's unwillingness to refrain from escalation (for different reasons) increases the risk of escalation.

Scenario 4: Cyber attack to damage confidence in nuclear capabilities

The likelihood that a nuclear weapons system that works as it is expected and supposed to work and a decision-maker's confidence that it will do so are not independent of each other. Confidence is psychological, however, and although the technical reality of a weapons system's reliability may have some influence on it, it is by no means the only one. Political and military leaders nonetheless make decisions based on their confidence that their systems will operate properly. A leader with doubts about the ability of system X to operate properly in combat may well choose an option involving system Y, even if in fact system X would operate properly under the required circumstances.

Although there is no known instance in which a cyber attack on military systems has had such effects, it is instructive to recall the debacle of the Intel FDIV bug of 1994: the early Intel Pentium processor had a bug in its floating-point unit that sometimes led to incorrect results when one floating point number was divided into another (the FDIV instruction). Responding to reports of this bug, Intel released a technical analysis indicating that about 1 in 9 billion floating point divides with random parameters would produce inaccurate results, which under conservative operating assumptions would result in a failure once in 27,000 years of operation.[12] In other words, most users would never experience such a failure.

At first, Intel offered to replace processors for users who could prove that they were affected. This announcement failed to reassure and placate the user community, and within a few months, Intel offered to replace any flawed Pentium processor upon request. Intel eventually took a $475 million pre-tax charge to cover "replacement and write-off" for all flawed processors,[13] thus demonstrating the inadequacy of an engineering analysis of failure in addressing psychological doubts engendered by such failure.

This point is often overlooked in analyses of vulnerability to cyber attack. In many scenarios, the target of a hostile cyber attack is assumed to be the computers and networks that control many military systems. A great deal of analytical work addresses the extent to which such an attack might seriously compromise the actual ability of these systems to deliver the services on which military forces rely. Of particular concern is that a cyber attack might compromise these systems on a large scale—leaving most of them incapable of performing properly.

But if a decision-maker *believes*—with or without proper foundation—that the systems in question may not work when needed, that decision-maker's abilities to direct the use of those systems have been compromised. Mistaken beliefs might be induced by false reports given to the decision-maker by staff analysts, by rumors heard on social media, or by adversary claims. For example, if an adversary was able to demonstrably compromise one weapons system and then claim that it had compromised all similar systems (irrespective of whether it had in fact done so), the impact on a leader's decision-making might be similar to an actual compromise on all of such systems. A loss of confidence could also result a leader taking more time that would otherwise be needed to arrive at a decision.[14]

The point is significant because compromising one or two systems may well be a much less demanding task from an operational point of view than compromising hundreds of such systems, and thus "certain types of attack that do not cause extensive actual damage must be considered to have some catastrophic potential."[15]

Nation A inserts malware (or hardware vulnerabilities) in a number of Nation B's nuclear weapon delivery platforms with the intent of compromising Nation B's adversary's nuclear forces. For operational reasons, A may have found it easier to compromise the supply chains of B's acquisition processes. During an escalating crisis, A communicates to B that it has done so and demonstrates that it has done so by providing clues that allow B to discover these vulnerabilities—and then informs B that A has done so on many more of B's platforms. Indeed, Nation A may not even have to actually do anything real to Nation B—it may suffice for A to simply act as though it has successfully compromised B's weapons system.[16]

B's leaders must then consider whether A's claim is genuine, whether the problem is widespread, whether A has access to additional vulnerabilities that A did not announce , and how to react.

Scenario 5—Social media corruption of the information ecosystem in which nuclear decision-makers receive and process information

Today's information environment—which includes social media, always-on mobile communications, personal information feeds customized and tailored to the interests and desires of those who receive them, and the availability of enormous amounts of data to divine those preferences and desires—is characterized by a volume and velocity of communication that is orders of magnitude greater than in past decades. More information reaches more people in more places than ever before, but that information is in large part unverified and unanalyzed. Social media, in particular, are designed for short, simple messages that play to emotions rather than analytical thinking, and often lack context and authentication.

Traditional media intermediaries once curated information for importance, accuracy, and credibility. However, in the past few decades, these roles have shrunk significantly, while individual preferences now play a significantly increased role in determining the volume and character of the information people receive today.[17] Uninformed individuals can develop voices on any topic that are as loud as those of recognized experts. Voices heard in today's information environment may receive money for carrying or creating particular content. For example, the 2019 Mueller report investigating Russian interference in the 2016 election found that a Russian organization called the Internet Research Agency conducted a social media campaign "designed to provoke and amplify political and social discord in the United States" and received funding from an ally of Russian President Vladimir Putin.[18] A number of entrepreneurs have also discovered some level of public demand for information critical of people they do not like and have learned to monetize that demand.[19]

Today's information environment affects both political leaders and publics. National leaders use official and personal social media to diminish and to woo partners and adversaries, to announce presidential policy intentions, to boast about military capabilities both new and old. They monitor media streams of foreign leaders and their subordinates. Publics are also affected, often demanding action in response to provocation,[20] and the simplistic and repetitive nature of modern social media communication is likely to reinforce such sentiments.

In this loud and chaotic information environment, discourse—such as it is—lacks nuance and subtlety. A lack of tact and diplomacy—indeed, insults and other disrespectful communications—are common, and such communications, displayed for all to see, may inadvertently harden the attitudes of previously ambivalent parties, turning them into committed and resolved enemies, while at the same time making face-saving de-escalation by both sides more difficult. They may also create conditions under which the various parties are more likely to believe even wholly unsubstantiated information and act upon it.[21]

Compounding problems of information overload, the psychological evidence to date suggests that people systematically deviate from rationality in decision-making,[22] thus calling into question the rationality of decision-makers assumed in classical nuclear deterrence theory. Under stress, people are more likely to employ fast, intuitive, and reactive decision-making rather than slower, more reflective and deliberate decision-making.[23]

Imagine the Cuban Missile Crisis playing out in today's global information environment.[24] In 1962, President Kennedy had several days to deliberate before making a carefully calibrated speech announcing the discovery of Soviet medium- and intermediate-range nuclear-armed missiles in Cuba.[25] The U.S. government had a monopoly on overhead imagery, providing to President Kennedy and his staff—and only them—with vital information about how close the missiles were to becoming operational. The Joint Chiefs of Staff unanimously recommended an airstrike, followed by a ground invasion of Cuba, but President Kennedy chose instead to order a blockade. As noted in chapter 3, Khrushchev sent two letters to Kennedy, who chose to respond to only the first, which was less demanding than the second, a decision that history shows helped to de-escalate the crisis.[26]

Today, commercially available satellite imagery could have detected the presence of these missiles and publicized them to the world days sooner than the president actually did. Once such imagery was released, myriad voices would have begun to comment, with images of the missile sites going viral on social media, alarming millions and more in the United States. Concerned Americans, Internet Research Agency trolls, disarmament activists, gun rights proponents, survivalists across the political spectrum, retired military personnel, and relatives of active duty military personnel would all weigh in, causing confusion and discord in the Congress. Nor would these voices be exclusively American: citizens and political leaders would be weighing in from around the world. Unhappy Pentagon officials might have leaked the president's decision to overrule the JCS, increasing pressure for an invasion. Various senators and representatives would have called for the president to refrain from appeasement and to take a tough line in responding.

Perhaps most important, President Kennedy chose to take a measured and deliberative approach to the crisis. Central to his decision-making was information vetted and analyzed by U.S intelligence services. Today, U.S. and possibly Russian leaders would be awash in a sea of unverified or unverifiable, emotionally laden, and politically fraught information on their adversary's intentions and force postures. They would be confronting intense pressures from public opinion. Other temperamentally different presidents may be more impulsive in their decision-making, driven in part, perhaps, by listening directly to their political supporters urging them onward—with all of the attendant consequences for escalation.

Scenario 6—False social media messaging provoking war

In September 2017, multiple U.S. service members or their family members in Korea reported that they had received messages through text messages and Facebook notifications saying that a noncombatant evacuation order had been issued for the Korean Peninsula.[27] These messages and notifications were false. Had they been legitimate, such an order would have affected family members of 28,500 U.S. service members and essential nonemergency Defense Department civilian employees stationed in South Korea.

This particular fraud was quickly detected and quashed, and nothing resembling an actual evacuation occurred. But a significant security threat could have arisen, because a noncombatant evacuation from a potential zone of conflict could be interpreted as the prelude to hostilities—in that case, such an evacuation could be interpreted by North Korea as a signal that South Korean and U.S. forces were about to initiate military action against it.

A third party seeking to provoke conflict between two mutually hostile nations could build on a similar incident, flooding social media/text message communications with false reports of the noncombatant evacuation of a major city in Nation A, whose official channels that could be used to counter the false messaging would simultaneously be jammed or otherwise put out of action, at least temporarily, by means of various cyber attacks.

Executing such a plan would likely be unsuccessful under normal peacetime circumstances. However, an atmosphere of tension and rising crisis could prompt Nation B to pre-emptive military action based on the perception that an evacuation, especially one that was ordered by the government of Nation A, could indicate that Nation A was about to initiate hostilities. If A and B are nuclear powers, the increase in the risk of open conflict is all that much more concerning.

Common threads through the scenarios

The scenarios above span a broad range, suggesting the need to combine engineering, psychological, intelligence, and military operational and strategic expertise to anticipate what malevolent actors could do and how systems could fail in unexpected ways. Put differently, relegating the management of cyber risk only to the cyber specializations, without the involvement of those who understand strategic decision-making, military operations, or intelligence will guarantee a narrower perspective on those risks than would be wise, given the creativity that adversaries have repeatedly shown in cyberspace.

Box 5.1. The Fundamental Attribution Error and Able Archer 83

Psychologists have identified what is often called the "fundamental attribution error"—an unwarranted tendency to explain the behavior of others as the consequence of their underlying disposition and the identical behavior in oneself as the consequence of situational and circumstantial factors not within one's control.[1] Thus, shortly after President Ronald Reagan announced the Strategic Defense ("Star Wars") Initiative to develop a comprehensive defense against nuclear ballistic missiles in 1983, his secretary of defense went on the record to say: "They [the Soviets] know perfectly well that we will never launch a first strike against the Soviet Union. And all of their attacks, and all of their preparations—I should say, and all of their acquisitions in the military field in the last few years have been offensive in character."[2]

Against this backdrop, it is interesting to consider the Able Archer exercise of November 1983, a NATO command post exercise (i.e., one without troops on the ground) designed to "practice command and staff procedures, with particular emphasis on the transition from conventional to non-conventional operations, including the use of nuclear weapons."[3] One of its goals was to practice new nuclear weapons release procedures. Many analysts believe that at least some Soviet decision-makers had serious concerns that Able Archer 83 was in fact a cover for a nuclear attack on the Soviet Union.[4] Others doubt this.[5] However, regardless of what Soviet leaders actually believed in 1983, it is entirely plausible that they might have concluded that a real attack was imminent.

The United States knew its intentions were benign and believed that their adversaries must have known that too. But the Soviet leaders—or at least some senior decision-makers among them—had no such belief, especially after the United States had announced its intention to render its nuclear weapons impotent and obsolete. On the contrary, they might well have interpreted U.S. actions in the most hostile light possible, and have taken what they saw as appropriate actions in response. Such misperceptions are the soil out of which inadvertent and accidental escalation grows.

1. See, e.g., Lee Ross, "The Intuitive Psychologist and His Shortcomings: Distortions in the Attribution Process," *Advances in Experimental Social Psychology* 10 (January 1, 1977): 173–220, doi.org/10.1016/S0065-2601(08)60357-3.

2. Caspar Weinberger, interview on "Meet the Press," *NBC News*, March 27, 1983.

3. See NATO, "Exercise ABLE ARCHER 83: Information from SHAPE Historical Files," March 28, 2013, nsarchive2.gwu.edu/NSAEBB/NSAEBB427/docs/6.a.%20Exercise%20Able%20Archer%20SHAPE%20March%202013%20NATO.pdf.

4. See, e.g., National Security Archive, "The Soviet Side of the 1983 War Scare," November 5, 2018, nsarchive.gwu.edu/briefing-book/aa83/2018-11-05/soviet-side-1983-war-scare. Formerly classified documents released in 2021 are consistent with this view; see Nate Jones and David E. Hoffman, "Newly Released Documents Shed Light on 1983 Nuclear War Scare with Soviets," *Washington Post*, February 17, 2021, www.washingtonpost.com/national-security/soviet-nuclear-war-able-archer/2021/02/17/711fa9e2-7166-11eb-93be-c10813e358a2_story.html.

5. See, e.g., Gordon Barrass, "Able Archer 83: What Were the Soviets Thinking?" *Survival: Global Politics and Strategy* 58, no. 6 (November 1, 2016):7–30, doi.org/10.108 0/00396338.2016.1257176.

A second thread is the critical importance of the psychology of decision-makers. The psychology of decision-making is far from being an entirely rational process. A long history of research in social cognition has documented regular and systematic deviations rationality in many kinds of decision-making concerning the kinds of information to which decision-makers give credence and priority; for an example, see box 5.1. Individual differences also matter (e.g., one decision-maker may be more prone to accepting risk, compared to another more prone to reducing risk; one may be more impulsive than another; one may be more sensitive and aware of cyber risks than another; and so on). Taken together, such factors imply that these scenarios could play out in many different ways depending on the individuals involved. Catastrophic outcomes are thus not assured, but they are by no means ruled out either.

A related point is that the effect of adversary cyber operations on the perceptions and confidence of decision-makers is at least as important as their effect on the computer and communications systems that such operations target. That is, to a far greater degree than kinetic military operations, cyber operations force decision-makers to worry about what *might* be happening. The reason is rooted in the lack of obvious indications that a cyber attack was successful—and from the point of the targeted party, the lack of apparent damage may be illusory.

A third important common thread is that all of these scenarios depict adversary cyber operations playing out in times of tension or crisis or actual war. It is thus useful to consider the perspective of the adversary. As noted in chapter 1, from the adversary's point of view, cyber attacks are an uncertain instrument. Thus, attackers are not likely to depend exclusively on cyber attacks to prosecute key objectives during a kinetic war except under very unusual circumstances. A "bolt from the blue" attack on U.S. nuclear forces is in any event a possible but highly unlikely scenario, and it is even less likely that an adversary would launch such an attack using cyber weapons alone if it hoped for any reasonable measure of success.

Much more likely are scenarios in which offensive cyber activities are conducted as part of a wider nonnuclear military operation. In these scenarios, concerns about escalation are more likely to be associated with adversary cyber operations that are not necessarily directed at nuclear forces or capabilities but that have inadvertent or accidental cyber effects on them.[28] Under such circumstances, the psychological propensities of decision-makers may well assume larger importance.

U.S. military forces place high value on early action. For example, the *DOD Cyber Strategy* of 2015 explicitly stated that "During *heightened tensions* [emphasis added] or outright hostilities, DoD must be able to provide the President with a wide range of options for managing conflict escalation. If directed, DoD should be able to use cyber operations to disrupt an adversary's command and control networks, military-related critical infrastructure, and weapons capabilities."[29] A U.S. Cyber Command "Command Vision" statement asserts: "Our purpose is to achieve cyberspace superiority by *seizing and maintaining the tactical and operational initiative* [emphasis added] in cyberspace,"[30] and notes that Cyber Command will "[d]evelop advantages *in preparation for* [emphasis added] and during joint operations in conflict.[31]

References to actions in period of heightened tension, seizing the tactical initiative, and in preparation for conflict all imply that cyber activities are likely to be among the first capabilities used in the lead-up to and early phases of a conflict. Furthermore, once conflict is deemed inevitable, logic suggests the value of acting before an adversary can put its plans fully into motion. Of course, the adversary knows this as well, and acts on the same logic, with all of the instabilities that such mutual action imply.[32]

6

Designing the Cyber-Nuclear Future:
Observations and Imperatives

The previous chapters suggest a number of observations and associated imperatives for overseers of the U.S. nuclear enterprise that should guide the handling of cybersecurity (and cyber-related) issues associated with nuclear modernization. (Imperatives are listed in _italic underline_.) Table 1.1 provides a quick summary, and detailed discussion follows below.

Observation 1: Vulnerabilities of the U.S. nuclear enterprise to adversary cyber operations are not limited to technical attacks on NC3 components.

As the discussion of chapter 3 indicates, cyber technologies are deeply embedded in all elements of the nuclear enterprise—it is not just the NC3 system that is vulnerable to cyber compromises, although the potential impact on NC3 of adversary cyber operations is very important indeed. Nuclear delivery systems and platforms and the weapons themselves present additional targets for would-be cyber attackers. To the extent that they also engage in or support nonnuclear conflict, nuclear systems may well be affected by cyber attacks conducted in such conflict. Moreover, cybersecurity is not only a matter of reducing technical vulnerabilities to various elements of the nuclear enterprise. Finally, cybersecurity should be construed broadly rather than narrowly.

The imperative flowing from Observation 1 is that *efforts to enhance the cybersecurity posture of the U.S. nuclear enterprise must include all of its elements and address cybersecurity in both its acquisition and operational aspects*. Attention to acquisition is obvious—the various technical elements must be designed and implemented in ways that are as cybersecure as possible. But cybersecurity for the operational side also warrants substantial effort to ensure that good cybersecurity practices (e.g., cyber hygiene, regular backups) are followed. Maintaining the integrity of critical software and databases used for analysis and planning in nuclear scenarios and in nuclear weapons production is necessary as well.

Observation 2. Entanglement of conventional and nuclear functions in operational systems increases the risk of inadvertent nuclear escalation.

Entanglement of conventional and nuclear functions in operational systems, whether for NC3 or for weapons platforms, raises the risk of inadvertent nuclear escalation. It is undeniable that entanglement (or integration, if you prefer) of nuclear and conventional systems confers operational advantages in warfighting (e.g., communications or early-warning satellites that serve both nuclear and conventional needs as discussed in Scenario 4.2 above). But those advantages must be weighed against an increased possibility that cyber attacks directed against those systems will inevitably raise fears in U.S. decision-makers about nuclear systems being compromised, especially if conflict with another nuclear power is involved.

Three imperatives follow from this observation. The first is that in the interests of greater simplicity and thus greater security and reliability, *designers of modernized computer-driven systems, whether NC3 or weapons platforms, should moderate their appetites for increased functionality in the face of strong and hard-to-resist temptations to add such functionality for users*, especially as it relates to non-nuclear missions. (Box 6.1 presents some additional commentary on this imperative.) As noted earlier, NC3 modernization presents an opportunity to simplify the underlying NC3 architecture—but if users are unable to keep their desires for additional functionality in check, these gains in simplicity will be offset by additional complexity associated with these new requirements.

A key first step would be to define and then implement the *minimum* essential core functionality for nuclear operation, as recommended by the Defense Science Board (DSB) in 2017 as follows:

> We have to be confident that we have credible and capable systems to impose costs on adversaries. However, it is not feasible to protect all systems against the full-spectrum [i.e., the most sophisticated] capabilities of highly capable actors dedicated to compromising them.
>
> DoD must therefore devote urgent and sustained attention to boosting the cyber resilience of key U.S. strike systems (cyber, nuclear, non-nuclear)—including essential supporting forces and critical infrastructure to ensure we maintain credible response capabilities.[1]

In the case of NC3, the minimum essential functionality would cover the most important functions of the NC3 thin line. (As a hypothetical illustration of what might not be required, the minimum essential functionality required of NC3 might not include the capability for crewed bombers to report back to senior commanders on battle-damage assessment or other reconnaissance information gathered during their flight. Another example is that a nuclear-armed cruise missile would be designed without the capability to redirect it in flight to a new target. This latter example is not hypothetical—the Block IV version of the xGM-109 Tomahawk cruise missile can be aimed at an alternate, pre-planned target while in flight,[2] but it carries a conventional warhead; the nuclear version never had an inflight retargeting capability.) Architects of the NC3 system will have to make dozens or hundreds of such trade-off judgments to define the minimum essential functionality. This core functionality would be the basis for developing a relatively simple working system onto which additional functionality could be added.

Core functionality could also be embodied in an entirely independent

Box 6.1. An Engineering Perspective on Avoiding Inadvertent Nuclear War

In an important commentary on building nuclear weapons systems, including NC3 systems, Nancy Leveson, professor of aeronautics and astronautics at the Massachusetts Institute of Technology and perhaps the foremost expert on software safety in the world, points out that the most successful complex systems in the past were simple and used rigorous, straightforward processes.[1] For example, she notes that the use of software and more complex designs have been avoided in the design of strategies to prevent the accidental detonation of nuclear weapons.

She goes on to say that the more recently introduced software-intensive systems have been much less reliable, and that our ability to provide highly trustworthy systems has been compromised by gratuitous complexity in their design and inadequate development and maintenance processes. Maintaining the past high levels of reliability and safety of NC3 systems into the future will require a "back to basics" approaches to system, software, and security engineering. In addition, she argues, the security and reliability problems of complex software systems today are as much a product of our inability to manage these systems as they are of technological flaws. Social and organizational factors (including inadequate controls and flawed decision-making) are at least as responsible for failure as technical factors.

The essential underlying reason is that whereas the failure modes in older systems could reasonably be assumed to be the result of component failures, the same is no longer true today. Today's failures are as likely to be the result of system design flaws as component failure. We now build systems that cannot be exhaustively tested and for which it is impossible to anticipate, understand, plan, and guard against all potential adverse system behavior before operational use. Engineers are increasingly facing the potential for "unknown unknowns" in the behavior of the systems they are designing.

Moreover, system complexity is high enough that important system properties (such as safety, security, and reliability) are emergent—that is, they are related not only to the failure of individual system components but also to the interactions among the components that have not failed or even malfunctioned. That is, mishaps can occur due to unsafe interactions among individual components and subsystems that satisfy their requirements. Leveson identifies two approaches to deal with the problem of system complexity, which are not mutually exclusive. One is to reduce complexity in system design. However, relying on this alone runs the risk that it may then not be possible to satisfy certain mission requirements that decision-makers deem important. The second approach is to develop more powerful analysis and design techniques—that is, techniques that enable system designers and architects to handle complexity more effectively—that would enable them to increase the system complexity beyond what would be possible with simplification alone. Leveson's own research is oriented in this direction (and the source on which this box based provides a rough sketch of an approach growing out of system theory). Leveson stresses, however, that the second approach is not a free pass to ignore the imperative of simplification.

1. Nancy Leveson, *An Engineering Perspective on Avoiding Inadvertent Nuclear War*, NAPSNet Special Reports, July 25, 2019, nautilus.org/napsnet/napsnet-special-reports/an-engineering-perspective-on-avoiding-inadvertent-nuclear-war.

backup system for NC3 to provide that core should the primary systems be compromised. The deployment of an independent backup system to provide thin-line connectivity has the advantage that it can be kept relatively simple compared to the "full-up" system intended for day-to-day use. On the other hand, it has the distinct disadvantage that by definition, a backup system is not likely to be used on a day-to-day basis, and systems that are not exercised frequently (i.e., through day-to-day use) often do not work as intended. Any deployment of an independent backup NC3 system serving only thin-line purposes—desirable on strategic grounds as a way of increasing its insulation from cyber risk or from collateral damage in nonnuclear conflict—should be conditioned on viable and sustainable procedures that would exercise it nearly as often as it would be exercised if it were not a backup system.[3]

Similar comments apply to the nuclear force platforms and delivery vehicles. For example, the 2013 DSB report called for segmenting forces sufficient to assure mission execution in the face of concerted cyber attack and isolating them from everything but nuclear missions.[4]

Second, given that nuclear weapons are "the *foundation* (emphasis added) of our strategy to preserve peace and stability,"[5] the second imperative is that *the network infrastructure built to support conventional-nuclear integration should prioritize the needs of the nuclear enterprise first*. In practice, this would mean building the network infrastructure around the highest priority needs and then adding capacity for lower priorities as needed, always taking care to preserve the ability to carry the highest priority tasks as the number one goal. What it does not mean is to build a general-purpose network and then to take care of highest priority needs at the applications level—doing so would mean making hard-to-reverse compromises at the infrastructure level that will likely detract from fulfillment of the highest priority needs.

This goal will be difficult if, as is currently planned, NC3 acquisition is to be controlled by the services (that is, by the Air Force, the Navy, the Marine Corps, the Army, and the Space Force) rather than by U.S. Strategic Command.[6] For quite understandable reasons, service acquisition agencies are likely to give priority to the needs of their warfighting elements, which are for the most part nonnuclear. Giving U.S. Strategic Command a voice in decisions about dual-capable elements of NC3 is a positive step compared to the alternative, but the fact remains that the party with the actual acquisition authority to allocate budgets is in the driver's seat,[7] especially for "smaller" decisions that may nonetheless have a negative impact on others not so privileged.

Accordingly, a corollary of the second imperative is thus that U.S. Strategic Command's hand in making NC3 acquisition decisions, and indeed in any decisions that relate to acquisition of dual-capable weapons systems and platforms, should be strengthened, preferably with the ability to allocate funding that supports its nuclear mission, rather than only to oppose funding decisions that impede it. (Providing U.S. Strategic Command with acquisition authority would require legislative action.)

Third, entanglement between conventional and nuclear systems means that attacks on the former could affect or be perceived to be intended to affect the latter. And attacks, real or perceived, on a nation's nuclear systems are particularly escalatory if the nature of the conflict prior to that point has been confined to the conventional domain. This unavoidable fact of life drives the third imperative that _nuclear-armed nations should do what they can to minimize the possibility that cyber and other attacks on conventional assets will be seen as attacks on nuclear assets_.

This third imperative has implications for both offense and defense. For offense, commanders who order cyberattacks on entangled systems in the context of conventional conflict must be aware that such attacks are potentially escalatory on a ladder with nuclear rungs, as suggested in Scenario 2 above. Noting that all operational plans today are required to contain an annex describing the expected collateral damage that execution of the plan might entail, Paul Bracken has suggested that any operational plan that calls for attacks on adversary communications capabilities be required to include an annex that describes the likely impact of such attacks on the adversary's capabilities to communicate with its nuclear forces.[8] I propose a modest expansion of Bracken's proposal to include an assessment of the impact of an attack on any adversary assets that might provide NC3 capabilities (not just communications capabilities).

The imperative also requires both senior military commanders and civilian policy-makers to maintain situational awareness of what military cyber forces are doing that could have strategic consequences.[9] In practice, the operational footprint of kinetic forces in operation is much larger than that of cyber forces—kinetic forces entail large-scale movements that can be noticed and reported, and when they fire their weapons in anger, the resulting explosions are manifestly obvious to observers. By contrast, forces conducting offensive operations in cyberspace can do so without moving outside the building to which they report every day, and even the effects of a successful offensive operation in cyberspace may be invisible to observers physically present at the targets of the attack. Under these circumstances, senior military commanders and civilian policy-makers will need to take special care to maintain situational awareness and control of their own forces and to exercise a greater degree of oversight than might be necessary if only ordinary military forces were involved.

As an example, consider a cyber attack on the command and control network in the nationwide air defense system of an adversary.[10] While exploring the network, corrupting data, and issuing confusing or damaging commands, U.S. operators stumble onto a communications channel with the adversary's national command authorities. Exploitation of that channel might enable the United States to penetrate the command and control network of the adversary's national command authorities—but a decision to do so should not be made by the U.S. operators and commanders on the ground but rather by higher U.S. authorities. Thus, mechanisms must be established to provide such information up the chain of command when necessary, and other mechanisms established to act on such information should it be made available. This is not to say that the president must necessarily be involved in this process, but the decision to take such potentially escalatory action should be made at levels of authority high enough to weigh the risk of escalation—a point suggesting that some civilian oversight in such operational matters is not necessarily inappropriate.[11]

For defense, any U.S. system acquired that supports both conventional and nuclear capabilities is by definition entangled. Once the full functionality of the system is established, a "decision-making impact statement" analogous to an environmental impact statement could be required that describes the system's impact on nuclear decision-making by both adversary and U.S. decision-makers.

Part 1 of the statement would address the incentives and disincentives for adversary attacks on the entangled system in question. Part 2 of the statement would address how U.S. nuclear decision-makers would likely perceive and react to attacks on the system, even if conducted in the context of conventional conflict. Part 2 would recognize the possibility that U.S. nuclear decision-makers might themselves misinterpret adversary attacks on our own entangled systems—and a decision-making impact statement would provide some analysis of that possibility.

The point at which the requirements for a system are established is, in practice, not well defined. To be sure, the acquisition process demands a statement of requirements before acquisition can proceed. But after a system is deployed, it may be used to support a variety of missions not initially anticipated by system designers. These new uses of a system generate requirements in their own right and create additional operational risk, but without a process for reviewing all of the requirements imposed on a system at a given point in its deployment, that risk may well go unnoticed. For this reason, it may be appropriate for DoD to require that a decision-making impact statement be performed periodically for *all* entangled systems.

Finally, given the potential for misunderstandings about intent, several analysts have suggested that it might make sense for the United States to enter into agreements with adversaries to mutually refrain from conducting cyber intrusions into each other's NC3 infrastructure.[12] If A and B were to abide by such an agreement during conflict, such mutual restraint would help to reduce worst-case fears of A that B was trying to interfere with A's nuclear command and control, and vice versa, thereby promoting strategic stability for both sides.

Such an agreement would be difficult to negotiate. Richard Danzig points to one difficulty in coming to such an agreement, namely, the ambiguity between cyber intrusions for intelligence gathering and for potential sabotage, as discussed in Scenario 1. Both sides would have to agree not to conduct cyber intrusions for either purpose. In addition, the proposal rests on the idea that NC3 infrastructure can be cleanly separated from other systems that support nonnuclear command, control, and communications functions—a proposition that may be dubious in light of current trends in the opposite direction. The leverage possible by early targeting of NC3 (or of targeting conventional C3 at the onset of a conflict) may well be too lucrative in the short term for one side easily to forego it. And verification of such an agreement would be essentially impossible—both sides would continue to find security bugs and glitches in their NC3 systems, providing fodder for a constant stream of "maybe this one is deliberately planted" judgments.

On the other hand, the episodic functions of NC3 described in chapter 3 points out the need to maintain communications with adversary leaders, especially during conflict. If dedicated stand-alone communications links were established to facilitate crisis or wartime communications between leaders, neither side would have any particular incentive to target such links, whether by cyber or any other means.

Observation 3. Short timelines for decision-making increase cyber risk.

The use of computers in national security systems necessarily entails some degree of cyber risk. Cyber risk can be reduced in a variety of technical and procedural ways, but these are not the only ways of doing so. To some extent and in some cases, NC3 design choices that provide more decision time can compensate for increased cyber risk.

The imperative thus is that _to reduce cyber risk, NC3 systems should be designed to give senior leaders more time to make decisions of high consequence,_ which would in turn allow operators in the NC3 system to gather more information about the scope, nature, and reality of any threat event to which leaders must respond. Additional time can help to mitigate (though not eliminate) cyber risk by allowing system operators to confirm that information being provided by the NC3 system was not being corrupted or distorted as the result of adversary cyber activities. When a computer system crashes, it may take some investigation (and thus time) to determine if the crash was due to an attack or a benign failure. The same is true for any threat indication that appears—and the importance of knowing whether the indication is the consequence of a hostile attack or a benign failure increases as the stakes of any resulting decision increase.

As a principle for nuclear command and control, the imperative to provide the president with the maximum time possible to make consequential decisions is already well known to senior commanders and system designers and architects alike. Adding cyber threats to the various risks to mitigate by providing additional assessment and decision-making time is simply one more reason to do so. At the same time, many would argue that the timeline for decision-making is not defined by any features of the U.S. NC3 system but rather by the physical characteristics (in particular, speed) of adversary missiles and the distance from the point of hostile launch to impact on U.S. soil.

This argument is based on the fact that the flight time of Russian ICBMs from launch to impact on U.S. soil is about twenty-five minutes. In that time, the United States must detect a Russian ICBM launch, ascertain its intention, and if the conclusion is that they are aimed at U.S. ICBM fields, the president must, on the basis of the information provided by the NC3 system and other sources, decide whether or not to launch U.S. ICBMs before they are (or might be) destroyed—a so-called launch-on-warning (LOW) decision—and, if the decision is affirmative, launch them. Human beings are involved at many points in this timeline, but there is also a high degree of automation involved.

Another highly stressing scenario relates to the survivability of the NC3 system itself, which is likely to be degraded in a large-scale nuclear attack. A fully coordinated response to such an attack is most easily launched when the NC3 system is fully functional and not operating in a nuclear environment. But while it is essentially impossible that silo-based ICBMs would survive a large-scale attack to be used in a second strike, the essential components of the NC3 system are explicitly designed to survive such an attack, and are supposed to be even more survivable so if the planned NC3 modernization is successful.

The concern with LOW is that a launch might occur due to false indications of warning, and these false indications could be due to bugs in the system, to a deliberate cyber attack, or more likely, to the unintended side effects of some other adversary cyber intrusion. It makes no sense for Russia to conduct a cyber attack intended to result in the accidental launch of nuclear weapons towards it, but it is entirely possible that Russian (or Chinese) hacker activity in the U.S. NC3 system could have inadvertent side effects that result in false indications of attack.

The cyber risk to the U.S. NC3 system is fairly minimal today, as General John Hyten noted (see chapter 3 above). But minimal is not zero. Although the NC3 system is not directly connected to the Internet, various components have been upgraded since 1985. Even without being connected to the Internet themselves, the upgraded components are subject to some degree of cyber risk. A U.S. president today facing a decision to launch U.S. ICBMs on warning of attack should be advised to consider that the warning could be erroneous, for reasons including but not limited to the effects of a cyber compromise of some sort.

As the NC3 system is itself modernized, cyber risk is likely to increase—but by how much depends on what the system is designed to do. So, while it is true that no possible design of the U.S. NC3 system can change the time in which Russian ICBMs could land on U.S. soil, an NC3 system that did not have to provide the high-confidence tactical warning and attack assessment information needed to support a LOW decision would almost certainly be simpler, more reliable, and easier to build, maintain, and operate than one that did have to do so. In non-LOW scenarios, there would be considerably more time available for senior decision-makers to think about what should be done and for technical personnel to better understand the streams of incoming information.[13] Thus, the NC3 system would be less susceptible to the deliberate or inadvertent effects of adversary cyber operations directed against it.

On the other hand, the president could always decide to "ride out" the attack even if the NC3 system was designed to support a LOW decision. But since an adversary could not count on such a decision, the uncertainty thereby induced in a Russian adversary contemplating a large-scale attack on the United States would be increased, thus strengthening deterrence. An NC3 system not designed to support a LOW decision would enable an adversary to count on the lack of a LOW response, thus weakening deterrence.

Given the above, the issue is one of relative probabilities. If the probability of a large-scale surprise attack on U.S. ICBMs were sufficiently high, the additional deterrent value of maintaining a LOW capability could be valuable. But as the probability of such an attack drops, cyber risk becomes relatively more important and at a sufficiently low probability of surprise attack, the dangers of inadvertent or accidental cyber-induced war or escalation begin to dominate. Put differently, how does the additional value of enhancing deterrence through retention of a LOW capability compare to the possibility that a president would decide to launch U.S. ICBMs on the basis of false indications of warning (whether cyber-induced or otherwise), thus *initiating* a nuclear war or severely escalating a nuclear conflict unintentionally?

In short, though reducing cyber risk does add one point in favor of abandoning the capability for LOW, whether that additional risk should be dispositive is a different question. Those who are optimistic that cyber risks can be adequately mitigated (I am not among them) could reasonably believe that the NC3 system should maintain a LOW capability as a decision available to the president based on the usual strategic arguments for it.[14]

Finally, many analysts would argue that a decision to deploy an NC3 system with or without the capability to support a LOW decision cannot be separated from a decision about whether or not to have a silo-based ICBM force at all. If the United States chose to abandon such forces,[15] the decision to deploy an NC3 system without the capability to support LOW would be easier to make.

Observation 4. The legacy NC3 system has not failed catastrophically since 1985.

Significant changes in the NC3 infrastructure have occurred since 1985. Space-based infrared surveillance (SBIRS) satellites replaced older defense support program (DSP) satellites; advanced extremely high frequency (AEHF) satellites replaced MILSTAR communications satellites. But the organizational structure—the architecture—of the legacy NC3 overall system has remained more or less constant.

The lack of catastrophic failure of this system is one its major characteristics. Despite a number of close calls, there has been no accidental nuclear war, and corrective procedures and technology have been deployed to fix problems that have arisen. No similar claim can be made for any NC3 system that is further modernized, which will obviously take decades to develop decades of operational lessons.

The corresponding imperative is that *system architects and designers should establish as a requirement for a modernized system that it should do what the legacy system would do if faced with the same operational* _scenarios_. As the legacy system is modernized, legacy and modernized components should operate in parallel for an extended period of time, with the outputs of the modernized system checked against those of the legacy system. Admittedly, this practice would entail substantial additional costs and operational difficulties, but the consequences of catastrophic NC3 failure are so high that mitigating them should be worth it.

Observation 5. The tension between keeping up with a rapidly changing threat environment and maintaining an adequate cybersecurity posture cannot be resolved—only managed.

Taking at face value statements about the rapidly changing environment of military and geopolitical threats, system architects and designers must be able to modify, adapt, and evolve the systems they build to ensure that they have the functionality needed to respond to new threats as they emerge or are identified. Architecting and designing systems secure against cyber threats is an inherently time-consuming process, and it will be possible only if the time scale on which threats evolve is long compared to that in which adaptation can occur.

The time scale on which new threats evolve is not under the control of system architects and designers, and is unlikely to be under the control of political decision-makers. Only the time scale of adaptation is controllable. Customary DoD acquisition processes are cumbersome and slow, and because of changing threats (both changing threat actors and changing threat modes), these processes often result in the acquisition of systems that are obsolete even before initial deployment. A more responsive acquisition process is thus important for U.S. national security in the twenty-first century.

As the basis on which to build defense-specific applications, DoD relies on commercial off-the-shelf (COTS) software (e.g., operating systems). It is also investing in the development, adaptation, and use of modern software engineering techniques pioneered in Silicon Valley. For example, the Kessel Run program is a U.S. Air Force activity that "builds, tests, delivers, operates, and maintains cloud-based infrastructure and warfighting software applications, delivering them on time, as needed, and _with efficiency and cost-effectiveness_ *above other acquisition methods or practices in the Air Force and Department of Defense"* (emphasis added).[16]

However, the history in commercial software development shows that security considerations often—even usually—play second fiddle to delivery schedules, and there is no reason to expect that such pressures do not apply to military systems as well. As described in chapter 4, efforts devoted to enhancing cybersecurity generally slow schedules and delivery timelines. For example, products incorporating COTS technology may be more likely to contain security defects that would enable an adversary to mount a successful cyberattack as compared to products specifically designed to be secure, and thus in principle, it could be argued that the acquisition process should use only the latter products. But doing so would entail a large financial cost as well as a longer development process—so much larger and longer as to take that option off the table in almost all instances.

Further caution is warranted in adapting the software engineering and architectural development techniques of Silicon Valley for any aspect of the nuclear modernization program. These techniques have produced some of the most widely used commercial software in the world, and their power is not to be underestimated. Still, the stakes of the commercial world are much lower than those of national security, especially where nuclear weapons are concerned, and I can think of few things as scary as the unreserved widespread use of commercial Silicon Valley software development techniques for all aspects of the modernized NC3 system.

The corresponding imperative here is thus that both _users (including those at the most senior levels with the authority to specify the requirements for functionality related to nuclear weapons and operations) and system architects and designers must be prepared to make trade-offs between measures to reduce cyber risk and performance requirements_. Sacrifices needed to mitigate cyber risk may come in different forms, including lengthier acquisition schedules, reduced functionality, tighter access controls, or cumbersome nontechnological approaches. And since users are rarely willing to give up functionality for better cybersecurity, overseers of nuclear acquisition process (that is, civilians in the DoD and Congress) will have to ensure that they face those trade-offs honestly.

Observation 6. The cybersecurity posture across the U.S. nuclear enterprise is highly heterogeneous, with some elements having weaker cybersecurity than others.

Cyber vulnerabilities in the nuclear enterprise are almost certainly highly heterogeneous across its components, among the individual entities within each component, and indeed even across different operational scenarios. A detailed discussion of specific vulnerabilities in specific systems or operational scenarios is beyond the scope of this book and would be highly classified in any event. Nevertheless, it is worth noting that:

- Cyber vulnerabilities in the nuclear weapons complex are substantially different than those in nuclear delivery vehicles. For example, cyber risks for the networks of the nuclear weapons complex focus heavily on maintaining the confidentiality of secret information, whereas for delivery platforms the primary cyber risks relate to compromises of the integrity of flight-control software and weapons-systems control.
- Cyber vulnerabilities will be different for different delivery vehicles and platforms. Missiles, airplanes, and submarines have vastly different software and consequently different vulnerabilities. For example, SSBNs patrol at sea with minimal connectivity to higher authority as compared to the ICBM force. It is also much harder to imagine real-time control of malware placed on an SSBN than such control of a dual-capable fighter jet that is *designed* to operate as part of a network. Even airplanes that ostensibly perform the same mission—such as delivery of gravity nuclear bombs—will have different vendors, different teams of software developers, different software requirements, and so on, and hence will differ in their specific vulnerabilities.
- Cyber vulnerabilities will be different for different airframes even for the same type of aircraft, in part because updates cannot be delivered to every airframe simultaneously. Block (Version) 4 planes will have

different vulnerabilities than Block (Version) 2 planes (it may be hoped
that the software for Block 4 planes will fix the vulnerabilities found in
Block 2).

• Cyber vulnerabilities may vary by mission profile—even taking Route
A to the target rather than Route B could reveal a vulnerability present
on the first but not the second. The F-35 fighter is often regarded as a
flying cloud computing platform that can coordinate other air assets,
which may move in and out of communications view, thus dynamically
changing the network configuration. A vulnerability may appear mo-
mentarily and then disappear as distances between various air assets
change.

Heterogeneity in the cybersecurity posture of the nuclear enterprise is
a distinct advantage in the sense that a single cyber attack on the entire
enterprise is not likely to be fully successful, since some elements of the
enterprise will have a greater capacity to resist an attack than others.
Thus, a cyber attack may disrupt the optimal execution of a particular
option in the U.S. nuclear war plan, but it is highly unlikely to prevent its
execution entirely.

Whether suboptimal execution of a given option has strategic significance is impossible to determine in the absence of specifics about that
option and the intent behind ordering its execution, but as a general rule,
it should be expected that any given option builds in some room for failures that would result in some degree of suboptimality (e.g., it is designed
in a way that anticipates 30 percent of warheads not being delivered to
their targets). The operational question is whether an adversary cyber
operation would or could result in additional suboptimality sufficient to
deny the United States the ability to achieve its war aims as desired (e.g.,
an adversary cyber operation might result in an additional 25 percent of
warheads not being delivered).

At the same time, the imperative associated with Observation 6 is that
all operators should be taking the precautions that would be necessary if they
were using systems and networks known to be compromised by an adversary,
since systems with weaker cybersecurity postures are indeed more likely to

be compromised. These operating practices will be inconvenient, reduce productivity, and seem unnecessary, but employing them is the only way to limit the effects of a security compromise since operators generally do not know how secure their systems are.

Furthermore, humans should maintain the ability to perform at least a minimal set of these functions. Enabling humans in such a manner contributes to resiliency in two ways. First, it will to some extent give operators the ability to perform independent sanity checks on the computer-generated output they see. Second, and perhaps more important, human operators may well have to step into the breach if these automated functions are compromised for any reason. As an example, humans must retain the ability to plan in-flight refueling for bombers. Although such planning is made more efficient through the use of computerized databases, these might be corrupted in a cyber attack.

Imposing a requirement that humans be able to take over a minimal set of functions will require engineering the system in ways that actually provide for the possibility of manual control. Although this idea seems obvious, such engineering has not always been performed in both civilian and military systems alike. For example, in 2016, a software problem in an early version of the Nest electronic thermostat prevented home residents from being able to heat their homes during cold spells.[17] In 1998, a software problem aboard the U.S.S. *Yorktown*, a U.S. Navy warship designated as a test-bed for new technologies, left it unable to move for hours.[18] In neither case had system designers anticipated the need for manual control of basic functions such as turning on the heat or controlling ship propulsion.

Given these observations and corresponding imperatives, how should the nation proceed? What does it mean to take these observations and imperatives into account? This is the subject of the next and final chapter.

7

Moving Forward

This book was written at a time of transition between two presidential administrations. Of necessity, it relies on Trump administration documents, such as the 2017 *National Security Strategy of the United States of America* and the 2018 *Nuclear Posture Review*. New administrations seek to differentiate themselves from the outgoing one, but in the area of nuclear policy and practice, there has been remarkable continuity in the broad outlines over the years. Alas, the same is true for much of cybersecurity policy and practice within the defense establishment.

Thus, nothing in the policies of the incoming Biden administration should be expected to challenge the overarching premise of this book—that issues of cybersecurity are critical to the whole of the nuclear enterprise. It is possible that a Biden nuclear posture review could reduce or eliminate the role of nuclear weapons in deterring nonnuclear attacks on the United States or its allies and partners, but even such a change—radical though elimination would be in the context of the history of nuclear strategy—would not affect this premise very much. Furthermore, although issues of cyber risk impinge most strongly on the NC3 system, many of the cybersecurity issues facing NC3 modernization also apply in some form to other aspects of the nuclear modernization program.

A less likely change in policy would be abandoning those parts of policy calling for the president to have the unilateral and sole authority to order the use of nuclear weapons; at the time of this writing, a number of Democratic members of the House of Representatives have sent President Biden a letter requesting that he "consider modifying the decision-making process the United States uses in its command and control of nuclear forces," calling attention to the dangers of authority residing in the hands of one person, and suggesting the possibility that the concurrence of at least one other person should be required before such authority can be exercised.[1]

Should such a change of policy occur, the NC3 systems would face the additional stresses of coordinating that authority, possibly under great time pressure and thereby increasing the likelihood that nuclear weapons would not be used even if all required concurrences were available. This additional risk (of non-use when there was a consensus on use) must be weighed against the risk of use—perhaps by a president gone mad—when use would clearly be inappropriate. This is a judgment that this book does not address.

In considering the cyber-nuclear nexus, an important question is the following: since nearly all of the cybersecurity issues described in this book also apply to cyber threats faced by conventional general-purpose forces as well, what is so different about cyber threats to the nuclear enterprise? Is there anything special about these?

Interpreting the question narrowly, the answer has to be no. Like new nuclear weapons systems, new conventional weapons systems will be increasingly computerized and networked. Adversary hackers who target elements of the nuclear enterprise will by and large use the same tools, tactics, techniques, and procedures as those who target elements of the general-purpose forces. Malware useful for attacking systems used to deliver nuclear weapons is likely to be useful for similar systems delivering conventional explosives.

But the narrow interpretation here is misleading. Considering the larger context, the answer is yes—a cyber threat to the nuclear enterprise is very different. It is nuclear weapons, not conventional ones, that pose an existential threat to humanity. The stakes—including the cybersecurity stakes—are manifestly higher when nuclear weapons are involved, simply because the weapons are nuclear.

In the event that an adversary chooses to attack the U.S. nuclear enterprise with cyber weapons, it is likely that the adversary would use the skills of their first-line, top-caliber talent to undertake hacking operations against elements of the targeted nuclear enterprise and would be likely to resource them more generously than they would if the targets were simply the general-purpose forces. Greater skill of its cyber attackers plus additional resources for them means that the adversary would be less likely to make mistakes of tradecraft and more likely to imagine attack vectors unanticipated by the target.

Consequently, while the technical nature of cyber threats may be similar, the execution of adversary activities is likely to be much more competent and capable where nuclear weapons are involved, and the consequences of adversary success more dire. The policy significance is that under these circumstances, actions to mitigate cyber risks should be commensurate with the importance and significance of the assets being protected—and since, in the words of the 2018 *Nuclear Posture Review*, preventing adversary nuclear attacks "is the highest priority of the United States," the assets of the U.S. nuclear enterprise should be guarded in cyberspace accordingly.

Another possible manifestation of cyber risk is that an adversary may use cyber weapons against the United States for reasons other than targeting the U.S. nuclear enterprise, and that any effects on the nuclear enterprise will be accidental or inadvertent. Recall that by definition, inadvertent escalation can arise because one side interprets actions by the other in an entirely different light than the other side intends.

Protecting the U.S. nuclear enterprise against inadvertent escalation from a cyber attack directed elsewhere poses an additional and very different design problem than hardening it to frustrate a deliberate cyber attack on it. The former problem entails an architectural design that minimizes the possibility that U.S. decision-makers could misinterpret adversary cyberattacks directed elsewhere. That, in turn, places a high premium on separating U.S. nuclear and conventional assets and *refraining from the use of nuclear assets for conventional purposes even if they are technically capable of doing so.*

Furthermore, drawing on this book's framing of cyber risk as a holistic problem that entails a complex interaction between technology, people, and organization, it is highly desirable for the teams advising senior decision-makers about responding to cyber attack to include individuals whose role it is to challenge worst-case interpretations of adversary behavior, for example, by trying to understand and explain adversary behavior in terms of the *adversary's* interests. A partial precedent might be the use of "devil's advocates" as part of the ExCom structure set up by President Kennedy to advise him during the Cuban Missile Crisis. (Building advisory teams with such expertise that are able to command the necessary attention is likely to be more challenging than employing technology to harden the enterprise's cybersecurity posture.)

These remarks should not be taken to mean that reducing the likelihood of inadvertent escalation as the result of cyber attacks is more important than hardening key elements of the U.S. nuclear enterprise against deliberate cyber attacks—only that each task deserves significant attention in its own right.

To reduce cyber risks to the nuclear enterprise, it should be obvious that sustained, high-level attention to cybersecurity issues will be necessary. Many senior decision-makers are on board with the idea that cybersecurity poses many important challenges that must be addressed in nuclear modernization, and a number of activities, both classified and unclassified, are under way to ensure that the observations and corresponding recommendations described above are followed to some extent. But trade-offs between additional system functionality and enhanced cybersecurity are particularly painful to make, and experience with cybersecurity issues in system acquisition, both civilian and military, suggests that program managers rarely make compromises on other system functionality to improve cybersecurity.

Moreover, high-level policy attention to cybersecurity issues does not necessarily translate into improved cybersecurity practices on the ground. Senior decision-makers and those overseeing nuclear modernization in both the executive and legislative branches will have to keep in mind the large gap that often—indeed, usually—exists between the stated goals of an activity or a program and what actually happens on the ground. This is especially so when, for a given set of requirements, successfully enhancing security means reducing productivity, increasing cost, lengthening timelines, and causing additional inconvenience for operators and users. Experience suggests the likelihood, for example, that at least some important databases will be contained in unprotected and unauthenticated Excel files on someone's PC at work. That PC is probably on a protected classified network somewhere, but may well be otherwise undefended, leaving the database spreadsheets open to alteration should an adversary penetrate the network.

To illustrate, it is virtually certain that every official involved with the weapons systems examined by the GAO report referenced in chapter 3 would agree that cybersecurity was and is an important issue to take into account in the acquisition of that system. And yet, they were confident that their efforts were adequate, and they discounted GAO's findings. Accordingly, some methodology is needed to establish on-the-ground truth—and experience teaches that one of the best ways to do that is to make frequent use of red teaming that is permitted to conduct its activities as a sophisticated, well-resourced, and determined adversary would conduct them, and that the reports of such red team exercises be made broadly available to program overseers.

The importance of using red teams is underscored by the FY 2019 report of Director of Operational Testing and Evaluation (DOT&E), which noted that "no-fail" missions of the Combatant Commands, of which the mission of nuclear deterrence is surely one, should be stressed by the best approximation of advanced adversaries.[2] However, the report found that most of the red teams available operated at only the moderate-threat level or below, and none routinely operated at the advanced nation-state level. DOT&E indicated that due to a lack of expertise and resources, the skills and expertise of several National Security Agency-certified red teams had atrophied to the point of ineffectiveness, and that restoring them to a mission-ready status would require the armed services supporting these teams to significantly increase their support to them.

As this book goes to press, another Government Accountability Office report on weapons systems cybersecurity issued in March 2021 notes that DoD has made progress incorporating cybersecurity into the contracting and acquisition process since its last report on the same topic in 2018.[3] Nevertheless, this report did not examine in depth mission-level analyses of cybersecurity vulnerabilities, alignment of cybersecurity activities to acquisition milestones, or the effectiveness of testing procedures, all of which would have been necessary to update the 2018 report fully. These latter issues are more closely related to the operational cybersecurity posture of weapons systems, and are thus even more important than contracting issues in improving said posture.

As for setting priorities for DoD cybersecurity, one aspect is clear from the above—as a rule of thumb and given the central importance of the nuclear forces in the U.S. national security posture, reducing cyber risk to the nuclear enterprise should generally take precedence over similar efforts regarding the general-purpose forces. Within the nuclear enterprise, reducing cyber risk to the NC3 system should probably take priority over reducing cyber risk to other elements. The reason is that it is the NC3 system that ensures that the president has positive control over the nuclear forces. Authority for nuclear operations is thus more highly centralized as contrasted with authority for most conventional operations, where a commander's intent often provides guidance sufficient to allow decentralized execution of operational plans. (It is far less plausible to imagine nuclear forces striking targets of opportunity without presidential approval than to imagine conventional forces doing so.)

As far as I can tell, the cybersecurity posture of the nuclear weapons complex—especially at the nuclear weapons laboratories—appears to be considerably stronger and more robust than that of most DoD elements in the nuclear enterprise. This is not to say that it could not be improved, but effort and resources devoted to improving cybersecurity are likely to be better spent on DoD elements.

Recognition of the observations and respect for the imperatives described in chapter 6 above is intended to be a first step in addressing cybersecurity vulnerabilities as the nuclear modernization effort moves forward. Such recognition and respect will not guarantee its cybersecurity posture in the face of future cyber threats, but ignoring them or giving them inadequate attention will surely increase the likelihood of serious failure in some element of the nuclear enterprise.

Notes

Preface

1. U.S. Department of Defense, Office of the Deputy Assistant Secretary of Defense for Nuclear Matters, *Nuclear Matters Handbook 2020*, fas.org/man/eprint/nmhb2020.pdf.

2. See, e.g., Scott Sagan, *The Limits of Safety: Organizations, Accidents, and Nuclear Weapons*(Princeton, NJ: Princeton University Press, 1993, press.princeton.edu/books/paperback/9780691021010/the-limits-of-safety; *Managing Nuclear Operations*, ed. John Steinbruner, Ashton Carter, and Charles Zraket (Washington, DC: Brookings Institution, 1987; Paul Bracken, *The Command and Control of Nuclear Forces* (New Haven, CT: Yale University Press, 1983); Bruce Blair, *Strategic Command and Control: Redefining the Nuclear Threat* (Washington, DC: Brookings Institution, 1985; Paul Bracken, *The Second Nuclear Age: Strategy, Danger, and the New Power Politics,* (New York: Times Books, 2012); Eric Schlosser, *Command and Control: Nuclear Weapons, the Damascus Accident, and the Illusion of Safety* (New York: Penguin Books, 2014),

3. U.S. Department of Defense, Air Force, *LGM-30G Minuteman III Fact Sheet*, September 30, 2015, www.af.mil/About-Us/Fact-Sheets/Display/Article/104466/lgm-30g-minuteman-iii.

Chapter 1: Introduction and Background

1. Daniel Ford, *The Button: The Pentagon Command and Control System—Does It Work?* (New York: Simon & Schuster, 1985), 28.

2. U.S. Cybersecurity and Infrastructure Security Agency, "Joint Statement by the

Federal Bureau of Investigation (FBI), the Cybersecurity and Infrastructure Security Agency (CISA), the Office of the Director of National Intelligence (ODNI), and the National Security Agency (NSA)," Department of Homeland Security, January 5, 2021,www.cisa.gov/news/2021/01/05/joint-statement-federal-bureau-investigation-fbi-cybersecurity-and-infrastructure.

3. Jordan Williams, "Durbin Says Alleged Russian Hack 'Virtually a Declaration of War,'" *The Hill*, December 16, 2020, thehill.com/policy/cybersecurity/530461-durbin-says-alleged-russian-hack-virtually-a-declaration-of-war.

4. Colin Dwyer, "Pompeo Says Russia 'Pretty Clearly' behind Cyberattack, Prompting Pushback from Trump." NPR, December 19, 2020, www.npr.org/2020/12/19/948318197/pompeo-russia-pretty-clearly-behind-massive-solarwinds-cyberattack.

5. Andrea Mitchell, "Sen. Coons: 'This Is a Chilling Example of How Aggressive Russian Cyber Activities Have Become,'" MSNBC, December 17, 2020, www.msnbc.com/andrea-mitchell-reports/watch/sen-coons-this-is-a-chilling-example-of-how-aggressive-russian-cyber-activities-have-become-97931333651.

6. Thomas Bossert, "I Was the Homeland Security Adviser to Trump. We're Being Hacked," *New York Times*, December 17, 2020, www.nytimes.com/2020/12/16/opinion/fireeye-solarwinds-russia-hack.html.

7. Bill Whitaker, "SolarWinds: How Russian Spies Hacked the Justice, State, Treasury, Energy and Commerce Departments," CBS News, *60 Minutes*, February 14, 2021, www.cbsnews.com/news/solarwinds-hack-russia-cyberattack-60-minutes-2021-02-14.

8. Material in this section is derived largely from National Research Council (NRC), *Toward a Safer and More Secure Cyberspace*, ed. Seymour Goodman and Herbert Lin (Washington, DC: National Academies Press, 2007), doi.org/10.17226/11925; NRC, *A 21st Century Cyber-Physical Systems Education* (Washington, DC: National Academies Press, 2016), doi.org/10.17226/23686; and NRC, *At the Nexus of Cybersecurity and Public Policy: Some Basic Concepts and Issues*, ed. David Clark, Thomas Berson, and Herbert Lin (Washington, DC: National Academies Press, 2014), doi.org/10.17226/18749.

9. National Research Council, *Toward a Safer and More Secure Cyberspace*, ed. Goodman and Lin.

10. For more on supply chain vulnerabilities, see, e.g., U.S. Office of the Director of National Intelligence, National Counterintelligence and Security Center, "Supply Chain Risk Management" (n.d.), www.dni.gov/index.php/ncsc-what-we-do/ncsc-supply-chain-threats.

11. Jason Breslow, "How Edward Snowden Leaked 'Thousands' of NSA Documents," PBS, *Frontline*, May 13, 2014, www.pbs.org/wgbh/frontline/article/how-edward-snowden-leaked-thousands-of-nsa-documents; Sarah Childress, "Bradley Manning Sentenced to 35 Years for WikiLeaks," PBS, *Frontline*, August 21, 2013, www.pbs.org/wgbh/frontline/article/bradley-manning-sentenced-to-35-years-for-wikileaks.

12. See Steve Stasiukonis, "Social Engineering, the USB Way," June 7, 2006, www.darkreading.com/attacks-breaches/social-engineering-the-usb-way/d/d-id/1128081.

13. Andy Greenberg, "Hackers Remotely Kill a Jeep on the Highway—with Me in It," *WIRED*, July 21, 2015, www.wired.com/2015/07/hackers-remotely-kill-jeep-highway.

14. For more discussion of this point, see National Research Council, *Technology, Policy, Law, and Ethics Regarding U.S. Acquisition and Use of Cyberattack Capabilities*, ed. William Owens, Kenneth Dam, and Herbert Lin (Washington, DC: National Academies Press, 2009), chaps. 2 and 3, doi.org/10.17226/12651.

15. This brief discussion of attribution is condensed from a much more extended discussion of attribution found in Herbert Lin, "Attribution of Malicious Cyber Incidents: From Soup to Nuts," *Journal of International Affairs* 70, no. 1 (Winter 2016): 75-137, jia.sipa.columbia.edu/attribution-malicious-cyber-incidents.

16. U.S. Department of Defense, *Nuclear Posture Review*, February 2018, 21, media.defense.gov/2018/Feb/02/2001872886/-1/-1/1/2018-NUCLEAR-POSTURE-REVIEW-FINAL-REPORT.PDF.

17. The literature on nuclear deterrence is extensive. A primer on deterrence from which some of this discussion is derived can be found in Michael Mazarr, *Understanding Deterrence* (Santa Monica, CA: RAND Corporation, 2018), www.rand.org/pubs/perspectives/PE295.html.

18. U.S. Department of State, Bureau of Arms Control, Verification and Compliance Fact Sheet, "New START Treaty Aggregate Numbers of Strategic Offensive Arms," September 1, 2019, www.state.gov/wp-content/uploads/2019/12/AVC-New-START-Jan-2020.pdf.

19. Arms Control Association. "U.S. Strategic Nuclear Forces Under New START" (Washington, DC: Arms Control Association, 2020), www.armscontrol.org/factsheets/USStratNukeForceNewSTART#:~:text=As%20of%20March%20201%2C%202020,capable%20bombers%2C%20and%20240%20SLBMs.

20. U.S. Congressional Budget Office, *The Potential Costs of Expanding U.S. Strategic Nuclear Forces If the New START Treaty Expires* (August 2020), www.cbo.gov/publication/56524.

21. U.S. Department of Defense, "Statement on the Fielding of the W76-2 Low-Yield Submarine Launched Ballistic Missile Warhead," attributed to Under Secretary of Defense for Policy John Rood, February 4, 2020, www.defense.gov/Newsroom/Releases/Release/Article/2073532/statement-on-the-fielding-of-the-w76-2-low-yield-submarine-launched-ballistic-m.

22. See, e.g., Hans Kristensen and Matthew McKinzie, *Reducing Alert Rates of Nuclear Weapons* (Geneva: United Nations Institute for Disarmament Research, 2012), www.unidir.org/files/publications/pdfs/reducing-alert-rates-of-nuclear-weapons-400.pdf.

23. U.S. General Accounting Office, *Triad Summary*, PEMD-92-36R, September 28, 1992, www.gao.gov/assets/90/82669.pdf.

24. Elaine Grossman, "DoD Defends New Sub-Launched Missiles," *InsideDefense.Com*, March 10, 2006, archived at web.archive.org/web/20121011044135/www.military.com/features/0,15240,90477,00.html.

25. U.S. Congressional Research Service, *Nonstrategic Nuclear Weapons*, by Amy Woolf (2020, updated 2021), RL32572, fas.org/sgp/crs/nuke/RL32572.pdf.

26. U.S. Department of Defense, "Air Force Nuclear Command, Control, and Communications (NC3)," Air Force Instruction (AFI) 13-550, April 16, 2019, fas.org/irp/doddir/usaf/afi13-550.pdf.

27. Jeffrey Larsen, "Nuclear Command, Control, and Communications: US Country Profile," NAPSNet Special Reports, August 22, 2019, nautilus.org/napsnet/napsnet-special-reports/nuclear-command-control-and-communications-us-country-profile.

28. David A. Deptula, Robert Haddick, and William A. LaPlante, "Time to Update NC3," *Air Force Magazine*, March 22, 2019, www.airforcemag.com/article/time-to-update-nc3. The array of NC3 communications systems is known in the U.S. Air Force as the AN/USQ-225 weapons system, consisting of "AF [Air Force] communications systems and components (radios, terminals, messaging, and conferencing systems that establish and function across the NC3 networks) through which the President exercises nuclear command and control"; see U.S. Department of Defense. "Air Force Nuclear Command, Control, and Communications (NC3)," Air Force Instruction (AFI) 13-550, April 16, 2019, fas.org/irp/doddir/usaf/afi13-550.pdf.

29. Larsen, "Nuclear Command, Control, and Communications: US Country Profile."

30. For some discussion on the relationship between cyber operations and escalation dynamics based on war-gaming experience, see Jacquelyn Schneider, "What War Games Tell Us About the Use of Cyber Weapons in a Crisis," Council on Foreign Relations, June 21, 2018, www.cfr.org/blog/what-war-games-tell-us-about-use-of-cyber-weapons-crisis.

31. Paul Bracken, *The Hunt for Mobile Missiles: Nuclear Weapons, AI, and the New Arms Race* (Philadelphia: Foreign Policy Research Institute, 2020), www.fpri.org/wp-content/uploads/2020/09/the-hunt-for-mobile-missiles.pdf.

32. See, e.g., Adam Lowther and Curtis McGiffin, "America Needs a 'Dead Hand,'" Maxwell Air Force Base, August 23, 2019, www.maxwell.af.mil/News/Commentaries/Display/Article/1942374/america-needs-a-dead-hand.

Chapter 2: The Cyber-Nuclear Connection

1. Fred Kaplan, "'WarGames' and Cybersecurity's Debt to a Hollywood Hack," *New York Times*, February 19, 2016, www.nytimes.com/2016/02/21/movies/wargames-and-cybersecuritys-debt-to-a-hollywood-hack.html.

2. U.S. Department of Defense, *Nuclear Posture Review*, February 2018, 21.

3. U.S. Department of Defense, *Nuclear Posture Review Report*, April 2010, viii, dod.defense.gov/Portals/1/features/defenseReviews/Nuclear Posture Review/2010_ Nuclear_Posture_Review_Report.pdf.

4. Christopher Ford, *International Security in Cyberspace: New Models for Reducing Risk*, U.S. Department of State Arms Control and International Security Papers 1, no. 20 (2020), www.state.gov/wp-content/uploads/2020/10/T-paper-series-Cybersecurity-Format-508.pdf.

5. U.S. Department of Defense, Joint Chiefs of Staff, *The National Military Strategy of the United States of America—A Strategy for Today, a Vision for Tomorrow* (Office of the Joint Chiefs of Staff, 2004), archive.defense.gov/news/Mar2005/d20050318nms.pdf.

6. For more discussion, see Herbert Lin, "Anything New under the Sun? Nuclear Responses to Cyberattacks," Lawfare, January 19, 2018, www.lawfareblog.com/anything-new-under-sun-nuclear-responses-cyberattacks.

7. David Sanger and William Broad, "Pentagon Suggests Countering Devastating Cyberattacks with Nuclear Arms," *New York Times,* January 16, 2018, www.nytimes.com/2018/01/16/us/politics/pentagon-nuclear-review-cyberattack-trump.html; Patrick Tucker, "No, the US Won't Respond to a Cyber Attack with Nukes," *Defense One*, February 2, 2018, www.defenseone.com/technology/2018/02/no-us-wont-respond-cyber-attack-nukes/145700; Shaun Waterman, "Experts Push Back on Trump Administration's Call to Respond to Cyberattacks with Nukes," *CyberScoop*, February 13, 2018, www.cyberscoop.com/nuclear-posture-review-cyberattacks-nukes-donald-trump; George Perkovich, "Really? We're Gonna Nuke Russia for a Cyberattack?" *Politico,* January18, 2018, www.politico.com/magazine/story/2018/01/18/donald-trump-russia-nuclear-cyberattack-216477.

8. William Lynn, "Defending a New Domain: The Pentagon's Cyberstrategy," *Foreign Affairs,* September/October 2010, www.foreignaffairs.com/articles/united-states/2010-09-01/defending-new-domain, provides more details of the hack that prompted Operation Buckshot Yankee and explains its significance in inspiring U.S. government responses, including the creation of the U.S. Cyber Command.

9. Ellen Nakashima, "Cyber-Intruder Sparks Response, Debate," *Washington Post*, December 8, 2011, www.washingtonpost.com/national/national-security/cyber-intruder-sparks-response-debate/2011/12/06/gIQAxLuFgO_story.html.

10. Drew Harwell and Ellen Nakashima, "Hackers' Threats Prompt Sony Pictures to Shelve Christmas Release of 'The Interview,'" *Washington* Post, December 17, 2014, www.washingtonpost.com/business/economy/top-movie-theater-chains-cancel-premiere-showings-of-the-interview/2014/12/17/dd1bdb2a-8608-11e4-9534-f79a23c40e6c_story.html.

11. For a more comprehensive overview of the Sony Pictures incident, North Korean cyber capabilities, and their implications for U.S. national security, see U.S.

Congressional Research Service, *North Korean Cyber Capabilities: In Brief*, by Emma Chanlett-Avery, John Rollins, Liana Rosen, and Catherine Theohary (2017), R44912, crsreports.congress.gov/product/pdf/R/R44912.

12. For detailed investigation and analysis into the OPM hack and its effects on U.S. national security, see U.S. Congress, House, Committee on Oversight and Government, *The OPM Data Breach: How the Government Jeopardized National Security for More than a Generation*, Majority Staff Report, by Jason Chaffetz, Mark Meadows, Will Hurd et al. September 7, 2016, https://republicans-oversight.house. gov/wp-content/uploads/2016/09/The-OPM-Data-Breach-How-the-Government-Jeopardized-Our-National-Security-for-More-than-a-Generation.pdf.

13. See, e.g., U.S. Department of Justice, Office of Special Counsel, Robert Mueller, III, *Report on the Investigation into Russian Interference in the 2016 Presidential Election* (Washington, DC: Department of Justice, 2019), www.justice.gov/storage/report. pdf. For more context on the 2016 election interference and prescriptions ahead of the 2020 election, see *Securing American Elections: Prescriptions for Enhancing the Integrity and Independence of the 2020 U.S. Presidential Election and Beyond*, ed. Michael McFaul (Stanford: Stanford Cyber Policy Center, Freeman Spogli Institute, 2019), stanford.box.com/shared/static/xd35pzvlnl2konx16suee7mqvjvk6nrb.pdf.

14. National Intelligence Council, *Foreign Threats to the 2020 U.S. Federal Elections*, ICA-2020-00078D, March 15, 2021, www.dni.gov/files/ODNI/documents/assessments/ICA-declass-16MAR21.pdf.

15. SolarWinds Corporation, Form 8-K, Current Report Pursuant to Section 13 or 15(d) of the Securities Exchange Act of 1934, U.S. Securities and Exchange Commission, Washington, DC, December 14, 2020 (date of earliest event reported), www.sec.gov/Archives/edgar/data/0001739942/000162828020017451/swi-20201214.htm.

16. For early reports on the SolarWinds incident and its implications for U.S. national security, see "Highly Evasive Attacker Leverages SolarWinds Supply Chain to Compromise Multiple Global Victims with SUNBURST Backdoor," FireEye Threat Research Blog, Milpitas, CA, December 13, 2020, www.fireeye.com/blog/threat-research/2020/12/evasive-attacker-leverages-solarwinds-supply-chain-compromises-with-sunburst-backdoor.html; see also U.S. Congressional Research Service, "SolarWinds Attack—No Easy Fix," by Chris Jaikaran (updated January 6, 2021), CRS report IN11559, crsreports.congress.gov/product/pdf/IN/IN11559. A later report published on NPR.org provides more recently obtained information (see Dina Temple-Raston. "A 'Worst Nightmare' Cyberattack: The Untold Story of the Solar-Winds Hack," NPR.org., April 16, 2021, www.npr.org/2021/04/16/985439655/a-worst-nightmare-cyberattack-the-untold-story-of-the-solarwinds-hack), but the investigation is still ongoing at the time of this writing.

17. U.S. White House, "FACT SHEET: Imposing Costs for Harmful Foreign

Activities by the Russian Government," April 15, 2021, www.whitehouse.gov/brief-ing-room/statements-releases/2021/04/15/fact-sheet-imposing-costs-for-harmful-foreign-activities-by-the-russian-government.

18. U.S. Department of Defense, Defense Science Board, *Resilient Military Systems and the Advanced Cyber Threat*, January 2013, 42, apps.dtic.mil/dtic/tr/fulltext/u2/a569975.pdf.

19. U.S. Department of Defense, Defense Science Board, "Task Force Report on Cyber Deterrence." February 2017. dsb.cto.mil/reports/2010s/DSB-CyberDeterrenceReport_02-28-17_Final.pdf.

20. Stanislav Abaimov and Paul Ingram, *Hacking UK Trident: A Growing Threat* (London: British American Security Information Council, June 2017), basicint.org/wp-content/uploads/2018/06/HACKING_UK_TRIDENT.pdf.

21. Andrew Futter, *Hacking the Bomb: Cyber Threats and Nuclear Weapons* (Washington, DC: Georgetown University Press, 2018), http://press.georgetown.edu/book/georgetown/hacking-bomb.

22. Page Stoutland and Samantha Pitts-Kiefer, *Nuclear Weapons in the New Cyber Age: Report of the Cyber-Nuclear Weapons Study Group* (Washington, DC: Nuclear Threat Initiative, 2018), media.nti.org/documents/Cyber_report_finalsmall.pdf.

23. Michael Klare, "Cyber Battles, Nuclear Outcomes? Dangerous New Pathways to Escalation," *Arms Control Today* (Washington, DC: Arms Control Association, 2019), www.armscontrol.org/act/2019-11/features/cyber-battles-nuclear-outcomes-dangerous-new-pathways-escalation.

24. Jon Lindsay, "Cyber Operations and Nuclear Weapons," NAPSNet Special Reports, June 20, 2019, nautilus.org/napsnet/napsnet-special-reports/cyber-operations-and-nuclear-weapons.

25. David C. Gompert and Martin C. Libicki, "Cyber War and Nuclear Peace," *Survival: Global Politics and Strategy* 61, no. 4 (2019): 45–62, doi.org/10.1080/00396338.2019.1637122.

26. James Acton, "Cyber Warfare & Inadvertent Escalation," *Dædalus* 149, no. 2 (Spring 2020): 133–49, www.amacad.org/publication/cyber-warfare-inadvertent-escalation. For discussion of the impact on escalation dynamics of conventional war on nuclear assets in a non-cyber context, Barry Posen, *Inadvertent Escalation: Conventional War and Nuclear Risks* (Ithaca, NY: Cornell University Press, 1991).

Chapter 3: The U.S. Nuclear Enterprise

1. U.S. Department of Energy, National Nuclear Security Administration, "Maintaining the Stockpile," www.energy.gov/nnsa/missions/maintaining-stockpile.

2. U.S. Department of Energy, National Nuclear Security Administration, "Stockpile Stewardship and Management Plan (SSMP)," www.energy.gov/nnsa/downloads/stockpile-stewardship-and-management-plan-ssmp.

3. Ibid.

4. U.S. Department of Energy, National Nuclear Security Administration, "Maintaining the Stockpile."

5. Shaya Potter, Steven Bellovin, and Jason Nieh, "Two-Person Control Administration: Preventing Administration Faults through Duplication," in *Proceedings of the 23rd Large Installation System Administration Conference (LISA '09)*, Baltimore, November 1–6, 2009 (Berkeley, CA: USENIX Association, 2009), 15–27, academiccommons.columbia.edu/doi/10.7916/D8HQ45MK.

6. Bill Chappell, Greg Myre, and Laurel Wamsley, "What We Know About Russia's Alleged Hack of the U.S. Government and Tech Companies," NPR, December 21, 2020, www.npr.org/2020/12/15/946776718/u-s-scrambles-to-understand-major-computer-hack-but-says-little.

7. U.S. Department of Energy, "DOE Update on Cyber Incident Related to SolarWinds Compromise," December 18, 2020, www.energy.gov/articles/doe-update-cyber-incident-related-solar-winds-compromise.

8. Natasha Bertrand and Eric Wolff, "Nuclear Weapons Agency Breached amid Massive Cyber Onslaught," *Politico*, December 17, 2020, www.politico.com/news/2020/12/17/nuclear-agency-hacked-officials-inform-congress-447855.

9. Lockheed Martin, "F-35 Software Development: A Digital Jet for the Modern Battlespace," https://web.archive.org/web/20210123100734/https://www.f35.com/about/life-cycle/software.

10. Clay Dillow, "Only One of Six Air Force F-35s Could Take Off during Testing," *Fortune*, April 28, 2016, fortune.com/2016/04/28/f-35-fails-testing-air-force.

11. Mingxu Yi, Lifeng Wang, and Jun Huang, "Active Cancellation Analysis Based on the Radar Detection Probability," *Aerospace Science and Technology* 46 (November 2015): 273–81, doi.org/10.1016/j.ast.2015.07.018.

12. Brian Krebs, "Target Hackers Broke in via HVAC Company," *Krebs on Security*, February 5, 2014, krebsonsecurity.com/2014/02/target-hackers-broke-in-via-hvac-company.

13. Kim Zetter, "An Unprecedented Look at Stuxnet, the World's First Digital Weapon," *Wired*, November 3, 2014, www.wired.com/2014/11/countdown-to-zero-day-stuxnet/.

14. U.S. Government Accountability Office, *Weapon Systems Cybersecurity: DOD Just Beginning to Grapple with Scale of Vulnerabilities*, GAO 19-128, October 9, 2018, www.gao.gov/products/GAO-19-128.

15. David Sanger and William Broad, "New U.S. Weapons Systems Are a Hackers' Bonanza, Investigators Find," *New York Times*, October 10, 2018, www.nytimes.com/2018/10/10/us/politics/hackers-pentagon-weapons-systems.html.

16. Siobhan Gorman, August Cole, and Yochi Dreazen, "Computer Spies Breach Fighter-Jet Project," *Wall Street Journal*, April 21, 2009, www.wsj.com/articles/SB124027491029837401.

17. Robert Koch and Mario Golling, "Weapons Systems and Cyber Security—a Challenging Union," in *2016 8th International Conference on Cyber Conflict* [CyCon, Tallinn, Estonia], 191–203, ccdcoe.org/uploads/2018/10/Art-12-Weapons-Systems-and-Cyber-Security-A-Challenging-Union.pdf.

18. Sally Adee, "The Hunt for the Kill Switch," *IEEE Spectrum*, May 1, 2008, spectrum.ieee.org/semiconductors/design/the-hunt-for-the-kill-switch.

19. U.S. Senate, Committee on Armed Services, *Inquiry into Counterfeit Electronic Parts in the Department of Defense Supply Chain. Report of the Committee on Armed Services*, Report 112–167 (Washington, DC: U.S. Government Printing Office, 2012), www.armed-services.senate.gov/imo/media/doc/Counterfeit-Electronic-Parts.pdf.

20. U.S. Department of Defense, Inspector General, "Audit of the DOD's Management of the Cybersecurity Risks for Government Purchase Card Purchases of Commercial Off-the-Shelf Items," July 26, 2019, media.defense.gov/2019/Jul/30/2002164272/-1/-1/1/DODIG-2019-106.PDF.

21. U.S. Department of Homeland Security, Cybersecurity & Infrastructure Security Agency, Craig Miller, "Security Considerations in Managing COTS Software," December 14, 2006, us-cert.cisa.gov/bsi/articles/best-practices/legacy-systems/security-considerations-in-managing-cots-software.

22. U.S. Department of Defense, Inspector General, "Audit of the DoD's Management."

23. Barls Egemen Özkan and Serol Bulkan, "Hidden Risks to Cyberspace Security from Obsolete COTS Software," in *2019 11th International Conference on Cyber Conflict* [CyCon, Tallinn, Estonia], 1–19, doi.org/10.23919/CYCON.2019.8756990.

24. U.S. Department of Defense, Inspector General, "Audit of the DoD's Management."

25. U.S. Department of Defense, Director, Operational Test and Evaluation, "F-35 Joint Strike Fighter (JSF)," FY19 DoD Programs, www.dote.osd.mil/Portals/97/pub/reports/FY2019/dod/2019f35jsf.pdf?ver=2020-01-30-115432-173.

26. Daniel Lydiate, "Military Aviation's Cyber Challenge: Are Cyber-Vulnerabilities a Credible Threat to a Modern Air Force?" Strategy and Security Institute, University of Exeter, Exeter, England, N.d., www.raf.mod.uk/what-we-do/centre-for-air-and-space-power-studies/documents1/dissertation-lydiate-dan-mstrat-dissertational1.

27. Shaun Nichols, "Easy-to-Hack Combat Systems, Years-Old Flaws and a Massive Bill—Yup, That's America's F-35," *The Register*, March 28, 2019, www.theregister.com/2019/03/28/f35_software_fail.

28. U.S. Government Accountability Office, "F-35 Joint Strike Fighter: Actions Needed to Address Manufacturing and Modernization Risks," May 12, 2020, www.gao.gov/assets/710/706815.pdf.

29. U.S. Department of Defense, Director, Operational Test and Evaluation, "F-35 Joint Strike Fighter (JSF)."

30. "North Korea Jams South's Guided Missiles," UPI, March 8, 2011, www.upi.com/Defense-News/2011/03/08/North-Korea-jams-Souths-guided-missiles/49341299621609.

31. Lockheed Martin, "GPS Spatial Temporal Anti-Jam Receiver (GSTAR) System to Be Integrated in F-35 Modernization," October 29, 2019, news.lockheedmartin.com/lockheed-martin-gps-spatial-temporal-anti-jam-receiver-gstar-system-integrated-f35-modernization.

32. Darlene Storm, "Did Hackers Remotely Execute 'unexplained' Commands on German Patriot Missile Battery?" *Computerworld*, July 8, 2015, www.computerworld.com/article/2945383/did-hackers-remotely-execute-unexplained-commands-on-german-patriot-missile-battery.html.

33. U.S. Department of Defense Inspector General, "Security Controls at DoD Facilities for Protecting Ballistic Missile Defense System Technical Information," media.defense.gov/2018/Dec/14/2002072642/-1/-1/1/DODIG-2019-034.PDF.

34. Paul Kocher et al., "Security as a New Dimension in Embedded System Design," in *DAC '04: Proceedings of the 41st Annual Design Automation Conference* (June 7–11, 2004), 753–60 (San Diego, CA: ACM Press, 2004),doi.org/10.1145/996566.996771.

35. U.S. Strategic Command, Planning and Command and Control, "ALERT/RECALL PROCEDURES," Strategic Instruction (SI) 506–02, April 20, 2017, released under USFOIA request to Nautilus Institute, PDF in the author's possession, publication pending at nautilus.org/publications/foia-document-search. Hat tip to Peter Hayes, who supplied this and a number of other declassified U.S. Strategic Command Strategic Instructions.

36. A very useful discussion of the broad topic of NC3 and strategic stability can be found in Peter Hayes, Binoy Kampmark, Philip Reiner, and Deborah Gordon, "Synthesis Report–NC3 Systems and Strategic Stability: A Global Overview." NAPSNet Special Reports, May 5, 2019, nautilus.org/?p=97769.

37. Hans Kristensen, "US Nuclear War Plan Updated amidst Nuclear Policy Review," Federation of American Scientists, April 4, 2013, fas.org/blogs/security/2013/04/oplan8010-12.

38. Corrie Poland, "The Air Force Is Becoming More Agile—One Project at a Time," *Installations, Environment, & Energy*, April 24, 2019, www.safie.hq.af.mil/News/Article-Display/Article/1823169/the-air-force-is-becoming-more-agile-one-project-at-a-time; Rachel Cohen, "Second Tanker Planning Software Project Enters Testing," *Air Force Magazine*, July 8, 2019, www.airforcemag.com/second-tanker-planning-software-project-enters-testing.

39. Bruce Katz and Peter Ising, "Kessel Run Deploys KRADOS to Air Operations

Center," January 12, 2021, kesselrun.af.mil/news/Kessel-Run-Deploys-KRADOS. html.

40. U.S. Strategic Command, Strategic Instruction (SI) 512–06, June 15, 2018, "Guidelines for Reporting Pre-Launch Survivability," released under USFOIA request to Nautilus Institute, PDF in the author's possession, publication pending, nautilus.org/publications/foia-document-search.

41. See, e.g., U.S. Department of Defense, "Air Force Nuclear Command, Control, and Communications (NC3)," Air Force Instruction (AFI) 13-550.

42. Peter Grier, "Misplaced Nukes," *Air Force Magazine*, June 26, 2017, www.airforcemag.com/article/misplacednukes. The official (but redacted) Air Force report is "Commander-Directed Report of Investigation Prepared by Major General Douglas L. Raaberg, Investigating Officer, Concerning an Unauthorized Transfer of Nuclear Warheads between Minot AFB, North Dakota and Barksdale AFB, Louisiana, August 30, 2007, scholar.harvard.edu/files/jvaynman/files/minot_afb_report.pdf.

43. U.S. Department of Defense, Secretary of Defense Task Force on DoD Nuclear Weapons Management, "Phase I: The Air Force's Nuclear Mission," September 2008, www.globalsecurity.org/wmd/library/report/2008/nuclear-weapons_phase-1_2008-09-10.pdf.

44. U.S. Department of Defense, "Air Force Nuclear Command, Control, and Communications (NC3)," Air Force Instruction (AFI) 13-550.

45. Ashton Carter, "Sources of Error and Uncertainty," in *Managing Nuclear Operations*, ed. Steinbruner, 630.

46. Alan Borning, "Computer System Reliability and Nuclear War," *Communications of the ACM* 30, no. 2 (February 1, 1987): 112–31, doi.org/10.1145/12527.12528.

47. Sagan, *Limits of Safety*, 176–77.

48. Ibid., 130–31.

49. Ibid., 99–100.

50. U.S. Congress, Senate, Committee on Armed Services, *Recent False Alerts from the Nation's Missile Attack Warning System,* report by Senators Barry Goldwater and Gary Hart (Washington, DC: Government Printing Office, 1980).

51. William Burr, "False Warnings of Soviet Missile Attacks Put U.S. Forces on Alert in 1979–1980," National Security Archive, March 16, 2020, nsarchive.gwu.edu/briefing-book/nuclear-vault/2020-03-16/false-warnings-soviet-missile-attacks-during-1979-80-led-alert-actions-us-strategic-forces.

52. See, e.g., James Johnson, "'Catalytic Nuclear War in the Age of Artificial Intelligence & Autonomy: Emerging Military Technology and Escalation Risk between Nuclear-Armed States," *Journal of Strategic Studies*, January 13, 2021, 1–41, doi.org/10.1080/01402390.2020.1867541.

53. U.S. Congress, 526 Congressional Investigation Pearl Harbor Attack.

"Testimony of First Lt. Joseph Lockard, Signal Corps, United States Army," www. ibiblio.org/pha/myths/radar/lockard3.html.

54. U.S. Department of Defense, "Air Force Nuclear Command, Control, and Communications (NC3)," Air Force Instruction (AFI) 13-550.

55. Michael Beschloss, *The Crisis Years: Kennedy and Khrushchev, 1960–1963* (New York: Edward Burlingame Books, 1991), 524.

56. William Arkin and Robert Windrem, "Secrets of 9/11: New Details of Chaos, Confusion Emerge," NBC News, September 11, 2016, www.nbcnews.com/storyline/9-11-anniversary/secrets-9-11-new-details-chaos-nukes-emerge-n645711.

57. Nautilus Institute, Stanley Center for Peace and Security, and Technology for Global Security, *Last Chance: Communicating at the Nuclear Brink. Scenarios and Solutions Workshop Synthesis Report* (Berkeley, CA: Nautilus Institute, 2020), nautilus. org/wp-content/uploads/2020/05/Last-Chance-Synthesis-Report-May-14-2020.pdf.

58. U.S. Department of Defense, "Air Force Nuclear Command, Control, and Communications (NC3)," Air Force Instruction (AFI) 13-550.

59. A useful primer on presidential authority for using nuclear weapons is Jeffrey G. Lewis and Bruno Tertrais, *The Finger on the Button: The Authority to Use Nuclear Weapons in Nuclear-Armed States,* CNS Occasional Paper 45 (Monterey, CA: James Martin Center for Nonproliferation Studies, Middlebury Institute of International Studies, 2019), www.nonproliferation.org/wp-content/uploads/2019/02/Finger-on-the-Nuclear-Button.pdf.

60. See U.S. Congress, House, Subcommittee on International Security and Scientific Affairs of the Committee on International Relations, testimony of Vice Admiral Gerald Miller, "First Use of Nuclear Weapons: Preserving Responsible Control," March 15–16, 1976, 55, http://blog.nuclearsecrecy.com/wp-content/uploads/2017/04/hrg-1976-hir-0038_from_1_to_251.pdf. Cited in Lewis and Tertrais, *Finger on the Button.* Miller's testimony does not refer to the 1965 date, which appears to come from Lewis and Tertrais.

61. John Harvey, *U.S. Nuclear Command and Control for the 21st Century,* NAPSNet Special Reports, May 24, 2019, nautilus.org/napsnet/napsnet-special-reports/u-s-nuclear-command-and-control-for-the-21st-Century.

62. The always/never distinction is explicated in much greater detail in Peter Feaver, *Guarding the Guardians: Civilian Control of Nuclear Weapons in the United States* (Ithaca, NY: Cornell University Press, 1992). Note, however, that deterrence does not necessarily require the "always" part be true. An adversary may well be dissuaded from striking the United States with nuclear weapons even if there is only a 80 percent or 90 percent, rather than 100 percent, likelihood of a U.S. nuclear response.

63. Several of the scenarios for attacks on "always" and "never" are found in Harvey, *U.S. Nuclear Command and Control.*

64. The relevant parameter is "Command and Control Procedures (CCP) reliability" and is found in U.S. Strategic Command, Strategic Instruction (SI) 526–01, June 30, 2020, "Guidelines for Nuclear Weapon System Operational Testing and Reporting," Strategic Instruction (SI) 526–01, June 30, 2020, released under USFOIA request to Nautilus Institute, PDF in the author's possession, publication pending. Curiously, U.S. Strategic Command's guidance for calculating damage expectancy (the likelihood that a target will be adequately damaged by a nuclear strike) takes into account the probability that a weapon will arrive at the target and the probability that the weapon will be damaged given that the weapon explodes. One would expect the probability of weapon arrival to include the CCP parameter, which measures the likelihood of NC3 working properly, but according to U.S. Strategic Command Strategic Instruction SI 512–06 "Guidelines for Reporting Pre-Launch Survivability" (cited in n. 40 above), it does not. On the other hand, it may be that the CCP parameter is taken into account elsewhere in the nuclear strike planning process. Thanks to Peter Hayes for the reference to the CCP parameter.

65. Gabriel Myers, "Missileers Receive New Computer Capabilities," *U.S. Air Force*, June 8, 2006, www.af.mil/News/Article-Display/Article/130775/missileers-receive-new-computer-capabilities; Joseph Page II, Mark Bigley, and Douglas Angell, "Launch Control Center NetLink," *High Frontier* 3, no. 2 (March 2007): 66–69, https://web.archive.org/web/20081029190633/http://www.afspc.af.mil/shared/media/document/AFD-070322-103.pdf; *Air Force Times,* "Air Force Missile Sites to Get Wi-Fi," August 7, 2017. www.airforcetimes.com/news/your-air-force/2014/11/04/air-force-missile-sites-to-get-wi-fi.

66. A. W. Geiger, "Key Findings about the Online News Landscape in America," *Pew Research Center*, September 11, 2019, www.pewresearch.org/fact-tank/2019/09/11/key-findings-about-the-online-news-landscape-in-america.

67. Geoff Brumfiel, "How to Order Pizza from a Nuclear Command Bunker," NPR, July 31, 2014, www.npr.org/sections/thesalt/2014/07/31/336614501/how-to-order-pizza-from-a-nuclear-command-bunker.

68. Henry Shelton, with Ronald Levinson, and Malcolm McConnell, *Without Hesitation: The Odyssey of an American Warrior* (New York: St. Martin's Press, 2011)

69. Harvey, *U.S. Nuclear Command and Control*; Ariel E. Levite, Lyu Jinghua, George Perkovich et al., *China-U.S. Cyber-Nuclear C3 Stability* (Washington, DC: Carnegie Endowment for International Peace, 2021), https://carnegieendowment.org/2021/04/08/china-u.s.-cyber-nuclear-c3-stability-pub-84182.

70. Bruce Blair, "Keeping Presidents in the Nuclear Dark (Episode #1: The Case of the Missing Permissive Action Links)," *Bruce Blair's Nuclear Column*, Center for Defense Information, February 11, 2004, www.globalzero.org/wp-content/uploads/2019/03/BB_Keeping-Presidents-in-the-Nuclear-Dark-Episode-1-The-Case-of-the-Missing-Permissive-Action-Links_02.11.2004.pdf. This would hardly

surprise cybersecurity specialists familiar with passwords on sticky notes stuck on monitors and dumb passwords such as "password123."

71. Mel Lyman, "Crimson Tide: They Got It All Wrong," *Comparative Strategy* 18, no. 4 (1999): 309–12, https://doi.org/10.1080/01495939908403188.

72. U.S. Congress, Senate, Committee on Armed Services, testimony of Admiral Cecil D. Haney, commander, U.S. Strategic Command, February 27, 2014, www.hsdl.org/?view&did=751682.

73. U.S. Congress, Senate, Committee on Armed Services, testimony of General John Hyten, commander, U.S. Strategic Command, March 1, 2019, www.stratcom.mil/Media/Speeches/Article/1771903/us-strategic-command-and-us-northern-command-sasc-testimony.

74. U.S. Government Accountability Office, "Nuclear Command, Control, and Communications: Review of DOD's Current Modernization Efforts," GAO-14–414R, March 18, 2014, www.gao.gov/assets/670/661752.pdf.

75. See, e.g., Hyten testimony cited in n. 73 above. See also David A. Deptula, William A. LaPlante, and Robert Haddick, *Modernizing U.S. Nuclear Command, Control, and Communications* (Arlington, VA: Mitchell Institute for Aerospace Studies, Air Force Association, 2019), 26 and 31, http://docs.wixstatic.com/ugd/a2dd91_ed45cfd71de2457eba3bcce4d0657196.pdf.

76. Marc Ambinder, "Failure Shuts Down Squadron of Nuclear Missiles," *The Atlantic*, October 26, 2010, www.theatlantic.com/politics/archive/2010/10/failure-shuts-down-squadron-of-nuclear-missiles/65207; Noah Shachtman, "Communication with 50 Nuke Missiles Dropped in ICBM Snafu," *WIRED*, October 26, 2010, www.wired.com/2010/10/communications-dropped-to-50-nuke-missiles-in-icbm-snafu.

77. Bruce Blair, "Could Terrorists Launch America's Nuclear Missiles?" *Time*, November 11, 2010, http://content.time.com/time/nation/article/0,8599,2030685,00.html.

78. Keegan Hamilton, "The Plan to Make America's Nukes Great Again Could Go Horribly Wrong," *VICE*, April 20, 2017, www.vice.com/en/article/a3j9mg/the-plan-to-make-americas-nukes-great-again-could-go-horribly-wrong.

79. Bruce Blair, "Why Our Nuclear Weapons Can Be Hacked," *New York Times*, March 14, 2017, www.nytimes.com/2017/03/14/opinion/why-our-nuclear-weapons-can-be-hacked.html.

80. Bruce Blair, "Rogue States: Nuclear Red-Herrings," December 5, 2003, https://web.archive.org/web/20031223085259/www.cdi.org/blair/russia-targeting.cfm. This document's time frame is reported in Blair's 2010 *Time* magazine article "Could Terrorists Launch America's Nuclear Missiles?" The report itself is almost certainly the *Final Report of the Federal Advisory Committee on Nuclear Failsafe and Risk Reduction*, written in 1990–92. A heavily redacted version of this document released under FOIA is https://documents.theblackvault.com/documents/dod/readingroom/15/622.pdf.

81. Blair, "Why Our Nuclear Weapons Can Be Hacked."

82. Larsen, "Nuclear Command, Control, and Communications: US Country Profile."

83. Jim Winchester, *The Encyclopedia of Modern Aircraft* (San Diego, CA: Thunder Bay Press) 2006), 264.

84. The Nautilus Institute has published NC3 reports for China (https://nautilus.org/napsnet/napsnet-special-reports/nuclear-command-control-and-communications-systems-of-the-peoples-republic-of-china); France (https://nautilus.org/napsnet/napsnet-special-reports/france-nuclear-command-control-and-communications); India (https://nautilus.org/napsnet/napsnet-special-reports/command-and-control-of-nuclear-weapons-in-india); Israel (https://nautilus.org/napsnet/napsnet-special-reports/israels-nc3-profile-opaque-nuclear-governance); Pakistan (https://nautilus.org/napsnet/napsnet-special-reports/nuclear-command-control-and-communications-nc3-the-case-of-pakistan); North Korea (https://nautilus.org/napsnet/napsnet-special-reports/dprks-nc3-system); Russia (https://nautilus.org/napsnet/napsnet-special-reports/russias-nc3-and-early-warning-systems); and the United Kingdom (https://nautilus.org/napsnet/napsnet-special-reports/united-kingdom-nuclear-weapon-command-control-and-communications).

85. U.S. Department of Defense, *Nuclear Posture Review*, February 2018, 57.

86. Hyten testimony cited in n. 73 above.

87. Harvey, *U.S. Nuclear Command and Control.*

88. Deptula et al., *Modernizing U.S. Nuclear Command, Control, and Communications,* 27.

89. See Harvey, *U.S. Nuclear Command and Control.*

90. The notion that strategic assets might be used to support conventional (tactical) military operations is not new. Indeed, the program known as TENCAP (Tactical Exploitation of National Capabilities) has for years facilitated the use of national strategic assets such as satellites to provide imagery and other products to tactical military commanders. A primer on TENCAP can be found at "Tactical Exploitation of National Capabilities (TENCAP)," Military Space Programs (n.d.), www.globalsecurity.org/intell/systems/tencap.htm.

91. Ashton Carter, "Remarks by Secretary Carter to Troops at Minot Air Force Base, North Dakota" (September, 26, 2016), www.defense.gov/Newsroom/Transcripts/Transcript/Article/956079/remarks-by-secretary-carter-to-troops-at-minot-air-force-base-north-dakota.

92. U.S. Congress, Senate, Committee on Armed Services, Assistant Secretary of Defense for Strategy, Plans, and Capabilities Robert Scher, testimony before the Senate Armed Services Subcommittee on Strategic Forces, February 9, 2016, www.armed-services.senate.gov/imo/media/doc/Scher_02-09-16.pdf.

93. "The DoD ensures the communications architecture for the nuclear deterrent can serve as the core component of a broader national command, control,

communications, computers, and intelligence (C4I) system supporting the President." See U.S. Department of Defense, *Nuclear Matters Handbook 2016*, chap. 6, "Nuclear Command and Control," 74, www.lasg.org/Nuclear-Matters-2016.pdf. John Harvey notes: "Today's NC2 system is a legacy of the Cold War. . . . Portions of the system are dedicated to the nuclear mission. Other portions are multiple-use and employed during general purpose military operations" (Harvey, *U.S. Nuclear Command and Control*).

94. U.S. Department of Defense, *Nuclear Posture Review*, February 2018, 21.

95. Colin Clark, "Nuclear C3 Goes All Domain: Gen. Hyten," *Breaking Defense*, February 20, 2020, https://breakingdefense.com/2020/02/nuclear-c3-goes-all-domain-gen-hyten.

96. Haney testimony cited in n. 72 above.

97. U.S. Congress, Senate, Committee on Armed Services, testimony of General John Hyten, commander, U.S. Strategic Command, February 26, 2019, www.armed-services.senate.gov/imo/media/doc/Hyten_02-26-19.pdf.

98. Sandra Erwin, "Q&A: Air Force Gen. John Hyten Says U.S. Space Strategy, Budget Moving 'down the Right Path,'" *SpaceNews*, April 3, 2018, https://spacenews.com/qa-air-force-gen-john-hyten-says-u-s-space-strategy-budget-moving-down-the-right-path.

99. See Patrick Tucker, "Will America's Nuclear Weapons Always Be Safe From Hackers?" *The Atlantic*, December 30, 2016, https://amp.theatlantic.com/amp/article/511904.

100. Adam Lowther and Shane Grosso, "Understanding Nuclear Command, Control, and Communications," in *Guide to Nuclear Deterrence in the Age of Great-Power Competition*, ed. Adam B. Lowther (Bossier City, LA: Louisiana Tech Research Institute, 2020), 315–29, www.academia.edu/43929785/Guide_to_Nuclear_Deterrence_in_the_Age_of_Great_Power_Competition.

101. U.S. Government Accountability Office, "Critical Infrastructure Protection: Commercial Satellite Security Should Be More Fully Addressed" (August 2002), www.gao.gov/products/gao-02-781.

102. Harvey, *U.S. Nuclear Command and Control*.

103. Hyten testimony cited in n. 73 above.

104. U.S. Congress, Senate, Committee on Armed Services, testimony of Admiral Charles Richard, commander, U.S. Strategic Command, February 13, 2020, www.stratcom.mil/Portals/8/Documents/2020_USSTRATCOM_Posture_Statement_SASC_Final.pdf.

105. U.S. Department of Defense, Office of the Undersecretary of Defense for Acquisition and Sustainment, "Thomas F. Greenfield, Director, Nuclear Command, Control, and Communications." www.acq.osd.mil/asda/iipm/greenfield.html.

106. Sandra Erwin, "STRATCOM to Design Blueprint for Nuclear Command,

Control and Communications," *SpaceNews*, March 29, 2019, https://spacenews.com/stratcom-to-design-blueprint-for-nuclear-command-control-and-communications.

107. The use of qualifier "primarily" reflects the fact that DoD does have some responsibility for some portions of some nuclear weapons as such. For example, it supplies the tail kit assembly for the B-61 Mod 12 to the DoE, which performs final integration for the completed device. See U.S. Department of Defense, Director, Operational Testing and Evaluation, "B61 Mod 12 Life Extension Program Tail Kit Assembly," www.dote.osd.mil/Portals/97/pub/reports/FY2018/af/2018b61.pdf?ver=2019-08-21-155843-557, and U.S. Department of Energy, National Nuclear Security Administration, "B61–12 Life Extension Program Fact Sheet" (June 1, 2020), www.energy.gov/nnsa/articles/b61-12-life-extension-program-lep-fact-sheet.

108. Richard testimony cited in n. 104 above.

109. U.S. Department of Defense, Office of the Deputy Assistant Secretary of Defense for Nuclear Matters, *Nuclear Matters Handbook 2020*, 27. Page iii of this document notes that it is an unofficial handbook, published by the DoD Office of the Deputy Assistant Secretary of Defense for Nuclear Matters, that offers an overview of the U.S. nuclear enterprise. As an unofficial guide, it is "neither authoritative nor directive, although every effort has been made to ensure that it is accurate and comprehensive."

110. The "thin line" of NC3 is commonly understood to be the part of NC3 minimally providing "assured, unbroken, redundant, survivable, secure, and enduring connectivity to and among the President, the Secretary of Defense, the CJCS, and designated commanders through all threat environments [including nuclear environments] to perform all necessary command and control functions" (see, e.g., U.S. Department of Defense, Office of the Deputy Assistant Secretary of Defense for Nuclear Matters, *Nuclear Matters Handbook 2020*, 26). The Defense Science Board's 2017 "Task Force Report on Cyber Deterrence" extended the definition of "thin line" to go beyond NC3 alone.

111. U.S. Department of Defense, Defense Science Board, "Defense Science Board Task Force Report on Cyber Deterrence," 24.

112. U.S. National Defense Authorization Act for Fiscal Year 2018, Public Law 115–91, December 12, 2017, www.congress.gov/115/plaws/publ91/PLAW-115publ91.pdf.

113. Cornell Law School, Legal Information Institute, "10 U.S. Code § 2366 – Major Systems and Munitions Programs: Survivability Testing and Lethality Testing Required before Full-Scale Production." www.law.cornell.edu/uscode/text/10/2366.

114. U.S. Congress, Joint Explanatory Statement of the Committee of Conference for the National Defense Authorization Act for Fiscal Year 2018, www.armed-services.senate.gov/imo/media/doc/JOINT%20EXPLANATORY%20STATE-MENT%20OF%20THE%20COMMITTEE%20OF%20CONFERENCE.pdf.

115. U.S. National Defense Authorization Act for Fiscal Year 2018, Public

Law 115–91, December 12, 2017, www.congress.gov/115/plaws/publ91/PLAW-115publ91.pdf.

116. Mark Pomerleau, "The Pentagon's Plan to Secure Sensitive Systems," *Fifth Domain*, December 11, 2018, www.fifthdomain.com/industry/2018/12/11/the-pentagons-plan-to-secure-sensitive-systems.

117. U.S. Department of Defense, Director, Operational Test and Evaluation, "Cyber Assessments," FY19 Cybersecurity, 2019, www.dote.osd.mil/Portals/97/pub/reports/FY2019/other/2019cyber-assessments.pdf.

118. U.S. National Defense Authorization Act for Fiscal Year 2021, HR 6395, January 3, 2020, www.congress.gov/116/bills/hr6395/BILLS-116hr6395enr.pdf.

Chapter 4: Cybersecurity Lessons for Nuclear Modernization

1. Tibi Puiu, "Your Smartphone Is Millions of Times More Powerful Than All of NASA's Combined Computing in 1969," *ZME Science*, February 11, 2020, www.zmescience.com/science/news-science/smartphone-power-compared-to-apollo-432.

2. Charles A. R. Hoare, "The Emperor's Old Clothes," *Communications of the ACM* 24, no. 2 (February 1981): 75–83, https://dl.acm.org/doi/10.1145/358549.358561.

3. Bruce Schneier, "A Plea for Simplicity," in *Schneier on Security*, November 19, 1999, www.schneier.com/essays/archives/1999/11/a_plea_for_simplicit.html; Nancy Leveson, *An Engineering Perspective on Avoiding Inadvertent Nuclear War*, NAPSNet Special Reports, July 25, 2019, https://nautilus.org/napsnet/napsnet-special-reports/an-engineering-perspective-on-avoiding-inadvertent-nuclear-war. From time to time, it is asserted that complexity can improve security when that complexity is associated with the addition of security measures. For example, using longer and more complex passwords can improve security. The observation is true but limited in scope, because the complexity referenced in the claim is the complexity of *overall system* functionality.

4. For more discussion of this point, see Frederick Brooks, *The Mythical Man-Month: Essays on Software Engineering* (Reading, MA: Addison-Wesley, 1995).

5. "Next Generation NC3 Enterprise Challenge," beta.sam.gov, November 27, 2018, https://beta.sam.gov/opp/390609791364842047d3ab34aa7d1441/view.

6. McKinsey and Company, "Modernizing the US Nuclear Deterrent: An Interview with Elizabeth Durham-Ruiz," June 20, 2019, www.mckinsey.com/industries/aerospace-and-defense/our-insights/modernizing-the-us-nuclear-deterrent-an-interview-with-elizabeth-durham-ruiz.

7. U.S. Congress, Senate, Committee on Armed Services, testimony of Admiral Charles Richard, February 13, 2020.

8. U.S. Government Accountability Office, *Weapon Systems Cybersecurity: Guidance Would Help DOD Programs Better Communicate Requirements to Contractors*, GAO 21-179, March 2021, www.gao.gov/assets/gao-21-179.pdf.

9. Herbert Lin, "Army Combat Exercise in Hawaii Plays Down Cyber Threat," Lawfare, February 6, 2016. www.lawfareblog.com/army-combat-exercise-hawaii-plays-down-cyber-threat.

10. For Google outages, see Carly Page, "Gmail Down: Google Services Suffer Global Outage," *Forbes*, August 20, 2020,www.forbes.com/sites/carlypage/2020/08/20/gmail-down-google-services-suffer-global-outage; Abner Li, "YouTube Is Currently Down amid Widespread Outage," *9to5Google*, November 11, 2020, https://9to5google.com/2020/11/11/youtube-tv-down-2/; and Greg Kumparak, "Gmail Is Broken Right Now, One Day after a Massive Outage," *TechCrunch*, December 15, 2020, https://social.techcrunch.com/2020/12/15/gmail-is-a-little-broken-right-now-one-day-after-a-massive-outage-errors. For Amazon, see Jay Peters, "Prolonged AWS Outage Takes Down a Big Chunk of the Internet," *The Verge*, November 25, 2020, www.theverge.com/2020/11/25/21719396/amazon-web-services-aws-outage-down-internet.

11. Donald Norman, "When Security Gets in the Way," *Interactions* 16, no. 6 (2010): 60–63, https://jnd.org/when_security_gets_in_the_way.

12. National Research Council, *Toward a Safer and More Secure Cyberspace*, ed. Goodman and Lin, 127.

13. Butler Lampson, "Usable Security: How to Get It," *Communications of the ACM* 52, no. 11 (November 1, 2009): 25–27, https://doi.org/10.1145/1592761.1592773. On obliging users to adopt opaque, difficult-to-use security, see Anne Adams and Martina Angela Sasse, "Users Are Not the Enemy," *Communications of the ACM* 42, no. 12 (December 1, 1999): 40–46, https://doi.org/10.1145/322796.322806.

14. Blair, "Keeping Presidents in the Nuclear Dark (Episode #1: The Case of the Missing Permissive Action Links)," n. 72 in chap. 3.

15. Much of this discussion is derived from box 2.4 in National Research Council, *Toward a Safer and More Secure Cyberspace*, ed. Goodman and Lin. 124–25.

16. Ken Thompson, "Reflections on Trusting Trust," *Communications of the ACM* 27, no. 8 (August 1, 1984): 761–63, https://doi.org/10.1145/358198.358210. See also Paul Karger and Roger Schell, "Thirty Years Later: Lessons from the Multics Security Evaluation," in *Proceedings of the 18th Annual Computer Security Applications Conference* (Las Vegas: IEEE Computer Society, 2002), 119–26, https://doi.org/10.1109/CSAC.2002.1176285.

Chapter 5: Cyber Risks in Selected Nuclear Scenarios

1. A much wider range of scenarios that involve cyber-nuclear interactions can be found in Jon Lindsay, "Cyber Operations and Nuclear Escalation: The Diversity of Danger," in *Nuclear Command, Control, and Communications: Strategies for a Digital Age*, ed. James Wirtz and Jeffrey Larsen (Washington, DC: Georgetown University Press, forthcoming.

2. Max Frankel, *High Noon in the Cold War: Kennedy, Khrushchev, and the Cuban Missile Crisis* (New York: Random House, 2005).

3. The ambiguity between cyber espionage and attack is the first concern raised in Acton, "Cyber Warfare & Inadvertent Escalation," n. 26 in chap. 2. It is also addressed in a U.S.-China context by Ben Buchanan and Fiona Cunningham, "Preparing the Cyber Battlefield: Assessing a Novel Escalation Risk in a Sino-American Crisis," *Texas National Security Review* 3, no. 4 (Fall 2020): 55–81, https://tnsr. org/2020/10/preparing-the-cyber-battlefield-assessing-a-novel-escalation-risk-in-a-sino-american-crisis, who also conclude that the risk of inadvertent escalation due to cyber capabilities in a future Sino-American crisis cannot be dismissed. Additional analysis of this type can be found in Martin Libicki, "Drawing Inferences from Cyber Espionage," in *2018 10th International Conference on Cyber Conflict* [CyCon, Tallinn, Estonia], 109–22, doi: 10.23919/CYCON.2018.8405013.

4. U.S. Department of Defense, Marine Corps, *Command and Control* (Washington, DC: Department of the Navy, 2018), www.marines.mil/Portals/1/Publications/ MCDP%206.pdf?ver=2019-07-18-093633-990.

5. See, e.g., James Miller Jr. and Richard Fontaine, *A New Era in U.S.-Russian Strategic Stability* (Washington, DC: Center for a New American Security, 2017), 18, www.cnas.org/publications/reports/a-new-era-in-u-s-russian-strategic-stability.

6. This argument is elaborated in James Acton, "Escalation through Entanglement: How the Vulnerability of Command-and-Control Systems Raises the Risks of an Inadvertent Nuclear War," *International Security* 43, no. 1 (Summer 2018): 56–99, https://doi.org/10.1162/isec_a_00320.

7. Sandra Erwin, "U.S. Early Warning Satellites Helped Avert Casualties from Iran's Missile Attack," *SpaceNews*, January 8, 2020, https://spacenews.com/u-s-early-warning-satellites-helped-avert-casualties-from-irans-missile-attack; see also General John Hyten, commander, U.S.Strategic Command, testimony at Hearing on Military Assessment of Nuclear Deterrence Requirements, March 17, 2017, dod.defense.gov/Portals/1/features/2017/0917_nuclear-deterrence/docs/Transcript-HASC-Hearing-on-Nuclear-Deterrence-8-March-2017.pdf.

8. Harvey, *U.S. Nuclear Command and Control*.

9. Brendan Rittenhouse Green and Austin Long, "Conceal or Reveal? Managing Clandestine Military Capabilities in Peacetime Competition," *International Security* 44, no. 3 (Winter 2019/20): 48–83, https://doi.org/10.1162/isec_a_00367. On the other hand, a reputation for cyber expertise may have some value in convincing adversaries that a nation has potent cyber capabilities.

10. Stanley Kubrick, dir., *The Doomsday Machine in Dr. Strangelove*, YouTube video, November 24, 2008, www.youtube.com/watch?v=cmCKJi3CKGE&t=226s.

11. The scenario is based on a discussion in Erik Gartzke and Jon Lindsay, "The Cyber Commitment Problem and the Destabilization of Nuclear Deterrence," in

Bytes, Bombs, and Spies: The Strategic Dimensions of Offensive Cyber Operations, ed. Herbert Lin and Amy Zegart (Washington, DC: Brookings Institution, 2018).

12. Intel Corporation, *Statistical Analysis of Floating Point Flaw*, July 8, 2004, archived at https://web.archive.org/web/20160406055056/http://download.intel.com/support/processors/pentium/sb/FDIV_Floating_Point_Flaw_Pentium_Processor.pdf.

13. Intel Corporation, *1994 – Annual Report*, www.intel.com/content/www/us/en/history/history-1994-annual-report.html.

14. Roozbeh Kiani, Leah Corthell, and Michael N. Shadlen. "Choice Certainty Is Informed by Both Evidence and Decision Time." *Neuron* 84, no. 6 (2014): 1329–42, www.cell.com/neuron/fulltext/S0896-6273(14)01096-4.

15. National Research Council, *Information Technology for Counterterrorism: Immediate Actions and Future Possibilities*, ed. John L. Hennessy, David A. Patterson, and Herbert S. Lin (Washington, DC: National Academies Press, 2003), https://doi.org/10.17226/10640.

16. See, e.g., Martin Libicki, *Brandishing Cyberattack Capabilities* (Santa Monica, CA: RAND Corporation, 2013), 19–28, www.rand.org/pubs/research_reports/RR175.html.

17. Philip Napoli, "Social Media and the Public Interest: Governance of News Platforms in the Realm of Individual and Algorithmic Gatekeepers," *Telecommunications Policy* 39, no. 9 (October 2015): 751–60, https://doi.org/10.1016/j.telpol.2014.12.003.

18. See U.S. Department of Justice, Robert S. Mueller III, *Report*.

19. See, e.g., Samanth Subramanian, "Inside the Macedonian Fake-News Complex," *Wired*, February 15, 2017, www.wired.com/2017/02/veles-macedonia-fake-news.

20. See, e.g., Jessica Chen Weiss and Allan Dafoe, "Authoritarian Audiences, Rhetoric, and Propaganda in International Crises: Evidence from China," *International Studies Quarterly* 63, no. 4 (December 2019): 963–73, https://doi.org/10.1093/isq/sqz059.

21. Kelly Greenhill, "Of Wars and Rumors of Wars: Extra-Factual Information and (In)Advertent Escalation," in *Three Tweets to Midnight: Effects of the Global Information Ecosystem on the Risk of Nuclear Conflict*, ed. Harold Trinkunas, Herbert Lin, and Benjamin Loehrke, 113–36 (Stanford: Hoover Institution Press, 2020), www.hoover.org/sites/default/files/research/docs/trinkunas_threetweetstomidnight_113-136_ch.6.pdf.

22. See, for example, Daniel Kahneman, *Thinking, Fast and Slow* (New York: Farrar, Straus & Giroux), 2011.

23. Rongjun Yu, "Stress Potentiates Decision Biases: A Stress Induced Deliberation-to-Intuition (SIDI) Model." *Neurobiology of Stress* 3 (February 12, 2016): 83–95. https://doi.org/10.1016/j.ynstr.2015.12.006.

24. Danielle Jablanski, Herbert Lin, and Harold Trinkunas, "Retweets to

Midnight: Assessing the Effects of the Information Ecosystem on Crisis Decision Making between Nuclear Weapons States," in *Three Tweets to Midnight: Effects of the Global Information Ecosystem on the Risk of Nuclear Conflict*, ed. Harold Trinkunas, Herbert Lin, and Benjamin Loehrke, 1–16 (Stanford: Hoover Institution Press, 2020), www.hoover.org/sites/default/files/research/docs/trinkunas_threetweetstomidnight_1-16_ch.1.pdf.

25. Len Scott and Steve Smith, "Lessons of October: Historians, Political Scientists, Policy-Makers and the Cuban Missile Crisis," *International Affairs* 70, no. 4 (October 1, 1994): 659–84, https://doi.org/10.2307/2624552.

26. See, e.g., Beschloss, *Crisis Years: Kennedy and Khrushchev*, chap. 18.

27. Kim Gamel, "US Forces Korea Warns of Fake Evacuation Messages," *Stars and Stripes*, September 21, 2017, www.stripes.com/news/pacific/us-forces-korea-warns-of-fake-evacuation-messages-1.488792.

28. To illustrate the difference between inadvertent and accidental escalation, consider a situation in which a communications satellite owned by Nation A supports both conventional and nuclear operations. Inadvertent escalation could occur if B attacks the satellite. A could well be concerned that its nuclear communications channels being compromised (thus seeing the cyber attack as an attack on A's strategic capabilities), whereas B could be attacking the satellite with the sole intention of degrading the effectiveness of A's conventional operations. Accidental escalation could occur if B's attack specifically targeted a conventional communications channel but by mistake had unanticipated bleed-over effects on a nuclear communications channel. Different mechanisms would be in play for each, but the outcome would likely be the same. In both cases, B's actions would raise concerns in A's decision makers about the security of their nuclear capabilities and could lead to escalation.

29. U.S. Department of Defense, *Department of Defense Cyber Strategy*, April 2015, 14, archive.defense.gov/home/features/2015/0415_cyber-strategy/final_2015_dod_cyber_strategy_for_web.pdf.

30. U.S. Department of Defense, Cyber Command, *Achieve and Maintain Cyberspace Superiority: Command Vision for US Cyber Command* (2018), 7, www.cybercom.mil/Portals/56/Documents/USCYBERCOM%20Vision%20April%202018.pdf.

31. Ibid., 8.

32. The seminal article on this phenomenon, often known as the security dilemma, is Robert Jervis, "Cooperation under the Security Dilemma," *World Politics* 30, no. 2 (1978): 167–214, www.jstor.org/stable/2009958. Charles Glaser elaborates on this in *Rational Theory of International Politics: The Logic of Competition and Cooperation* (Princeton, NJ: Princeton University Press, 2010). How the security dilemma plays out in cyberspace is addressed in Ben Buchanan, *The Cybersecurity Dilemma: Hacking, Trust and Fear between Nations* (New York: Oxford University Press, 2017).

Chapter 6: Designing the Cyber-Nuclear Future: Observations and Imperatives

1. U.S. Department of Defense, Defense Science Board, "Defense Science Board Task Force Report on Cyber Deterrence," 17.

2. "Tomahawk's Chops: xGM-109 Block IV Cruise Missiles," *Defense Industry Daily,* December 8, 2020, www.defenseindustrydaily.com/block-iv-xgm-109-tomahawk-chopped-07423/.

3. I am indebted to David Clark of the Massachusetts Institute of Technology for the observation about frequent system exercise.

4. U.S. Department of Defense, Defense Science Board, *Resilient Military Systems and the Advanced Cyber Threat*, 43.

5. U.S. White House, *National Security Strategy of the United States of America* (2017), 30, trumpwhitehouse.archives.gov/wp-content/uploads/2017/12/NSS-Final-12-18-2017-0905.pdf.

6. By law, the military services (Army, Navy, Air Force, Marine Corps, and Space Force) organize, train and equip personnel and units for operational use. But the services do not exercise operational control over these personnel—rather, the services provide personnel and equipment to the various combatant commands, of which U.S. Strategic Command is one. In general, combatant commands do not exercise acquisition authority, although Space Command and Special Operations Command are notable exceptions.

7. This, of course, is just a different version of the Golden Rule: Whoever has the gold makes the rules. An early articulation of this Golden Rule can be found at www.comics.org/issue/395133.

8. Paul Bracken, "Communication Disruption Attacks in NC3," paper prepared for the Workshop on Antidotes for Emerging NC3 Technical Vulnerabilities, Stanford University, October 21–22, 2019, convened by the Nautilus Institute for Security and Sustainability, Technology for Global Security, the Stanley Center for Peace and Security, and the Stanford Center for International Security and Cooperation; also Paul Bracken, "The Risk of New Military Technologies Must Be Properly Assessed," *The Hill,* March 18, 2021, thehill.com/opinion/national-security/543023-the-risk-of-new-military-technologies-must-be-properly-assessed.

9. For more discussion of this point, see National Research Council, *Technology, Policy, Law, and Ethics Regarding U.S. Acquisition and Use of Cyberattack Capabilities*, ed. Owens et al., 50, doi.org/10.17226/12651.

10. Ibid., 65.

11. A report from the Carnegie Endowment for International Peace goes further, recommending that cyber operations targeting NC3 should require authorization by senior leadership. See Levite et al., "China-U.S. Cyber-Nuclear C3 Stability."

12. See, e.g., Richard Danzig, "Surviving on a Diet of Poisoned Fruit: Reducing the National Security Risks of America's Cyber Dependencies," Center for a New American Security, July 2014, s3.us-east-1.amazonaws.com/files.cnas.org/

documents/CNAS_PoisonedFruit_Danzig.pdf, and Gompert and Libicki, "Cyber War and Nuclear Peace." Jinghua Lyu and Ariel Levite of the Carnegie Endowment for International Peace advance this proposal in the context of U.S.-Chinese relations in cyberspace. See Jinghua Lyu and Ariel (Eli) Levite, "Chinese-American Relations in Cyberspace: Toward Collaboration or Confrontation?" Carnegie Endowment for International Peace, January 24, 2019, carnegieendowment.org/2019/01/24/chinese-american-relations-in-cyberspace-toward-collaboration-or-confrontation-pub-78213.

13. In April 2015, James Cartwright, former commander of U.S. Strategic Command, argued that taking the ICBM force off high alert levels (and thus precluding LOW) would reduce cyber risk; see Robert Burns, "Ex-Commander: Nukes on High Alert Are Vulnerable to Error," *AP News*, April 30, 2015, apnews.com/article/e970363945364db79dff94240956e2c4. Cartwright cited a report on which he was the lead author, *De-Alerting and Stabilizing the World's Nuclear Force Postures* (Washington, DC: Global Zero, 2015), 31, www.globalzero.org/wp-content/uploads/2018/09/global_zero_commission_on_nuclear_risk_reduction_report_0.pdf.

14. For an argument in favor of retaining the capability to launch ICBMs on receipt of tactical warning, see Matthew Kroenig, "The Case for the US ICBM Force," *Strategic Studies Quarterly* 12, no. 3 (Fall 2018): 50–69, www.jstor.org/stable/10.2307/26481909. For an argument opposing retention of such a capability, see David Wright, William D. Hartung, and Lisbeth Gronlund, *Rethinking Land-Based Nuclear Missiles: Sensible Risk-Reduction Practices for US ICBMs* (Cambridge, MA: Union of Concerned Scientists, 2020), chap. 6,www.ucsusa.org/resources/rethinking-icbms. For a formerly classified analysis, see National Security Archive, "The 'Launch on Warning' Nuclear Strategy and Its Insider Critics," June 19, 2019, nsarchive.gwu.edu/briefing-book/nuclear-vault/2019-06-11/launch-warning-nuclear-strategy-its-insider-critics.

15. The least expensive way to eliminate silo-based ICBMs is to abandon ICBMs entirely, which would entail cancelling the GBSD portion of the modernization program. More expensive possibilities that preserve an ICBM force include shallow underwater missile basing and deep underground missile basing, two possibilities that would decouple ICBM survivability and LOW, but might also entail some loss of responsiveness and/or communications reliability, have been discussed: see U.S. Office of Technology Assessment, *MX Missile Basing* (Washington, DC: U.S. Government Printing Office, 1981), ota.fas.org/reports/8116.pdf.

16. U.S. Department of Defense, Air Force, "Kessel Run" (n.d.), kesselrun.af.mil/mission.

17. Nick Bilton, "Nest Thermostat Glitch Leaves Users in the Cold," *New York Times*, January 13, 2016, www.nytimes.com/2016/01/14/fashion/nest-thermostat-glitch-battery-dies-software-freeze.html.

18. Gregory Slabodkin, "Software Glitches Leave Navy Smart Ship Dead in the Water," *Government Computing News*, July 13, 1998, gcn.com/articles/1998/07/13/software-glitches-leave-navy-smart-ship-dead-in-the-water.aspx.

Chapter 7: Moving Forward

1. Emily Jacobs, "House Democrats Ask Biden to Give up Sole Power to Launch Nuclear Bomb," *New York Post* (blog), February 25, 2021. nypost.com/2021/02/25/democrats-ask-biden-to-give-up-power-to-launch-nuclear-bomb.

2. U.S. Department of Defense, Director, Operational Test and Evaluation, "Cyber Assessments."

3. U.S. Government Accountability Office, *Weapon Systems Cybersecurity: Guidance Would Help DOD Programs Better Communicate Requirements to Contractors*, GAO 21-179 (March 2021), 26–27, www.gao.gov/assets/gao-21-179.pdf.

Bibliography

Abaimov, Stanislav, and Paul Ingram. "Hacking UK Trident: A Growing Threat." London: British American Security Information Council (BASIC), 2017. https://basicint.org/wp-content/uploads/2018/06/HACKING_UK_TRIDENT.pdf.

Acton, James M. "Cyber Warfare & Inadvertent Escalation." *Dædalus* 149, no. 2 (Spring 2020): 133–49. www.amacad.org/publication/cyber-warfare-inadvertent-escalation.

———. "Escalation through Entanglement: How the Vulnerability of Command-and-Control Systems Raises the Risks of an Inadvertent Nuclear War." *International Security* 43, no. 1 (Summer 2018): 56–99. https://doi.org/10.1162/isec_a_00320.

Adams, Anne, and Martina Angela Sasse. "Users Are Not the Enemy." *Communications of the ACM* 42, no. 12 (December 1, 1999): 40–46. https://doi.org/10.1145/322796.322806.

Adee, Sally. "The Hunt for the Kill Switch." *IEEE Spectrum*, May 1, 2008, https://spectrum.ieee.org/semiconductors/design/the-hunt-for-the-kill-switch.

"Air Force Missile Sites to Get Wi-Fi." *Air Force Times,* August 7, 2017. www.airforce-times.com/news/your-air-force/2014/11/04/air-force-missile-sites-to-get-wi-fi.

Ambinder, Marc. "Failure Shuts Down Squadron of Nuclear Missiles." *The Atlantic*, October 26, 2010. www.theatlantic.com/politics/archive/2010/10/failure-shuts-down-squadron-of-nuclear-missiles/65207.

Arkin, William, and Robert Windrem. "Secrets of 9/11: New Details of Chaos, Confusion Emerge." *NBC News,* September 11, 2016. www.nbcnews.com/storyline/9-11-anniversary/secrets-9-11-new-details-chaos-nukes-emerge-n645711.

Arms Control Association. "U.S. Strategic Nuclear Forces Under New START." Fact Sheet. Washington, DC: Arms Control Association, 2020. www.armscontrol.

org/factsheets/USStratNukeForceNewSTART#:~:text=As%20of%20March%20
1%2C%202020,capable%20bombers%2C%20and%2040%20SLBMs.

Barrass, Gordon. "Able Archer 83: What Were the Soviets Thinking?" *Survival: Global Politics and Strategy* 58, no. 6 (November 1, 2016): 7–30. https://doi.org/1
0.1080/00396338.2016.1257176.

Bertrand, Natasha, and Eric Wolff. "Nuclear Weapons Agency Breached amid Massive Cyber Onslaught." *Politico,* December 17, 2020. www.politico.com/
news/2020/12/17/nuclear-agency-hacked-officials-inform-congress-447855.

Beschloss, Michael. *The Crisis Years: Kennedy and Khrushchev, 1960–1963.* New York: Edward Burlingame Books, 1991.

Bilton, Nick. "Nest Thermostat Glitch Leaves Users in the Cold." *New York Times,* January 13, 2016. www.nytimes.com/2016/01/14/fashion/nest-thermostat-glitch-battery-dies-software-freeze.html.

Blair, Bruce. "Could Terrorists Launch America's Nuclear Missiles?" *Time,* November 11, 2010. http://content.time.com/time/nation/article/0,8599,2030685,00.
html.

———. "Keeping Presidents in the Nuclear Dark (Episode #1: The Case of the Missing Permissive Action Links)." *Bruce Blair's Nuclear Column,* Center for Defense Information, February 11, 2004. www.globalzero.org/wp-content/uploads/2019/03/BB_Keeping-Presidents-in-the-Nuclear-Dark-Episode-1-The-Case-of-the-Missing-Permissive-Action-Links_02.11.2004.pdf.

———. "Rogue States: Nuclear Red-Herrings." December 5, 2003. https://web.archive.org/web/20031223085259/www.cdi.org/blair/russia-targeting.cfm.

———. *Strategic Command and Control: Redefining the Nuclear Threat.* Washington, DC: Brookings Institution, 1985

———. "Why Our Nuclear Weapons Can Be Hacked." *New York Times,* March 14, 2017. www.nytimes.com/2017/03/14/opinion/why-our-nuclear-weapons-can-be-hacked.html.

Borning, Alan. "Computer System Reliability and Nuclear War." *Communications of the ACM* 30, no. 2 (February 1, 1987): 112–31. https://doi.org/10.1145/12527.12528.

Bossert, Thomas. "I Was the Homeland Security Adviser to Trump. We're Being Hacked." *New York Times,* December 17, 2020. www.nytimes.com/2020/12/16/
opinion/fireeye-solarwinds-russia-hack.html.

Bracken, Paul. *The Command and Control of Nuclear Forces.* New Haven, CT: Yale University Press, 1983.

———. "Communication Disruption Attacks in NC3." Paper for the Workshop on Antidotes for Emerging NC3 Technical Vulnerabilities, Stanford University, October 21–22, 2019, convened by the Nautilus Institute for Security and Sustainability, Technology for Global Security, the Stanley Center for Peace and Security, and the Stanford Center for International Security and Cooperation.

———. *The Hunt for Mobile Missiles: Nuclear Weapons, AI, and the New Arms Race.* Philadelphia: Foreign Policy Research Institute, 2020. www.fpri.org/wp-content/uploads/2020/09/the-hunt-for-mobile-missiles.pdf.

———. "The Risk of New Military Technologies Must Be Properly Assessed." *The Hill*, March 18, 2021. https://thehill.com/opinion/national-security/543023-the-risk-of-new-military-technologies-must-be-properly-assessed.

———. *The Second Nuclear Age: Strategy, Danger, and the New Power Politics*, New York: Times Books, 2012.

Breslow, Jason. "How Edward Snowden Leaked 'Thousands' of NSA Documents." PBS. *Frontline*, May 13, 2014. www.pbs.org/wgbh/frontline/article/how-edward-snowden-leaked-thousands-of-nsa-documents.

Brooks, Frederick. *The Mythical Man-Month: Essays on Software Engineering.* Reading, MA: Addison-Wesley, 1995.

Brumfiel, Geoff. "How to Order Pizza from a Nuclear Command Bunker." July 31, 2014. www.npr.org/sections/thesalt/2014/07/31/336614501/how-to-order-pizza-from-a-nuclear-command-bunker.

Buchanan, Ben. *The Cybersecurity Dilemma: Hacking, Trust and Fear between Nations.* New York: Oxford University Press, 2017.

Buchanan, Ben, and Fiona Cunningham. "Preparing the Cyber Battlefield: Assessing a Novel Escalation Risk in a Sino-American Crisis." *Texas National Security Review* 3, no. 4 (Fall 2020): 55–81. https://tnsr.org/2020/10/preparing-the-cyber-battlefield-assessing-a-novel-escalation-risk-in-a-sino-american-crisis.

Burns, Robert. "Ex-Commander: Nukes on High Alert Are Vulnerable to Error." AP News, April 30, 2015. https://apnews.com/article/e970363945364db79dff94240956e2c4.

Burr, William. "False Warnings of Soviet Missile Attacks Put U.S. Forces on Alert in 1979–1980." March 16, 2020. https://nsarchive.gwu.edu/briefing-book/nuclear-vault/2020-03-16/false-warnings-soviet-missile-attacks-during-1979-80-led-alert-actions-us-strategic-forces.

Carter, Ashton. "Communications Technologies." In *Managing Nuclear Operations*, ed. John Steinbruner, Ashton Carter, and Charles Zraket, 223. Washington, DC: Brookings Institution, 1987.

———. "Remarks by Secretary Carter to Troops at Minot Air Force Base, North Dakota." September 26, 2016. www.defense.gov/Newsroom/Transcripts/Transcript/Article/956079/remarks-by-secretary-carter-to-troops-at-minot-air-force-base-north-dakota.

———. "Sources of Error and Uncertainty." In *Managing Nuclear Operations*, ed. John Steinbruner, Ashton Carter, and Charles Zraket. Washington, DC: Brookings Institution,1987.

Chappell, Bill, Greg Myre, and Laura Wamsley. "What We Know about Russia's Alleged Hack of the U.S. Government and Tech Companies." *NPR*, December 21, 2020. www.npr.org/2020/12/15/946776718/u-s-scrambles-to-understand-major-computer-hack-but-says-little.

Childress, Sarah. "Bradley Manning Sentenced to 35 Years for WikiLeaks." PBS, *Frontline*, August 21, 2013. www.pbs.org/wgbh/frontline/article/bradley-manning-sentenced-to-35-years-for-wikileaks.

Clark, Colin. "Nuclear C3 Goes All Domain: Gen. Hyten." *Breaking Defense*, February 20, 2020. https://breakingdefense.com/2020/02/nuclear-c3-goes-all-domain-gen-hyten.

Cohen, Rachel. "Second Tanker Planning Software Project Enters Testing." *Air Force Magazine*, July 8, 2019. www.airforcemag.com/second-tanker-planning-software-project-enters-testing.

Cornell Law School. Legal Information Institute. "U.S. Code, 10 U.S. Code § 2366—Major Systems and Munitions Programs: Survivability Testing and Lethality Testing Required before Full-Scale Production." www.law.cornell.edu/uscode/text/10/2366.

Danzig, Richard. "Surviving on a Diet of Poisoned Fruit: Reducing the National Security Risks of America's Cyber Dependencies." Center for a New American Security. July 2014, https://s3.us-east-1.amazonaws.com/files.cnas.org/documents/CNAS_PoisonedFruit_Danzig.pdf.

Deptula, David A., Robert Haddick, and William A. LaPlante. *Modernizing U.S. Nuclear Command, Control, and Communications*. Arlington, VA: Mitchell Institute for Aerospace Studies, Air Force Association, February 2019. http://docs.wixstatic.com/ugd/a2dd91_ed45cfd71de2457eba3bcce4d0657196.pdf.

———. "Time to Update NC3." *Air Force Magazine*, March 22, 2019. www.airforcemag.com/article/time-to-update-nc3.

Dillow, Clay. "Only One of Six Air Force F-35s Could Take Off during Testing." *Fortune*, April 28, 2016. https://fortune.com/2016/04/28/f-35-fails-testing-air-force.

Dwyer, Colin. "Pompeo Says Russia 'Pretty Clearly' behind Cyberattack, Prompting Pushback from Trump." NPR, December 19, 2020. www.npr.org/2020/12/19/948318197/pompeo-russia-pretty-clearly-behind-massive-solarwinds-cyberattack.

Erwin, Sandra. "Q&A: Air Force Gen. John Hyten Says U.S. Space Strategy, Budget Moving 'down the Right Path.'" *SpaceNews*, April 3, 2018. https://spacenews.com/qa-air-force-gen-john-hyten-says-u-s-space-strategy-budget-moving-down-the-right-path.

———. "STRATCOM to Design Blueprint for Nuclear Command, Control and Communications." *SpaceNews*, March 29, 2019. https://spacenews.com/stratcom-to-design-blueprint-for-nuclear-command-control-and-communications.

———. "U.S. Early Warning Satellites Helped Avert Casualties from Iran's Missile

Attack." *SpaceNews*, January 8, 2020. https://spacenews.com/u-s-early-warning-satellites-helped-avert-casualties-from-irans-missile-attack.

Feaver, Peter, *Guarding the Guardians: Civilian Control of Nuclear Weapons in the United States*. Ithaca, NY: Cornell University Press, 1992.

Final Report of the Federal Advisory Committee on Nuclear Failsafe and Risk Reduction. 1992. https://documents.theblackvault.com/documents/dod/reading-room/15/622.pdf

Ford, Christopher. *International Security in Cyberspace: New Models for Reducing Risk.* U.S. Department of State Arms Control and International Security Papers, 1, no. 20 (2020). www.state.gov/wp-content/uploads/2020/10/T-paper-series-Cybersecurity-Format-508.pdf.

Ford, Daniel. *The Button: The Pentagon's Strategic Command and Control System.* New York: Simon & Schuster, 1985.

Frankel, Max. *High Noon in the Cold War: Kennedy, Khrushchev, and the Cuban Missile Crisis.* New York: Random House, 2005.

Futter, Andrew, *Hacking the Bomb: Cyber Threats and Nuclear Weapons.* Washington, DC: Georgetown University Press, 2018.

Gamel, Kim. "US Forces Korea Warns of Fake Evacuation Messages." *Stars and Stripes*, September 21, 2017. www.stripes.com/news/pacific/us-forces-korea-warns-of-fake-evacuation-messages-1.488792.

Gartzke, Erik, and Jon Lindsay. "The Cyber Commitment Problem and the Destabilization of Nuclear Deterrence." In *Bytes, Bombs, and Spies: The Strategic Dimensions of Offensive Cyber Operations*, ed. Herbert Lin and Amy Zegart. Washington, DC: Brookings Institution, 2018.

Geiger, A. W. "Key Findings about the Online News Landscape in America." Pew Research Center, September 11, 2019. www.pewresearch.org/fact-tank/2019/09/11/key-findings-about-the-online-news-landscape-in-america.

Glaser, Charles. *Rational Theory of International Politics: The Logic of Competition and Cooperation.* Princeton, NJ: Princeton University Press, 2010.

Global Zero Commission on Nuclear Risk Reduction. *De-Alerting and Stabilizing the World's Nuclear Force Postures.* Washington, DC: Global Zero, 2015. www.globalzero.org/wp-content/uploads/2018/09/global_zero_commission_on_nuclear_risk_reduction_report_0.pdf.

Gompert, David C., and Martin C. Libicki. "Cyber War and Nuclear Peace." *Survival: Global Politics and Strategy* 61, no. 4 (2019): 45–62. https://doi.org/10.1080/003 96338.2019.1637122.

Gorman, Siobhan, August Cole, and Yochi Dreazen. "Computer Spies Breach Fighter-Jet Project." *Wall Street Journal*, April 21, 2009. www.wsj.com/articles/SB124027491029837401.

Green, Brendan Rittenhouse, and Austin Long. "Conceal or Reveal? Managing Clandestine Military Capabilities in Peacetime Competition." *International Security* 44, no. 3 (Winter 2019/20): 48–83. https://doi.org/10.1162/isec_a_00367.

Greenberg, Andy. "Hackers Remotely Kill a Jeep on the Highway—with Me in It," *WIRED*, July 21, 2015. www.wired.com/2015/07/hackers-remotely-kill-jeep-highway.

Greenhill, Kelly M. "Of Wars and Rumors of Wars: Extra-Factual Information and (In)Advertent Escalation." In *Three Tweets to Midnight: Effects of the Global Information Ecosystem on the Risk of Nuclear Conflict*, ed. Harold Trinkunas, Herbert Lin, and Benjamin Loehrke, 113–36. Stanford: Hoover Institution Press, 2020. www.hoover.org/sites/default/files/research/docs/trinkunas_threetweetstomidnight_113-136_ch.6.pdf.

Grier, Peter. "Misplaced Nukes." *Air Force Magazine*, June 26, 2017. www.airforcemag.com/article/misplacednukes. The underlying official (but redacted) Air Force report is "Commander Directed Report of Investigation Prepared by Major General Douglas L. Raaberg Investigating Officer Concerning an Unauthorized Transfer of Nuclear Warheads between Minot AFB, North Dakota and Barksdale AFB, Louisiana, 30 August 2007" (https://scholar.harvard.edu/files/jvaynman/files/minot_afb_report.pdf).

Grossman, Elaine. "DoD Defends New Sub-Launched Missiles." *InsideDefense.Com*, March 10, 2006. https://web.archive.org/web/20121011044135/http://www.military.com/features/0,15240,90477,00.html.

Hamilton, Keegan. "The Plan to Make America's Nukes Great Again Could Go Horribly Wrong." *VICE* News, April 20, 2017. www.vice.com/en/article/a3j9mg/the-plan-to-make-americas-nukes-great-again-could-go-horribly-wrong.

Harvey, John R. "U.S. Nuclear Command and Control for the 21st Century." NAP-SNet Special Reports, May 24, 2019. https://nautilus.org/napsnet/napsnet-special-reports/u-s-nuclear-command-and-control-for-the-21st-Century.

Harwell, Drew, and Ellen Nakashima. "Hackers' Threats Prompt Sony Pictures to Shelve Christmas Release of 'The Interview.'" *Washington Post*, December 17, 2014. www.washingtonpost.com/business/economy/top-movie-theater-chains-cancel-premiere-showings-of-the-interview/2014/12/17/dd1bdb2a-8608-11e4-9534-f79a23c40e6c_story.html

Hayes, Peter, Binoy Kampmark, Philip Reiner, and Deborah Gordon. "Synthesis Report–NC3 Systems and Strategic Stability: A Global Overview." NAPSNet Special Reports, May 5, 2019. https://nautilus.org/napsnet/napsnet-special-reports/synthesis-report-nc3-systems-and-strategic-stability-a-global-overview.

"Highly Evasive Attacker Leverages SolarWinds Supply Chain to Compromise Multiple Global Victims with SUNBURST Backdoor." FireEye Threat Research Blog, Milpitas, CA. December 13, 2020. www.fireeye.com/blog/threat-research/2020/12/evasive-attacker-leverages-solarwinds-supply-chain-compromises-with-sunburst-backdoor.html.

Hoare, Charles A. R. "The Emperor's Old Clothes." *Communications of the ACM* 24, no. 2 (February 1981): 75–83. https://dl.acm.org/doi/10.1145/358549.358561.

Hoffman, David. "I Had a Funny Feeling in My Gut." *Washington Post*, February 10, 1999. www.washingtonpost.com/wp-srv/inatl/longterm/coldwar/shatter021099b.htm.

Intel Corporation. *1994 – Annual Report*. www.intel.com/content/www/us/en/history/history-1994-annual-report.html.

———. *Statistical Analysis of Floating Point Flaw*. July 8, 2004. https://web.archive.org/web/20160406055056/http://download.intel.com/support/processors/pentium/sb/FDIV_Floating_Point_Flaw_Pentium_Processor.pdf.

Jablanski, Danielle, Herbert S. Lin, and Harold A. Trinkunas. "Retweets to Midnight: Assessing the Effects of the Information Ecosystem on Crisis Decision Making between Nuclear Weapons States." In *Three Tweets to Midnight: Effects of the Global Information Ecosystem on the Risk of Nuclear Conflict*, ed. Harold Trinkunas, Herbert Lin, and Benjamin Loehrke, 1–16. Stanford: Hoover Institution Press, 2020. www.hoover.org/sites/default/files/research/docs/trinkunas_threetweetstomidnight_1-16_ch.1.pdf.

Jacobs, Emily. "House Democrats Ask Biden to Give up Sole Power to Launch Nuclear Bomb." *New York Post* (blog), February 25, 2021. https://nypost.com/2021/02/25/democrats-ask-biden-to-give-up-power-to-launch-nuclear-bomb.

Jervis, Robert "Cooperation under the Security Dilemma." *World Politics* 30, no. 2 (1978): 167–214. www.jstor.org/stable/2009958.

Johnson, James. "'Catalytic Nuclear War' in the Age of Artificial Intelligence & Autonomy: Emerging Military Technology and Escalation Risk between Nuclear-Armed States." *Journal of Strategic Studies*, January 13, 2021, 1–41. https://doi.org/10.1080/01402390.2020.1867541.

Jones, Nate, and David Hoffman. "Newly Released Documents Shed Light on 1983 Nuclear War Scare with Soviets." *Washington Post*, February 17, 2021. www.washingtonpost.com/national-security/soviet-nuclear-war-able-archer/2021/02/17/711fa9e2-7166-11eb-93be-c10813e358a2_story.html.

Kahneman, Daniel. *Thinking, Fast and Slow*. New York: Farrar, Straus & Giroux, 2011.

Kaplan, Fred. "'WarGames' and Cybersecurity's Debt to a Hollywood Hack." *New York Times*, February 19, 2016. www.nytimes.com/2016/02/21/movies/wargames-and-cybersecuritys-debt-to-a-hollywood-hack.html.

Karger, Paul, and Roger Schell. "Thirty Years Later: Lessons from the Multics Security Evaluation." In *Proceedings of the 18th Annual Computer Security Applications Conference*, 119–26. Las Vegas: IEEE Computer Society, 2002. https://doi.org/10.1109/CSAC.2002.1176285.

Katz, Bruce, and Peter Ising. "Kessel Run Deploys KRADOS to Air Operations Center." January 12, 2021. https://kesselrun.af.mil/news/Kessel-Run-Deploys-KRADOS.html.

Kiani, Roozbeh, Leah Corthell, and Michael N. Shadlen. "Choice Certainty Is Informed by Both Evidence and Decision Time." *Neuron* 84, no. 6 (2014): 1329–42. www.cell.com/neuron/fulltext/S0896-6273(14)01096-4.

Klare, Michael. "Cyber Battles, Nuclear Outcomes? Dangerous New Pathways to Escalation." *Arms Control Today*. Washington, DC: Arms Control Association, 2019. www.armscontrol.org/act/2019-11/features/cyber-battles-nuclear-outcomes-dangerous-new-pathways-escalation.

Koch, Robert, and Mario Golling. "Weapons Systems and Cyber Security—a Challenging Union." In *2016 8th International Conference on Cyber Conflict* [CyCon, Tallinn, Estonia], 191–203. https://ccdcoe.org/uploads/2018/10/Art-12-Weapons-Systems-and-Cyber-Security-A-Challenging-Union.pdf.

Kocher, Paul, Ruby Lee, Gary McGraw, and Anand Raghunathan. "Security as a New Dimension in Embedded System Design." In *DAC '04: Proceedings of the 41st Annual Design Automation Conference* (June 7–11, 2004), 753–60. San Diego, CA: ACM Press, 2004. https://doi.org/10.1145/996566.996771.

Krebs, Brian. "Target Hackers Broke in via HVAC Company." *Krebs on Security*, February 5, 2014. https://krebsonsecurity.com/2014/02/target-hackers-broke-in-via-hvac-company.

Kristensen, Hans, and Matthew McKinzie. *Reducing Alert Rates of Nuclear Weapons*. Geneva: United Nations Institute for Disarmament Research, 2012 www.unidir.org/files/publications/pdfs/reducing-alert-rates-of-nuclear-weapons-400.pdf.

Kristensen, Hans. "US Nuclear War Plan Updated amidst Nuclear Policy Review." Federation of American Scientists, April 4, 2013. https://fas.org/blogs/security/2013/04/oplan8010-12.

Kroenig, Matthew. "The Case for the US ICBM Force." *Strategic Studies Quarterly* 12, no. 3 (Fall 2018): 50–69. www.jstor.org/stable/10.2307/26481909.

Kubrick, Stanley, dir. *The Doomsday Machine in Dr. Strangelove*. Excerpt from *Dr. Strangelove or: How I Learned to Stop Worrying and Love the Bomb* (1964). YouTube, November 24, 2008. www.youtube.com/watch?v=cmCKJi3CKGE&t=226s.

Kumparak, Greg. "Gmail Is Broken Right Now, One Day after a Massive Outage." *TechCrunch*, December 15, 2020. https://social.techcrunch.com/2020/12/15/gmail-is-a-little-broken-right-now-one-day-after-a-massive-outage-errors.

Lampson, Butler. "Usable Security: How to Get It." *Communications of the ACM* 52 (November 1, 2009): 25–27. https://doi.org/10.1145/1592761.1592773.

Larsen, Jeffrey. "Nuclear Command, Control, and Communications: US Country Profile." NAPSNet Special Reports, August 22, 2019. https://nautilus.org/napsnet/napsnet-special-reports/nuclear-command-control-and-communications-us-country-profile.

Leveson, Nancy. "An Engineering Perspective on Avoiding Inadvertent Nuclear War." NAPSNet Special Reports, July 25, 2019. https://nautilus.org/napsnet/napsnet-special-reports/an-engineering-perspective-on-avoiding-inadvertent-nuclear-war.

Levite, Ariel E., Lyu Jinghua, George Perkovich, Lu Chuanying, Xu Manshu, Li Bin, and Yang Fan., *China-U.S. Cyber-Nuclear C3 Stability*. Washington, DC: Carnegie Endowment for International Peace, April 2021. https://carnegieendowment.org/2021/04/08/china-u.s.-cyber-nuclear-c3-stability-pub-84182.

Lewis, Jeffrey G., and Bruno Tertrais. *The Finger on the Button: The Authority to Use Nuclear Weapons in Nuclear-Armed States*. Monterey, CA: James Martin Center for Nonproliferation Studies, Middlebury Institute of International Studies, 2019. CNS Occasional Paper 45. www.nonproliferation.org/wp-content/uploads/2019/02/Finger-on-the-Nuclear-Button.pdf.

Li, Abner. "YouTube Is Currently Down amid Widespread Outage." *9to5Google*, November 11, 2020. https://9to5google.com/2020/11/11/youtube-tv-down-2.

Libicki, Martin C., *Brandishing Cyberattack Capabilities*. Santa Monica, CA: RAND Corporation, 2013. www.rand.org/pubs/research_reports/RR175.html.

———. "Drawing Inferences from Cyber Espionage." In *2018 10th International Conference on Cyber Conflict* [CyCon, Tallinn, Estonia], 109–22. doi: 10.23919/CYCON.2018.8405013.

Lin, Herbert. "Anything New under the Sun? Nuclear Responses to Cyberattacks." Lawfare, January 19, 2018. www.lawfareblog.com/anything-new-under-sun-nuclear-responses-cyberattacks.

———. "Army Combat Exercise in Hawaii Plays Down Cyber Threat." Lawfare, February 6, 2016. www.lawfareblog.com/army-combat-exercise-hawaii-plays-down-cyber-threat.

———. "Attribution of Malicious Cyber Incidents: From Soup to Nuts." *Journal of International Affairs* 70 no. 1 (Winter 2016): 75–137. https://jia.sipa.columbia.edu/attribution-malicious-cyber-incidents.

Lindsay, Jon. "Cyber Operations and Nuclear Escalation: The Diversity of Danger." In *Nuclear Command, Control, and Communications: Strategies for a Digital Age*, ed. James Wirtz and Jeffrey Larsen. Washington, DC: Georgetown University Press, forthcoming.

———. "Cyber Operations and Nuclear Weapons." NAPSNet Special Report, June 20, 2019. https://nautilus.org/napsnet/napsnet-special-reports/cyber-operations-and-nuclear-weapons.

Lockheed Martin. "F-35 Software Development: A Digital Jet for the Modern Battlespace." https://web.archive.org/web/20210123100734/https://www.f35.com/about/life-cycle/software.

———. "GPS Spatial Temporal Anti-Jam Receiver (GSTAR) System to Be Integrated in F-35 Modernization." October 29, 2019. https://news.lockheedmartin.com/lockheed-martin-gps-spatial-temporal-anti-jam-receiver-gstar-system-integrated-f35-modernization.

Lowther, Adam, and Curtis McGiffin. "America Needs a 'Dead Hand.'" Maxwell Air Force Base, August 23, 2019. www.maxwell.af.mil/News/Commentaries/Display/Article/1942374/america-needs-a-dead-hand.

Lowther, Adam, and Shane Grosso. "Understanding Nuclear Command, Control, and Communications." In *Guide to Nuclear Deterrence in the Age of Great-Power Competition*, ed. Adam B. Lowther, 315–29. Bossier City, LA: Louisiana Tech Research Institute, 2020. www.academia.edu/43929785/ Guide_to_Nuclear_Deterrence_in_the_Age_of_Great_Power_Competition.

Lydiate, Daniel. "Military Aviation's Cyber Challenge: Are Cyber-Vulnerabilities a Credible Threat to a Modern Air Force?" Strategy and Security Institute, University of Exeter, Exeter, England. N.d. www.raf.mod. uk/what-we-do/centre-for-air-and-space-power-studies/documents1/ dissertation-lydiate-dan-mstrat-dissertational1.

Lyman, Mel. "Crimson Tide: They Got It All Wrong." *Comparative Strategy* 18, no. 4 (1999): 309–12. https://doi.org/10.1080/01495939908403188.

Lynn, William. "Defending a New Domain: The Pentagon's Cyberstrategy." *Foreign Affairs*, September/October 2010. www.foreignaffairs.com/articles/ united-states/2010-09-01/defending-new-domain.

Lyu, Jinghua, and Ariel (Eli) Levite "Chinese-American Relations in Cyberspace: Toward Collaboration or Confrontation?" Carnegie Endowment for International Peace, January 24, 2019. https://carnegieendowment.org/2019/01/24/chinese-american-relations-in-cyberspace-toward-collaboration-or-confrontation-pub-78213.

Macdonald, Eryn. "The Man Who Saved the World." In Union of Concerned Scientists, *All Things Nuclear* (blog), February 3, 2015. https://allthingsnuclear.org/ emacdonald/the-man-who-saved-the-world.

Mazarr, Michael. *Understanding Deterrence.* Santa Monica, CA: RAND Corporation, 2018. www.rand.org/pubs/perspectives/PE295.html.

McFaul, Michael, ed. *Securing American Elections: Prescriptions for Enhancing the Integrity and Independence of the 2020 U.S. Presidential Election and Beyond.* Stanford: Stanford Cyber Policy Center, Freeman Spogli Institute, 2019. https:// stanford.box.com/shared/static/xd35pzvlnl2konx16suee7mqvjvk6nrb.pdf.

McKinsey and Company. "Modernizing the US Nuclear Deterrent: An Interview with Elizabeth Durham-Ruiz." June 20, 2019. www.mckinsey.com/industries/ aerospace-and-defense/our-insights/modernizing-the-us-nuclear-deterrent-an-interview-with-elizabeth-durham-ruiz.

Miller, James N., Jr., and Richard Fontaine. *A New Era in U.S.-Russian Strategic Stability: How Changing Geopolitics and Emerging Technologies are Reshaping Pathways to Crisis and Conflict.* Harvard Kennedy School, Belfer Center for Science and International Affairs and the Center for a New American Security. Washington, DC: Center for a New American Security, 2017. www.cnas.org/publications/ reports/a-new-era-in-u-s-russian-strategic-stability.

Mitchell, Andrea. "Sen. Coons: 'This Is a Chilling Example of How Aggressive Russian Cyber Activities Have Become.'" MSNBC, December 17, 2020. www.msnbc. com/andrea-mitchell-reports/watch/sen-coons-this-is-a-chilling-example-of-how-aggressive-russian-cyber-activities-have-become-97931333651.

Mueller Report. See U.S. Department of Justice.

Myers, Gabriel. "Missileers Receive New Computer Capabilities." *U.S. Air Force*, June 8, 2006. www.af.mil/News/Article-Display/Article/130775/ missileers-receive-new-computer-capabilities.

Nakashima, Ellen. "Cyber-Intruder Sparks Response, Debate." *Washington Post*, December 8, 2011. www.washingtonpost.com/national/national-security/cyber-intruder-sparks-response-debate/2011/12/06/gIQAxLuFgO_story.html.

Napoli, Philip. "Social Media and the Public Interest: Governance of News Platforms in the Realm of Individual and Algorithmic Gatekeepers." *Telecommunications Policy* 39, no. 9 (October 2015): 751–60. https://doi.org/10.1016/j. telpol.2014.12.003.

National Research Council. Computer Science and Telecommunications Board. *A 21st Century Cyber-Physical Systems Education*. Washington, DC: National Academies Press, 2016. https://doi.org/10.17226/23686.

———. *At the Nexus of Cybersecurity and Public Policy: Some Basic Concepts and Issues*. Edited by David Clark, Thomas Berson, and Herbert Lin. Washington, DC: National Academies Press, 2014. https://doi.org/10.17226/18749.

———. *Information Technology for Counterterrorism: Immediate Actions and Future Possibilities*. Edited by John L. Hennessy, David A. Patterson, and Herbert S. Lin. Washington, DC: National Academies Press, 2003. https://doi. org/10.17226/10640.

———. *Technology, Policy, Law, and Ethics Regarding U.S. Acquisition and Use of Cyberattack Capabilities*. Edited by William Owens, Kenneth Dam, and Herbert Lin. Washington, DC: National Academies Press, 2009. https://doi. org/10.17226/12651.

———. *Toward a Safer and More Secure Cyberspace*. Edited by Seymour Goodman and Herbert Lin. Washington, DC: National Academies Press, 2007. https://doi. org/10.17226/11925.

National Security Archive. "The 'Launch on Warning' Nuclear Strategy and Its Insider Critics." June 19, 2019. https://nsarchive.gwu.edu/briefing-book/ nuclear-vault/2019-06-11/launch-warning-nuclear-strategy-its-insider-critics.

———. "The Soviet Side of the 1983 War Scare." November 5, 2018, https://nsar-chive.gwu.edu/briefing-book/aa83/2018-11-05/soviet-side-1983-war-scare.

NATO. See North Atlantic Treaty Organization.

Nautilus Institute, Stanley Center for Peace and Security, and Technology for Global Security. *Last Chance: Communicating at the Nuclear Brink. Scenarios and Solutions Workshop Synthesis Report*. Berkeley, CA: Nautilus Institute, May 14, 2020.

https://nautilus.org/napsnet/napsnet-special-reports/last-chance-communicat-ing-at-the-nuclear-brink-scenarios-and-solutions-workshop-synthesis-report/.

"Next Generation NC3 Enterprise Challenge." November 27, 2018. https://beta.sam.gov/opp/390609791364842047d3ab34aa7d1441/view.

Nichols, Shaun. "Easy-to-Hack Combat Systems, Years-Old Flaws and a Massive Bill—Yup, That's America's F-35." *The Register*, March 28, 2019. www.theregister.com/2019/03/28/f35_software_fail.

Norman, Donald. "When Security Gets in the Way." *Interactions* 16, no. 6 (2010): 60–63. Author's version, December 3, 2018, at https://jnd.org/when_security_gets_in_the_way.

North Atlantic Treaty Organization (NATO). "Exercise ABLE ARCHER 83: Information from SHAPE Historical File." March 28, 2013. https://nsarchive2.gwu.edu/NSAEBB/NSAEBB427/docs/6.a.%20Exercise%20Able%20Archer%20SHAPE%20March%202013%20NATO.pdf.

"North Korea Jams South's Guided Missiles." UPI, March 8, 2011. www.upi.com/Defense-News/2011/03/08/North-Korea-jams-Souths-guided-missiles/49341299621609.

Özkan, Barls Egemen, and Serol Bulkan. "Hidden Risks to Cyberspace Security from Obsolete COTS Software." In *2019 11th International Conference on Cyber Conflict* [CyCon, Tallinn, Estonia], 1–19. https://doi.org/10.23919/CYCON.2019.8756990.

Page, Carly. "Gmail Down: Google Services Suffer Global Outage." *Forbes*, August 20, 2020, www.forbes.com/sites/carlypage/2020/08/20/gmail-down-google-services-suffer-global-outage.

Page, Joseph T., II, Mark C. Bigley, and Douglas S. Angell. "Launch Control Center NetLink." *High Frontier* 3, no. 2 (March 2007): 66–69. https://web.archive.org/web/20081029190633/http://www.afspc.af.mil/shared/media/document/AFD-070322-103.pdf.

Perkovich, George. "Really? We're Gonna Nuke Russia for a Cyberattack?" *Politico*, January 18, 2018. www.politico.com/magazine/story/2018/01/18/donald-trump-russia-nuclear-cyberattack-216477.

Peters, Jay. "Prolonged AWS Outage Takes Down a Big Chunk of the Internet." *The Verge*, November 25, 2020. www.theverge.com/2020/11/25/21719396/amazon-web-services-aws-outage-down-internet.

Poland, Corrie. "The Air Force Is Becoming More Agile—One Project at a Time." *Installations, Environment, & Energy*, April 24, 2019. www.safie.hq.af.mil/News/Article-Display/Article/1823169/the-air-force-is-becoming-more-agile-one-project-at-a-time.

Pomerleau, Mark. "The Pentagon's Plan to Secure Sensitive Systems." *Fifth Domain*, December 11, 2018. www.fifthdomain.com/industry/2018/12/11/the-pentagons-plan-to-secure-sensitive-systems.

Posen, Barry. *Inadvertent Escalation: Conventional War and Nuclear Risks*. Ithaca, NY: Cornell University Press, 1991.

Potter, Shaya, Steven Michael Bellovin, and Jason Nieh. "Two-Person Control Administration: Preventing Administration Faults through Duplication." In *Proceedings of the 23rd Large Installation System Administration Conference (LISA '09)*, Baltimore, November 1–6, 2009, 15–27. Berkeley, CA: USENIX Association, 2009. https://academiccommons.columbia.edu/doi/10.7916/D8HQ45MK.

Puiu, Tibi. "Your Smartphone Is Millions of Times More Powerful Than All of NASA's Combined Computing in 1969." *ZME Science*, February 11, 2020. www.zmescience.com/science/news-science/smartphone-power-compared-to-apollo-432.

Ross, Lee. "The Intuitive Psychologist and His Shortcomings: Distortions in the Attribution Process." *Advances in Experimental Social Psychology* 10 (January 1, 1977): 173–220. https://doi.org/10.1016/S0065-2601(08)60357-3.

Sagan, Scott. *The Limits of Safety: Organizations, Accidents, and Nuclear Weapons*. Princeton, NJ: Princeton University Press, 1993. https://press.princeton.edu/books/paperback/9780691021010/the-limits-of-safety.

Sanger, David, and William Broad. "New U.S. Weapons Systems Are a Hackers' Bonanza, Investigators Find." *New York Times*, October 10, 2018. www.nytimes.com/2018/10/10/us/politics/hackers-pentagon-weapons-systems.html.

———. "Pentagon Suggests Countering Devastating Cyberattacks with Nuclear Arms." *New York Times,* January 16, 2018. www.nytimes.com/2018/01/16/us/politics/pentagon-nuclear-review-cyberattack-trump.html.

Schlosser, Eric. *Command and Control: Nuclear Weapons, the Damascus Accident, and the Illusion of Safety*. New York: Penguin Books, 2014,

Schneider, Fred, and Justin Sherman. "Bases for Trust in a Supply Chain." Lawfare, February 1, 2021. www.lawfareblog.com/bases-trust-supply-chain.

Schneider, Jacquelyn. "What War Games Tell Us about the Use of Cyber Weapons in a Crisis." Council on Foreign Relations, June 21, 2018. www.cfr.org/blog/what-war-games-tell-us-about-use-of-cyber-weapons-crisis.

Schneier, Bruce. "A Plea for Simplicity." *Schneier on Security*, November 19, 1999. www.schneier.com/essays/archives/1999/11/a_plea_for_simplicit.html.

Scott, Len, and Steve Smith. "Lessons of October: Historians, Political Scientists, Policy-Makers and the Cuban Missile Crisis." *International Affairs* 70, no. 4 (October 1, 1994): 659–84. https://doi.org/10.2307/2624552.

Shachtman, Noah. "Communication with 50 Nuke Missiles Dropped in ICBM Snafu." *WIRED*, October 26, 2010. www.wired.com/2010/10/communications-dropped-to-50-nuke-missiles-in-icbm-snafu.

Shelton, Henry, with Ronald Levinson and Malcolm McConnell. *Without Hesitation: The Odyssey of an American Warrior*. New York: St. Martin's Press, 2010.

Slabodkin, Gregory. "Software Glitches Leave Navy Smart Ship Dead in the Water." *Government Computing News*, July 13, 1998, https://gcn.com/articles/1998/07/13/software-glitches-leave-navy-smart-ship-dead-in-the-water.aspx.

SolarWinds Corporation. Form 8-K, Current Report Pursuant to Section 13 or 15(d) of the Securities Exchange Act of 1934, U.S. Securities and Exchange Commission, Washington, DC, December 14, 2020 (date of earliest event reported). www.sec.gov/Archives/edgar/data/0001739942/000162828020017451/swi-20201214.htm.

Stasiukonis, Steve. "Social Engineering, the USB Way." Dark Reading, June 7, 2006, www.darkreading.com/attacks-breaches/social-engineering-the-usb-way/d/d-id/1128081.

Steinbruner, John, Ashton Carter, and Charles Zraket, eds. *Managing Nuclear Operations*, Washington DC: Brookings Institution, 1987.

Storm, Darlene. "Did Hackers Remotely Execute 'unexplained' Commands on German Patriot Missile Battery?" *Computerworld*, July 8, 2015. www.computerworld.com/article/2945383/did-hackers-remotely-execute-unexplained-commands-on-german-patriot-missile-battery.html.

Stoutland, Page, and Samantha Pitts-Kiefer. *Nuclear Weapons in the New Cyber Age: Report of the Cyber-Nuclear Weapons Study Group*. Washington, DC: Nuclear Threat Initiative, 2018. https://media.nti.org/documents/Cyber_report_finalsmall.pdf.

"The Submarines of October: U.S. and Soviet Naval Encounters during the Cuban Missile Crisis." In *National Security Archive Electronic Briefing Book No. 75*, ed. William Burr and Thomas S. Blanton. October 31, 2002. https://nsarchive2.gwu.edu/NSAEBB/NSAEBB75.

Subramanian, Samanth. "Inside the Macedonian Fake-News Complex." *Wired*, February 15, 2017. www.wired.com/2017/02/veles-macedonia-fake-news.

"Tactical Exploitation of National Capabilities (TENCAP)." N.d. www.globalsecurity.org/intell/systems/tencap.htm.

Temple-Raston, Dina. "A 'Worst Nightmare' Cyberattack: The Untold Story Of The SolarWinds Hack." NPR.org. April 16, 2021. www.npr.org/2021/04/16/985439655/a-worst-nightmare-cyberattack-the-untold-story-of-the-solarwinds-hack.

Thompson, Ken. "Reflections on Trusting Trust." *Communications of the ACM* 27, no. 8 (August 1, 1984): 761–63. https://doi.org/10.1145/358198.358210.

"Tomahawk's Chops: xGM-109 Block IV Cruise Missiles." *Defense Industry Daily,* December 8, 2020. www.defenseindustrydaily.com/block-iv-xgm-109-tomahawk-chopped-07423.

Tuchman, Barbara W. *The Guns of August*. New York: Macmillan, 1962.

Tucker, Patrick. "No, the US Won't Respond to a Cyber Attack with Nukes." *De-

fense One, February 2, 2018. www.defenseone.com/technology/2018/02/
no-us-wont-respond-cyber-attack-nukes/145700.

——. "Will America's Nuclear Weapons Always Be Safe from Hackers?" *The Atlantic*, December 30, 2016. https://amp.theatlantic.com/amp/article/511904.

United States. Congress. 526 Congressional Investigation Pearl Harbor Attack. "Testimony of First Lt. Joseph Lockard, Signal Corps, United States Army." www.
ibiblio.org/pha/myths/radar/lockard3.html.

——. Joint Explanatory Statement of the Committee of Conference for the National Defense Authorization Act for Fiscal Year 2018. www.armed-services.
senate.gov/imo/media/doc/JOINT%20EXPLANATORY%20STATEMENT%20
OF%20THE%20COMMITTEE%20OF%20CONFERENCE.pdf.

——. Office of Technology Assessment. MX Missile Basing. Washington, DC: U.S.
Government Printing Office, 1981. https://ota.fas.org/reports/8116.pdf.

United States. Congress. House of Representatives. Committee on Armed Services.
National Defense Authorization Act for Fiscal Year 2018. Public Law 115–91.
December 12, 2017. H.R.2810. www.congress.gov/115/plaws/publ91/PLAW-
115publ91.pdf.

——. Committee on Oversight and Government. *The OPM Data Breach: How the
Government Jeopardized National Security for More than a Generation.* Majority Staff Report by Jason Chaffetz, Mark Meadows, Will Hurd et al., September
7, 2016. https://republicans-oversight.house.gov/wp-content/uploads/2016/09/
The-OPM-Data-Breach-How-the-Government-Jeopardized-Our-National-Se-
curity-for-More-than-a-Generation.pdf.

——. National Defense Authorization Act for Fiscal Year 2021. H.R. 6395. January
3, 2020. www.congress.gov/116/bills/hr6395/BILLS-116hr6395enr.pdf.

——. Subcommittee on International Security and Scientific Affairs of the Committee on International Relations. Vice Admiral Gerald Miller, "First Use of
Nuclear Weapons: Preserving Responsible Control." Hearings, March 15–16,
1976. http://blog.nuclearsecrecy.com/wp-content/uploads/2017/04/hrg-1976-
hir-0038_from_1_to_251.pdf. Cited in Jeffrey G. Lewis and Bruno Tertrais, *The
Finger on the Button: The Authority to Use Nuclear Weapons in Nuclear-Armed
States,* CNS Occasional Paper 45 (Monterey, CA: James Martin Center for Nonproliferation Studies, Middlebury Institute of International Studies, 2019), www.
nonproliferation.org/wp-content/uploads/2019/02/Finger-on-the-Nuclear-But-
ton.pdf.

United States. Congress. Senate. Committee on Armed Services. Admiral Cecil D.
Haney, commander, U.S. Strategic Command. U.S. Strategic Command and U.S.
Cyber Command. Testimony before the Senate Committee on Armed Services,
February 27, 2014. www.hsdl.org/?view&did=751682.

——. Admiral Charles Richard, commander, U.S. Strategic Command. Testimony before the Senate Committee on Armed Services, February 13, 2020. www. stratcom.mil/Portals/8/Documents/2020_USSTRATCOM_Posture_Statement_ SASC_Final.pdf.

———. Assistant Secretary of Defense for Strategy, Plans, and Capabilities Robert Scher. Testimony before the Senate Armed Services Subcommittee on Strategic Forces, February 9, 2016. www.armed-services.senate.gov/imo/media/doc/ Scher_02-09-16.pdf.

———. General John Hyten, commander, U.S. Strategic Command. Testimony Before the Senate Committee on Armed Services, February 26, 2019. www.armed-services.senate.gov/imo/media/doc/Hyten_02-26-19.pdf

———. General John Hyten, commander, U.S. Strategic Command. Testimony before the Senate Committee on Armed Services, March 1, 2019. www.stratcom.mil/Media/Speeches/ Article/1771903/us-strategic-command-and-us-northern-command-sasc-testimony.

———. General John Hyten, commander, U.S. Strategic Command. Testimony at Hearing on Military Assessment of Nuclear Deterrence Requirements, March 17, 2017. dod.defense.gov/Portals/1/features/2017/0917_nuclear-deterrence/ docs/Transcript-HASC-Hearing-on-Nuclear-Deterrence-8-March-2017.pdf.

———. Inquiry into Counterfeit Electronic Parts in the Department of Defense Supply Chain. Report of the Committee on Armed Services. Report 112–167.Washington, DC: U.S. Government Printing Office, 2012. www.armed-services.senate.gov/ imo/media/doc/Counterfeit-Electronic-Parts.pdf.

———. Recent False Alerts from the Nation's Missile Attack Warning System. Report to the Committee on Armed Services by Senators Barry Goldwater and Gary Hart. Washington, DC: Government Printing Office, 1980.

United States. Congressional Budget Office. The Potential Costs of Expanding U.S. Strategic Nuclear Forces If the New START Treaty Expires. August 2020. www.cbo. gov/publication/56524.

United States. Congressional Research Service. "Joint All-Domain Command and Control (JADC2)." In Focus, March 18, 2021. IF11493. Version 13. https://fas. org/sgp/crs/natsec/IF11493.pdf.

———. Nonstrategic Nuclear Weapons, by Amy F. Woolf. 2020, updated March 16, 2021. RL32572. https://fas.org/sgp/crs/nuke/RL32572.pdf.

———. North Korean Cyber Capabilities: In Brief, by Emma Chanlett-Avery, John Rollins, Liana Rosen, and Catherine Theohary. 2017. R44912. https://crsreports. congress.gov/product/pdf/R/R44912.

———. "SolarWinds Attack—No Easy Fix," by Chris Jaikaran. Updated January 6, 2021. CRS report IN11559 https://crsreports.congress.gov/product/pdf/IN/IN11559.

United States. Department of Defense. Air Force. "Air Force Nuclear Command, Control, and Communications (NC3)." Air Force Instruction (AFI) 13-550. April 16, 2019. https://fas.org/irp/doddir/usaf/afi13-550.pdf.

———. Director, Operational Test and Evaluation. "B61 Mod 12 Life Extension Program Tail Kit Assembly." FY18 Air Force Programs. www.dote.osd.mil/Portals/97/pub/reports/FY2018/af/2018b61.pdf?ver=2019–08–21–155843–557.

———. "F-35 Joint Strike Fighter (JSF)." FY19 DoD Programs. www.dote.osd.mil/Portals/97/pub/reports/FY2019/dod/2019f35jsf.pdf?ver=2020–01–30–115432–173.

———. "Kessel Run." N.d. https://kesselrun.af.mil.

———. LGM-30G Minuteman III Fact Sheet. September 30, 2015. www.af.mil/About-Us/Fact-Sheets/Display/Article/104466/lgm-30g-minuteman-iii.

United States. Department of Defense. Cyber Command. "Achieve and Maintain Cyberspace Superiority: Command Vision for US Cyber Command." 2018. www.cybercom.mil/Portals/56/Documents/USCYBERCOM%20Vision%20April%202018.pdf.

———. "Cyber Assessments." FY19 Cybersecurity, 2019. www.dote.osd.mil/Portals/97/pub/reports/FY2019/other/2019cyber-assessments.pdf.

———. *The Department of Defense Cyber Strategy*. April 2015. https://archive.defense.gov/home/features/2015/0415_cyber-strategy/final_2015_dod_cyber_strategy_for_web.pdf.

United States. Department of Defense. Defense Science Board. "Task Force Report on Cyber Deterrence." February 2017. https://dsb.cto.mil/reports/2010s/DSB-CyberDeterrenceReport_02-28-17_Final.pdf.

———. "Resilient Military Systems and the Advanced Cyber Threat." January 2013. https://apps.dtic.mil/dtic/tr/fulltext/u2/a569975.pdf.

United States. Department of Defense. Inspector General. "Audit of the DoD's Management of the Cybersecurity Risks for Government Purchase Card Purchases of Commercial Off-the-Shelf Items." July 26, 2019. https://media.defense.gov/2019/Jul/30/2002164272/-1/-1/1/DODIG-2019–106.PDF.

———. "Security Controls at DoD Facilities for Protecting Ballistic Missile Defense System Technical Information." December 10, 2018. https://media.defense.gov/2018/Dec/14/2002072642/-1/-1/1/DODIG-2019-034.PDF.

United States. Department of Defense. Joint Chiefs of Staff. *The National Military Strategy of the United States of America—A Strategy for Today, a Vision for Tomorrow*. Office of the Joint Chiefs of Staff, 2004. https://archive.defense.gov/news/Mar2005/d20050318nms.pdf.

United States. Department of Defense. Marine Corps. *Command and Control*. MCDP 6. Washington, DC: Department of the Navy, 2018. www.marines.mil/Portals/1/Publications/MCDP%206.pdf?ver=2019–07–18–093633–990.

United States. Department of Defense. *Nuclear Matters Handbook 2016*. www.lasg.org/Nuclear-Matters-2016.pdf.

———. *Nuclear Posture Review Report*, April 2010. https://dod.defense.gov/Portals/1/features/defenseReviews/Nuclear Posture Review/2010_Nuclear_Posture_Review_Report.pdf.

———. *Nuclear Posture Review*, February 2018, https://media.defense.gov/2018/ Feb/02/2001872886/-1/-1/1/2018-NUCLEAR-POSTURE-REVIEW-FINAL-REPORT.PDF.

———. Office of the Deputy Assistant Secretary of Defense for Nuclear Matters. *Nuclear Matters Handbook 2020*. https://fas.org/man/eprint/nmhb2020.pdf.

———. Office of the Undersecretary of Defense for Acquisition and Sustainment. "Thomas F. Greenfield, Director, Nuclear Command, Control, and Communications." www.acq.osd.mil/asda/iipm/greenfield.html.

———. Secretary of Defense Task Force on DoD Nuclear Weapons Management. "Phase I: The Air Force's Nuclear Mission," September 2008. www.globalsecurity. org/wmd/library/report/2008/nuclear-weapons_phase-1_2008-09-10.pdf.

———. "Statement on the Fielding of the W76–2 Low-Yield Submarine Launched Ballistic Missile Warhead." Attributed to Under Secretary of Defense for Policy John Rood. February 4, 2020. www.defense.gov/Newsroom/Releases/Release/ Article/2073532/statement-on-the-fielding-of-the-w76–2-low-yield-submarine-launched-ballistic-m.

United States. Department of Defense. Strategic Command. "ALERT/RECALL PROCEDURES." Strategic Instruction (SI) 506–02. April 20, 2017. Released under USFOIA request to Nautilus Institute. PDF in the author's possession. Publication pending at https://nautilus.org/publications/foia-document-search.

———. "Guidelines for Nuclear Weapon System Operational Testing and Reporting." Strategic Instruction (SI) 526–01. June 30, 2020. Released under USFOIA request to Nautilus Institute. PDF in the author's possession. Publication pending at https://nautilus.org/publications/foia-document-search.

———. "Guidelines for Reporting Pre-Launch Survivability." Strategic Instruction (SI) 512–06, June 15, 2018. Released under USFOIA request to Nautilus Institute. PDF in the author's possession. Publication pending at https://nautilus.org/ publications/foia-document-search.

United States. Department of Energy. "DoE Update on Cyber Incident Related to SolarWinds Compromise." December 18, 2020. www.energy.gov/articles/ doe-update-cyber-incident-related-to-solar-winds-compromise.

———. "Maintaining the Stockpile." www.energy.gov/nnsa/missions/maintaining-stockpile.

———. National Nuclear Security Administration. "B61–12 Life Extension Program Fact Sheet." June 1, 2020. www.energy.gov/nnsa/articles/b61-12-life-extension-program-lep-fact-sheet.

———. "Stockpile Stewardship and Management Plan (SSMP). www.energy.gov/ nnsa/downloads/stockpile-stewardship-and-management-plan-ssmp.

United States. Department of Homeland Security. Cybersecurity and Infrastructure Security Agency. "Joint Statement by the Federal Bureau of Investigation (FBI), the Cybersecurity and Infrastructure Security Agency (CISA), the Office of the Director of National Intelligence (ODNI), and the National Security Agency (NSA)." January 5, 2021. www.cisa.gov/news/2021/01/05/joint-statement-federal-bureau-investigation-fbi-cybersecurity-and-infrastructure.

———. Craig Miller. "Security Considerations in Managing COTS Software." December 14, 2006. https://us-cert.cisa.gov/bsi/articles/best-practices/legacy-systems/security-considerations-in-managing-cots-software.

United States. Department of Justice. Office of Special Counsel. Robert S. Mueller III. *Report on the Investigation into Russian Interference in the 2016 Presidential Election* Washington, D.C: U.S. Department of Justice, 2019. www.justice.gov/storage/report.pdf.

United States. Department of State. Bureau of Arms Control, Verification and Compliance. Fact sheet. "New START Treaty Aggregate Numbers of Strategic Offensive Arms." January 1, 2020. www.state.gov/wp-content/uploads/2019/12/AVC-New-START-Jan-2020.pdf.

United States. General Accounting Office. *Triad Summary.* PEMD-92–36R, September 28, 1992. www.gao.gov/assets/90/82669.pdf.

United States. Government Accountability Office (GAO). "Critical Infrastructure Protection: Commercial Satellite Security Should Be More Fully Addressed." August 2002. www.gao.gov/products/gao-02-781.

———. "F-35 Joint Strike Fighter: Actions Needed to Address Manufacturing and Modernization Risks." May 12, 2020. www.gao.gov/assets/710/706815.pdf.

———. "Nuclear Command, Control, and Communications: Review of DOD's Current Modernization Efforts." March 18, 2014. www.gao.gov/assets/670/661752.pdf.

———. *Weapon Systems Cybersecurity: DOD Just Beginning to Grapple with Scale of Vulnerabilities.* GAO 19-128. October 9, 2018. www.gao.gov/products/GAO-19-128.

———. *Weapon Systems Cybersecurity: Guidance Would Help DOD Programs Better Communicate Requirements to Contractors.* GAO 21-179. March 2021. www.gao.gov/assets/gao-21-179.pdf.

United States. National Counterintelligence and Security Center. Office of the Director of National Intelligence. "Supply Chain Risk Management." N.d. www.dni.gov/index.php/ncsc-what-we-do/ncsc-supply-chain-threats.

United States. National Intelligence Council. *Foreign Threats to the 2020 U.S. Federal Elections.* ICA-2020-00078D, March 15, 2021. www.dni.gov/files/ODNI/documents/assessments/ICA-declass-16MAR21.pdf.

United States. White House. "Imposing Costs for Harmful Foreign Activities by the Russian Government," April 15, 2021. Fact Sheet. www.whitehouse.gov/briefing-room/statements-releases/2021/04/15/fact-sheet-imposing-costs-for-harmful-foreign-activities-by-the-russian-government/.

———. *National Security Strategy of the United States of America*. December 2017. https://trumpwhitehouse.archives.gov/wp-content/uploads/2017/12/NSS-Final-12-18-2017-0905.pdf.

Waterman, Shaun. "Experts Push Back on Trump Administration's Call to Respond to Cyberattacks with Nukes." *CyberScoop*, February 13, 2018 www.cyberscoop.com/nuclear-posture-review-cyberattacks-nukes-donald-trump.

Weinberger, Caspar. Interview. "Meet the Press," *NBC News*, March 27, 1983.

Weiss, Jessica, and Allan Dafoe. "Authoritarian Audiences, Rhetoric, and Propaganda in International Crises: Evidence from China." *International Studies Quarterly* 63, no. 4 (December 2019): 963–73. https://doi.org/10.1093/isq/sqz059.

Whitaker, Bill. "SolarWinds: How Russian Spies Hacked the Justice, State, Treasury, Energy and Commerce Departments." CBS News, *60 Minutes*, February 14, 2021. www.cbsnews.com/news/solarwinds-hack-russia-cyberattack-60-minutes-2021-02-14.

Williams, Jordan. "Durbin Says Alleged Russian Hack 'Virtually a Declaration of War.'" *The Hill*, December 16, 2020. https://thehill.com/policy/cybersecurity/530461-durbin-says-alleged-russian-hack-virtually-a-declaration-of-war.

Winchester, Jim. *The Encyclopedia of Modern Aircraft*. San Diego, CA: Thunder Bay Press, 2006.

Wright, David, William D. Hartung, and Lisbeth Gronlund. *Rethinking Land-Based Nuclear Missiles: Sensible Risk-Reduction Practices for US ICBMs*. Cambridge, MA: Union of Concerned Scientists, 2020. www.ucsusa.org/resources/rethinking-icbms.

Yi, Mingxu, LifengWang, and Jun Huang. "Active Cancellation Analysis Based on the Radar Detection Probability." *Aerospace Science and Technology* 46 (November 2015): 273–81. https://doi.org/10.1016/j.ast.2015.07.018.

Yu, Rongjun. "Stress Potentiates Decision Biases: A Stress Induced Deliberation-to-Intuition (SIDI) Model." *Neurobiology of Stress* 3 (February 12, 2016): 83–95. https://doi.org/10.1016/j.ynstr.2015.12.006.

Zetter, Kim. "An Unprecedented Look at Stuxnet, the World's First Digital Weapon." *Wired*, November 3, 2014. www.wired.com/2014/11/countdown-to-zero-day-stuxnet.

Index

Lightning Source UK Ltd.
Milton Keynes UK
UKHW010422260921
391056UK00012B/545

9 781503 630390